Culturally Contested Literacies

Culturally Contested Literacies is a vivid ethnographic account of the everyday cross-cultural living and schooling experiences of six culturally diverse families in urban America. Documenting the ways in which these families learn about literacies and their meanings in relation to schools, inner-city environments, and other ethnic groups, Guofang Li's incisive analysis reveals the unique experiences of fractured urban America—the dynamics of how and in what conditions the families take up contradictory positions of conformity and resistance within and across various discourses and boundaries.

Unlike prior research that fragments various social categories, *Culturally Contested Literacies* explores the rich complexity within each family as it makes sense of its daily relations in terms of literacy, race, ethnicity, class, and gender. It juxtaposes the productions of such familial relations across different racial and cultural groups within the context of the larger socio-political and socio-economic formations. By presenting a realistic picture of the varying ways that America's "rainbow underclass" might encounter schooling, Li argues that urban education must be understood in relation not only to the individual's cultural and familial milieu, but also to the interactive context between the individual and schools.

Guofang Li is Associate Professor in the Department of Teacher Education at Michigan State University.

To the families in this study,
for their dreams beyond the city

Culturally Contested Literacies

America's "Rainbow Underclass" and Urban Schools

Guofang Li

Routledge
Taylor & Francis Group

NEW YORK AND LONDON

First published 2008
by Routledge
711 Third Avenue, New York, NY 10017

Simultaneously published in the UK
by Routledge
2 Park Square, Milton Park, Abingdon, Oxon OX14 4RN

*Routledge is an imprint of the Taylor & Francis Group, an
informa business*

© 2008 Taylor & Francis

Typeset in Minion Pro by Prepress Projects Ltd, Perth, UK

Library of Congress Cataloging-in-Publication Data
Li, Guofang.
    Culturally contested literacies: America's rainbow
    underclass and urban schools/by Guofang Li.
        p. cm.
    Includes bibliographical references and index.
    ISBN 978-0-415-95564-5 (hb: alk. paper) – ISBN 978-0-
    415-95565-2 (pb: alk. paper) 1. Multicultural education—
    United States—Case studies. 2. Education, Urban—United
    States—Case studies. 3. Literacy—Social aspects—United
    States—Case studies. I. Title.
    LC1099.3.L5 2008
    370.19′3480973–dc22
    2007019500

ISBN10: 0-415-95564-5 (hbk)
ISBN10: 0-415-95565-3 (pbk)
ISBN10: 0-203-93557-8 (ebk)

ISBN13: 978-0-415-95564-5 (hbk)
ISBN13: 978-0-415-95565-2 (pbk)
ISBN13: 978-0-203-93557-6 (ebk)

Contents

Acknowledgments   vi

1   Introduction: 1
America's *"Rainbow Underclass" and Inner City Schooling*

2   Where the Stories Began: 27
The City and its Schools

3   Being Vietnamese, Becoming Somebody   57

4   Being Sudanese, Being Black   93

5   Being White, Being the Majority in the Minority   127

6   Multicultural Families and Multiliteracies: 161
Tensions, Conformity, and Resistance to Urban Schooling

7   Culturally Contested Literacies and the Education of
America's "Rainbow Underclass"   183

Notes   199
References   201
Index   213

Acknowledgments

I am indebted to many individuals who provided me with support and assistance throughout this book project. The six families invited me into their homes and shared much of their histories, happy and unhappy life stories, worries, concerns, and triumphs with me, and, at times, generously offered me delicious food. The teachers and parent liaisons kindly dedicated their time to this project, sharing what they saw and experienced in the schools and their efforts to improve the education of the children they serve. I remain deeply appreciative of their support and participation, which have made this book possible.

I am also indebted to many of my graduate students at the University at Buffalo, where I completed the data collection, and in the Department of Teacher Education, Michigan State University, where I completed the writing of the project. Chizuko Konishi and Evelyn at the University at Buffalo were very instrumental in the data collection process. I am grateful for their time and dedication in assisting me in this project. I am also very grateful to Won Pyo Hong at the Michigan State University, who spent many hours listening to me work out my ideas, checking transcripts, and helping me refining the manuscript. I thank Kristen Perry for checking the transcripts and Jamie Puccioni for her editorial help.

I am deeply grateful to many of my colleagues and friends in the two universities. I owe a special thanks to Lois Weis at the University at Buffalo, who spent invaluable time reading and commenting on the manuscript. Her insightful comments have made this book a much stronger piece of scholarship.

My gratitude also goes to the staff at Routledge. I am deeply indebted to Catherine Bernard, who took a strong interest in the book when I first presented her with the project. I am grateful for her faith and belief in me. I also thank Heather Jarrow for her role in the production process and the two anonymous reviewers for their helpful suggestions and feedback on an earlier version of the manuscript.

My appreciation is also extended to many of my friends and colleagues who have helped me embrace life besides work—Xiufeng and Rui, Mary and Jian, Lynne and Shusheng, Tim for also reading some of my work, Diana and Geralyn, Weihong and Biao, Baolian, Dongping, and many others for providing much needed 'distraction' from writing. My final appreciation goes to my families in China and Canada for their continued support and love over the years.

1
Introduction:
America's "Rainbow Underclass" and Inner City Schooling

> Reality as it is thought does not correspond to the reality being lived objectively, but rather to the reality in which alienated man imagines himself to be.
>
> **–Paulo Freire, *Cultural Action for Freedom* (1975)**

It's a hot sunny summer afternoon in Buffalo,[1] a middle-sized city in western New York. Music is playing loudly on one of the front porches of West Lane Street in the heartland of the city's impoverished West Side. Accompanying the music, one can occasionally hear laughter amidst someone's teasing, men yelling, and kids screaming. It is too hot to stay inside. Many people sit around on deserted car seats on the front porches of their unkempt houses, either trying to enjoy the music while watching the cars pass by, or trying to ignore it.

A thirteen-year-old Sudanese refugee, Nina Torkeri, and her two younger sisters are tired of listening to the loud music the whole afternoon and they try to ignore it by playing with each other's hair while their eleven-year-old brother, Fred, is cruising up and down the street on his bicycle trying to see what's happening around the block. He is waiting for his older brother, Owen, to come home so that they can go play basketball. Upstairs in their two-bedroom apartment their mother Anne is preparing dinner with their eight-month-old baby sister strapped on her back, crying. She is sweating, rushing to get everything ready. It's too hot inside and the ear-pounding music makes her feel even hotter. She hopes that the music will stop soon. The unbearable noise that she has to endure daily makes her wish she could move to another area. However, she knows that this is an impossibility, for the rent is good here and she will not find any cheaper living accommodations for a family of eight.

Only several houses down, you will find the front porch of the Ton family is empty. The Ton family is the only Vietnamese family on this block. Twelve-year-old Mien sits intently in front of the computer in his room playing video games, while two of his Vietnamese buddies crouch beside him cheering and exclaiming as he moves the mouse. Downstairs in the big living room on the left side of the entrance, six-year-old Dan lies on the floor, eyes glued to the big 57-inch TV screen. He is playing the *Asian Empire* video game, while his ten-year-old sister, Nyen, watches him play and tries to play along, helping him as he cannot read or speak English. Excited by the game, he kicks, giggles, and shouts in Vietnamese to his sister, who tries hard to get him to listen to her. She is bored and thinks of going outside to look for her friend Mimi, a Lebanese girl attending the same school, to play. In the back, their grandmother, who can speak only Vietnamese, quietly prepares dinner. Their father, Lo, has just left for work in a factory in the south town for his second shift and their mother, Cam, will come home in a couple of hours from the same factory.

Two streets away, parallel to West Lane, the loud music can no longer be heard and the street is rather strangely quiet and empty. The house of another Sudanese refugee family, the Myers, is extremely quiet. A couple of family members watch TV just to stay occupied, while the others play in the backyard. Mother, Gloria, has not come back from her factory job, but all seven other family members are at home. They have to remain relatively quiet as their father, Mahdi, is taking a nap. He usually comes home early in the morning from his night shift at his meat-slicing job, catching sleep for a couple of hours before he drives his children to school during the school year. Now he can sleep one hour longer in the morning, as it is summer and the children do not go to school. He then attends classes at a local community college. In the afternoon after his classes are over, he tries to get a few more hours of sleep before he goes back to work again.

A few minutes away, another Vietnamese household, the Phan house, is equally quiet. The Phan parents are at work. The mother, Lynne, works in a nail salon and the father, Dao Phan, works as a mechanic. They will not come home until nearly 9:00 p.m. Sixteen-year-old Hanh sits in their dark living room trying to read, but she keeps thinking about the house chores she needs to do and the bills she must remind her parents to pay. Even on a beautiful day like this, she cannot go out of the house or talk to her friends over the phone because she is Vietnamese, and as a girl she is not allowed to do so. The living room curtain is tightly closed so that passers-by will think no one is at home. She can hear her brother, Chinh, shouting, chasing, and running with a group of boys outside the house. They are having a great time scourging the neighborhood. She hopes that he will soon come in and study English so that he can improve his reading and writing skills over the summer.

The neighborhood is composed not just of immigrants and refugees; several blocks away on Haven Street, the Claytons are one of the few white families in this area. Twenty-nine-year-old Pauline is a mother of three—two older children from a previous relationship and a baby son from her current boyfriend. She is pregnant with her fourth child, who is due in six months. As a single mother without a car, Pauline relies on welfare to get by. The family's current apartment is subsidized housing from the government. On a hot day like this, it is hard to stay inside. The Claytons' house is not quiet like some of the other houses. The phone is ringing. The baby is crying. Three-year-old Judd cannot stay still even for a second and is banging on the tables and chairs, running around and throwing things, while ten-year-old Kate runs after him to calm him down. Having a hard time talking on the phone, Pauline yells for her boyfriend, who is upstairs in their bedroom, to do something with the baby or with Judd.

On the outskirts of the neighborhood, the house of another white family, the Sassanos, is peaceful and quiet. Everyone is busy attending to their own matters. Ten-year-old Rod sits on the porch reading a new book he just borrowed from the public library, while his twelve-year-old brother Scott (who does not like books) hides himself in his room playing computer games. Their grandmother, who is hearing-impaired, lives upstairs and is always very quiet. Their father is a local jeweler and is still at work. Their mother, Loraine, happens to be at home after her shift at a local grocery store. She is busy organizing the upcoming Boy Scouts' camping activities for the next weekend. Their dining table is covered with charts, papers, and labels. She is pleased to see Rod reading, but is not happy with Scott, who dislikes reading books. However, since she has no time to think more about the children, she quickly ignores these thoughts and immerses herself in the tasks on hand. She needs to finish them soon, for her class at the local community college will be beginning soon, and she is studying to become a nurse.

All the families introduced above have two things in common in addition to living in the same neighborhood. They all have children who attend the nearby public school, Rainbow Elementary, and they all are committed to their children's schooling. The seemingly peaceful picture painted above, though a superficial sketch of their daily lives, reveals some serious undercurrents that run through these families' pathways to success in the inner-city neighborhood. As their stories will demonstrate in this book, despite their best efforts, many of these children are struggling in school, and only a few of them have achieved success. Even among the few success stories, serious socio-emotional stress seems to have masked the sense of pride and joy among the children.

These six different urban families are part of America's expanding "rainbow underclass," who are culturally diverse (hence the name "rainbow") and economically disadvantaged and who are often caught in downward social mobility (hence the term "underclass") (Portes & Zhou, 1993; Zuckerman, 2002). They, together with the poor and working-class African Americans remaining in inner cities, are part of a new class fraction in urban America that is often misunderstood and ignored in social science research and in the general public consciousness (Fine & Weis, 1998; Weis, 1990, 2004). Sitting at the bottom of the richest country in the world, they are often depicted as "the *cause* of national problems" and "the *reason* for the rise in urban crime, as embodying the *necessity* for welfare reform, and of sitting at the *heart* of moral decay" (Fine & Weis, 1998, p. 1, italics original). Yet, this group, especially the foreign-born immigrants and refugees, are often excluded in national conversations and ignored in the policy-making processes—their voices are often not heard and their experiences remain foreign to their middle-class neighbors and to the general public (Fine & Weis, 1998).

The intention of this book, therefore, is to bring the voices and experiences of this group, especially the foreign born, from the margin to the center. Extending prior research (e.g., Fine & Weis, 1998; Weis, 1990, 2004) that argues for the forging of this distinct social class under the new globalized economy, I explore literacy practices in this new class fraction as its members raise the next generation. That is, I examine the multifaceted literacies of this new class in their everyday cross-cultural living in an urban neighborhood as these literacies intersect with their schooling experiences. Specifically, I look at the multiple aspects of their daily literacy practices, as they cross the national, cultural, racial, and educational borders between their home countries and the US inner city and between their home and the school.

In this book, literacy means "an identity kit"—a discourse characterized by socially accepted ways of using language, of thinking, and of acting (Gee, 1991, p. 3). By literacies, I conceive that literacy discourses are intrinsically diverse, historically and culturally viable social practices (Collins & Blot, 2003). This book is about the "maps of meaning" (Hall & Jefferson, 1990) as experienced and understood by the six families—their "values and beliefs, dreams and struggles, newly discovered expectations and misunderstandings" (Valdés, 1996, p. 5). Like many other disadvantaged families, these families are also "consistently thwarted by institutional practices" (Rogers, 2003, p. 2). Therefore, I also analyze how the intricate institutional discourses (e.g., schooled literacy and educational policies) shape these families' everyday living and their children's schooling experiences. By bringing the everyday worlds of the families to the center stage, this book documents how culturally embedded literacies in the families are practiced, negotiated, and contested in the fabric of their urban living and schooling.

The families' everyday worlds of literacies are analyzed from a dialectical view of schooling that investigates the problems of minority experiences not just as isolated events of individuals or deficiencies in the social structure but more as part of the interactive context between the individual and the society (McLaren, 1988, 2003). I follow what Weis and Fine (2004) theorize as "a relational method" or "a compositional study" to understand how each family makes sense of its everyday literacy and living, and how the family members situate themselves in relation to a constructed Other (e.g., the African Americans). Unlike prior research that either essentializes or fragments various social categories, I examine not only the rich complexity within each family as they make sense of their daily relations in terms of race, ethnicity, class, and gender, but also the productions of such relations across cultural groups and within the context of the larger socio-political and socio-economic formations. Such a perspective allows me to examine not only the individual families' experiences but also the contradictions and asymmetries of power and privilege that both shape and problematize the meaning of these experiences. This dialectical thought will function to bring the power of human activity and knowledge to the surface and unmask the connections between the individual experiences and the cultural norms, values, and standards of the more powerful cultural sites such as the schools (Darder, 1995).

In this sense, this book is a study about discursive conditions surrounding the six families' literacy practices and their efforts to construct or take up their particular positions within and across various socio-cultural discourses. According to Foucault (1978), a discourse is not just a language system; it also constitutes power relations and invokes particular notions of truth and thus defines what is acceptable and unacceptable in a given context. As such, power is executed less through physical instruments than through discursive formations, especially in modern societies (Foucault, 1972). Foucault further argues that power relations in discourses are not unilateral or top-down, but dynamic and interactional:

> To be more precise, we must not imagine a world of discourse divided between accepted discourse and excluded discourse, or between the dominant discourse and the dominated one, but as a multiplicity of discursive elements that can come into play in various strategies.... We must make allowance for the complex and unstable process whereby discourse can be both an instrument and an effect of power, but also a hindrance, a stumbling block, a point of resistance and a starting point for an opposed strategy.
>
> (1978, pp. 100–101)

Thus, this book is also about the six families' dynamic and interactive experiences as they construct cultural/racial identities, make sense of their inner-city environments, and negotiate power relationships with more powerful institutions such as schools. As their stories will demonstrate, at times, these families accept/resign to the dominant discourses in literacy, culture, race, class, and gender prevalent in the inner city and in the wider society. Other times, they choose to reject them and try to create counter-narratives, alternative ways of speaking of and about themselves and their worlds. This book attempts to document their journeys and the complexities in their journeys as they take up particular and often contradictory positions in new and sometimes hard circumstances—the dynamics of how and in what conditions they connect/disconnect or double/split themselves within and across various discourses and boundaries.

In the chapters that follow, I will provide detailed accounts of the six culturally diverse families' experiences with literacies and schooling as they struggle to adjust and understand the American urban education system and/or to survive in an economically depressed, post-industrial city. I will describe the dynamics and complexities of each family's struggles and identity formations within an increasingly intricate situation in which literacy, culture, race, gender, and social class intertwine to make an impact on daily survival and the children's schooling experiences. I pay particular attention to the discursive elements that shape the families' contradictory social positioning characterized by both conformity and resistance to the dominant discourses and the consequences of such positioning—how they are both an effect of power and a hindrance in their everyday literacy practices and schooling.

Through a descriptive account of the culturally different literacy practices within the different households and of their symbolic struggles against institutional practices, I argue in this book that experiences in urban schooling must be understood as products of dialectical interaction in relation to not only the individual's cultural and familial milieu but also the interactive context between the individual and the more powerful cultural sites such as schools. In the current climate, minority school failure is often charged to the deficits of the disadvantaged families (and their children) (Whitehouse & Colvin, 2001) and the parenting practices that induce school failure (e.g., working-class parents believe in accomplishment of natural growth, in which a child's development unfolds spontaneously—as long as basic comfort, food, and shelter are provided) (Lareau, 2003). This study, in contrast, demonstrates that these inner-city working-class or underclass families are highly literate, committed to their children's success and capable of concerted cultivation that generates cultural capital. Yet, despite ample commitment, persistence, and cultural capital, "the sticky web of institutional discourses" (Rogers, 2003, p. 2) as well as the contradictions both within and between home and school cultural sites (Giroux, 2001) hold them in place of failure and disadvantage.

"New" Immigration Patterns and the Schooling of America's "Rainbow Underclass"

The United States is a nation of immigrants. In the past few decades, America has received different kinds of newcomers—professional immigrants (members of the professions of exceptional ability), entrepreneur immigrants (immigrants with substantial business expertise and capital), labor immigrants (illegal or contracted foreign workers for low-paying jobs), and refugees and asylees (people who escape their country of origin for fear of prosecution or physical harm) (Portes & Rumbaut, 1996). Just as they differ in their pathways into America, these groups also differ in their resettlement patterns, in their integration into the American cultural and economic structure, that result in segmentation in assimilation (Portes & Rumbaut, 1996, 2001). Whereas some groups have achieved upward social mobility and/or ethnic solidarity, many low-socio-economic status (SES) groups have experienced a downward spiral into poverty, often into an inner-city underclass (McBrien, 2005; Portes & Rumbaut, 1996, 2001).

Most refugees and asylees are vulnerable to this assimilation pattern and resettle in economically depressed urban areas with high rates of crime and unemployment (McBrien, 2005). National reports show that segmented assimilation among different immigrant groups is reflected in residential segregation across different regions of the nation (Healey, 2003). In general, new professional and entrepreneurial immigrants (e.g., those from Asia) are reported to settle in suburbs outside their urban ethnic enclaves (e.g., Monterey Park in California, nicknamed the "Chinese Beverly Hills") whereas many low-skilled primary labor immigrants and refugees (e.g., Vietnamese, African refugees, and Hispanic immigrants) settle in urban enclaves as they often receive government assistance or work in low-wage occupations (Healey, 2003; Li, 2005a; Portes & Rumbaut, 1996; Zhou, 2001). These newly arrived low-SES immigrants and refugees, together with the poor and working-class whites remaining in inner-city areas, have become America's "rainbow underclass." These "underclass" groups not only must contend with the low SES, they must also endure the impact of other social factors such as racism, negative reception, and language and cultural barriers (Portes & Zhou, 1993).

National statistics show that America has been highly segregated racially and economically across the nation since the 1980s. The US Census 2000 shows that growing ethnic diversity in the nation is accompanied by high residential segregation, especially between the black and the white. The average racial and economic composition of neighborhoods occupied by whites differs from that of neighborhoods occupied by blacks, Hispanics, Asians, or other ethnic groups. For example, on average, a typical white individual lives in a neighborhood in which 80.2 percent of residents are white, but only 6.7 percent are black, 7.9 percent are Hispanics, and 3.9 percent are Asian; whereas a typical black individual lives in a neighborhood that is made up of 51.4 percent blacks, 33.0 percent white, 11.4 percent Hispanic, and 3.3 percent Asian (Lewis Mumford Center, 2001). Since immigrants are often drawn to co-ethnic settlement, communities that are geographically separated but ethnically homogeneous are growing larger in immigrant-receiving states. Though there are many factors that contribute to the segregation (e.g., social preference, urban structure, and discrimination), socio-economic factors (e.g., affordability) are reported to exert the most significant impact (Clark,

1986; Krysan & Farley, 2002). Gimpel (1999) suggests that socio-economic mobility and geographic mobility are closely linked. People who have the means to move out of impoverished neighborhoods usually do so: moving up the economic ladder entails moving out. The relative immobility of the poor (including the recent low-SES immigrants and refugees) is part of the reason why poverty is geographically concentrated in certain neighborhoods and cities, as opposed to evenly dispersed across the nation.

Racial and economic segregation has significant impacts on the accultura-tion and integration of immigrant and minority groups. Gimpel (1999) points out that sometimes co-ethnic settlement provides social networks which can help new immigrants gain a foothold, but these networks are often situated within a context of urban poverty, violence, bad schools, and fierce competi-tion for scarce jobs and housing with rival groups. Hundreds of thousands of immigrants appear not to gain benefits via social networks and wind up in dead-end jobs paying the lowest wages without benefits, or worse still on social welfare. As a result, poverty is persistent in immigrant communities and it limits their geographic mobility as recent immigrants remain stuck in some of the worst labor markets in the country (Gimpel, 1999).

Every year, Buffalo admits over 5,000 refugees. Almost all of them, together with low-SES immigrants, settle in the central city area. Buffalo is a predominantly black and white town with a population of 292,648 in its metro area, 4.4 percent of whom are foreign born (US Census Bureau, 2000). In 2005, this population had dropped by about 3 percent to 279,745. The city sits in the Rust Belt and has experienced deindustrialization since the late 1970s (Fine & Weis, 1998). The poverty rate of the central city also almost doubled, from 14.8 percent in 1969 to 26.6 percent in 1999. In addition, the median family income decreased from $39,966 in 1969 to $30,614 in 1999. Because of the continued loss of jobs, the population of the city has been in steady decline. From 1990 to 2000, it is reported that the population dropped by 10.8 percent. Accompanying the economic downturn and the desegregation of city schools in 1977, the city has also experienced a rapid change in racial demographics, as many whites have chosen to move out of city to live in the suburbs. According to State of the Cities Data System (SOCDS) Census Data in 2000 (http://socds.huduser.org/Census/), between 1980 and 2000 the white population in the central city dropped from 69.6 to 51.8 percent, while the black or African American population increased from 26.3 to 36.6 percent, the Hispanic population rose from 2.7 to 7.5 percent, and the Asians and other races increased from 1.4 to 4.1 percent.

The segmented assimilation has a significant impact on what kinds of schools inner-city children attend and what kind of education they receive (Li, 2005b). The physical capital of schools such as available resources, the social organization of the student population, the teaching force, the learners, and the nature of curriculum and instruction differ in terms of the SES status of the community context of schools (Knapp & Woolverton, 2004; Li, 2005a). Schools in higher-SES communities possess more physical capital—they attract better-qualified teachers, receive more resources and funding, are better equipped with technology, and are in safer and more orderly environments. In contrast, schools serving students from low-income families have fewer resources, experience greater difficulties attracting qualified teachers, and face many more challenges in addressing students' needs (Lee & Burkam, 2002). In addition to the differences in physical capital, schools with different SES statuses also differ in their cultural and symbolic capital such as leadership, staff morale, expectations for students, and values placed on students' cultures and languages (Suárez-Orozco & Suárez-Orozco, 2001). Suárez-Orozco and Suárez-Orozco (2001) discovered that schools serving immigrant children range from high-functioning ones with high expectations and emphases on achievement to catastrophic ones characterized by the ever-present fear of violence, distrust, low expectations and institutional anomie. The latter kinds of schools, what they call "fields of endangerment," are usually located in neighborhoods troubled by drugs, prostitution, and gangs, and often focus on survival, not learning.

Poverty rate also correlates with students' achievement gaps. The NEAP (2005) report shows that the achievement gap between different SES groups has been persistent throughout the years. For example, as Table 1.1 shows, students who are eligible for free or reduced lunch programs (high poverty) and those who are not (low poverty) turn out to have substantial differences in their achievement.

Table 1.1 Achievement Gap between High-Poverty and Low-Poverty Students

			Scores		Group difference
	Grade	Year	High-poverty group	Low-poverty group	
Reading	4	2002	203	226	23
		2003	201	229	27
		2005	203	230	27
	8	2002	271	249	22
		2003	271	247	24
		2005	270	247	23
Math	4	2002	208	237	29
		2003	222	244	22
		2005	225	248	23
	8	2002	253	276	23
		2003	259	285	26
		2005	262	288	26

In addition to the community context and school factors, the schooling of America's "rainbow underclass" is also influenced by the acculturation process, that is, "their different patterns of learning the language and culture of the host society" (Portes & Rumbaut, 2001, p. 247). Two factors are important for this process. One is their adaptation to the culture of the host society, which is related to the community's context of reception—i.e., the degree of discrimination in the host community. Discrimination can arise from a variety of sources—historical, religious, racial, or political (e.g., seeing the immigrants as a real or symbolic threat). Communities that welcome diversity and have access to a variety of resources are more likely to foster upward social mobility among immigrants. In Centrie's (2004) study of Vietnamese youth's identity formation, for example, the school the students attend created a Vietnamese homeroom and study hall to assist their acculturation process. The homeroom and study hall allowed a free space for the affirmation of their Vietnamese values of collective learning, hard work, and appreciation of education and served as a safe and protected environment for them to learn English and American culture. The space therefore shielded the Vietnamese youth from harmful stereotypes and helped orient them to academic success.

On the other hand, if communities have negative responses to immigrants and have scarce resources, they are more likely to lead immigrants to downward assimilation, which is characterized by blocked entry into the American mainstream and socialization into the urban underclass. In contrast to the school in Centrie's (2004) study, the high school with a tradition of high academic achievement in Lee's (2005) research on Hmong students saw the minority students through the lens of difference and deficit and deemed them as "culturally, intellectually, and morally inferior to Whites" (p. 15). The school's approach to Hmong students perpetuates a racial structure that favors white students and their culture, fostering an adverse academic environment for the Hmong students. This reductionist approach therefore contributes to students' creation of oppositional identities and excludes them from academic excellence.

Communities' negative responses to minority groups have a profound influence on 1.5- or second-generation students' acculturation process. In her study of Vietnamese youth in San Diego, Zhou (2001) reports that, overall, perceptions among the Vietnamese adolescents about racial discrimination and white superiority were disturbing. Almost a third of the students held pessimistic views on racial discrimination and their economic opportunities in the US. Their perceptions about racial discrimination are often internalized, which often influences their adjustment and coping strategies (Alvarez & Helm, 2001). Similarly, Lam (2003) found that Vietnamese students who receive messages that emphasize positive images of being Asian American function better psycho-socially. In contrast, students who internalize the negative images of racial discrimination tend to demonstrate more social and psychological struggles. In a review of at-risk Asian students, Siu (1996) found that many Southeast Asian students reported having experienced different levels of racial discrimination (e.g., name calling or being insulted or ridiculed) at school and that these experiences were often manifested in various types of emotional harms such as depressive symptoms, withdrawn or deviant behaviors, and social problems.

The other significant factor in the acculturation process is the immigrant children's attitude and connection to their first language and culture of origin, or ethnicity. One possible tendency is a growing distance from their ethnic language and culture. This tendency, termed "ethnic flight" by Suárez-Orozco and Suárez-Orozco (2001), "often comes at a significant social and emotional cost," though it can help a person succeed by mainstream standards (p. 104). From early on, these children tend to reject their first language and culture and often refuse to speak it in their home. For these children, learning a second language means losing their first language (Li, 2006; Wong-Fillmore, 1991). The other tendency, ethnic identification, is an overt resistance to the school culture and practices in the host society (Gilmore, 1991). Children who have this attitude tend to develop adversarial identities toward the mainstream language and culture, particularly the schools' sanction against their first language in school (Suárez-Orozco & Suárez-Orozco, 2001). They often actively engage in resistance to the mainstream language and culture while persistently using their first language and adhering to their ethnic community. The resistance, however, often has a significant social and emotional cost. Li (2006) points out that their resistance may further prevent them from learning the official knowledge and the codes of power necessary for doing well in school and realizing their parents' expectations. Therefore, unless more positive attitudes to both their home and mainstream cultures are fostered, these adversarial identities may in the long run be self-defeating and counterproductive (Nieto, 2002). In their study of Vietnamese youth, for example, Zhou and Bankston (1998) find that students who remain closely connected to the support system within their family and the community and who succeed in maintaining a more positive academic orientation achieve better than those who are alienated from their families and communities and who construct oppositional identities to the values of mainstream society including resistance to the norms of achievement sanctioned in school.

Another notable issue among immigrant families is the growing generation gap between the parents and the children, which can make the process of acculturation more complicated. For immigrant children, segmented assimilation can also encourage values that are often at odds with those espoused by immigrant parents, creating further conditions for a problematic mode of dissonant acculturation that may lead to downward mobility (Portes

& Rumbaut, 2001). Portes and Zhou (1993) and Portes and Rumbaut (2001) theorize that possible relationships across generations during the process of acculturation include generational consonance and dissonance. Generational consonance occurs when both parents and children remain unacculturated, or acculturate at roughly the same rate, or when the immigrant community encourages selective second-generation acculturation. In the first case, both parents and children resist learning the mainstream culture and language, which often results in family isolation within the ethnic community. The last two cases are conducive to the families' search for integration and acceptance into the social mainstream as well as their preservation of their first language and culture. However, it is more common for low-SES immigrant and refugee families who arrive with limited English and with few economic resources, and who are often segmented into inner-city ghettos, to experience the first case of generational consonance or, more often, generational dissonance. Since the first-generation parents often lack sufficient education or integration into the mainstream culture, their children, who often acquire the new language and culture more quickly than their parents, increasingly become family spokespersons and assume the roles of interpreters and translators (McBrien, 2005; Suárez-Orozco & Suárez-Orozco, 2001). As these children increasingly adopt parental roles, parents gradually lose control and the ability to exercise guidance—developments that lead to intensified parent–child conflicts, role reversal, rupture of family ties, children's abandonment of ethnic language and culture, and ultimately the loss of parental authority (Portes & Rumbaut, 1996; Zhou, 2001).

Cultural dissonance among generations is believed to have a profound effect on children's psychosocial well-being. In a review of the literature on refugee children's needs, McBrien (2005) argues that, in addition to the socio-emotional difficulties of overcoming the traumatic memories of sudden exile from their homeland (e.g., Sokoloff, Carlin, & Pham, 1984), refugee and immigrant children often experience more psycho-social problems in cultural adaptation (e.g., Eisenbruch, 1988; Nguyen, Messe, & Stollak, 1999). The different life experiences of children and parents inevitably widen the generation gap, leading to intense bicultural conflicts that push children and parents into separate social worlds (Zhou, 2001). The substantial language gap between parents and adolescents, for example, is the most salient generational dissonance that creates acculturative stress. For many of these children, to conform or to reject family histories is also a matter of how to deal with cultural conflicts between native culture and mainstream American culture. Cultural clash between the old and the new is believed to be the most important factor that causes students' psychosocial stress and identity crises. Researchers have pointed out that the clashes of values, behaviors, and attitudes between home and school culture often produce serious internal struggles for immigrant students to balance the two (Lam, 2003; Lee & Wong, 2002; Tran, 2003). For example, Vietnamese culture often emphasizes obedience, discipline, and filial piety whereas the mainstream American culture values more individual autonomy and independence. Vietnamese students' efforts to be autonomous like their American peers can create family conflicts and internal disharmony (Lam, 2003). Many of them may feel the pressure to assimilate at the expense of their own cultural heritage, or reject being assimilated into American culture, or become apathetic to preserving their cultural identity (Zhou & Bankston, 1998).

The adversarial community and school condition and the disconcerting cultural dissonance, however, impact not only low-SES immigrant or refugee students, but also the poor white working-class children who are often neglected in educational research. In the changing global economic structure that is characterized by the rapid disappearance of working-class jobs in America, many have asserted the complete eclipse of this cultural group (Gorz, 1982; Weis, 2004). Sociologists such as Weis (2004) argue that the white working class is not only alive; it has become a newly settled, distinct class fraction that has rearticulated itself in relation to the familiar groups of color in post-industrial urban centers (such as the African Americans, Yemenis, and Vietnamese in Buffalo). Children from this group, like the other racial minorities in urban areas, also experience the painful cultural dissonance in a school system modeled after middle-class values and practices (Hicks, 2002). Hicks (2002) posits that the treatment of white working-class and poor children in school systems and in society at large is also oppressively hegemonic in ways that are submerged because of a lack of class awareness and cultural sensitivity to this group. Therefore, instead of simply writing this group off, there is a need to strive for a critical understanding of this group's experiences in relation to other groups of color and vice versa—"the varying diversity they might encounter—those involving relations of ethnicity, race, gender, *and* class" (Hicks, 2002, p. 4, italics original).

This book is an attempt to address the varying diversity in ways that the different racial groups might encounter by focusing on both the productions of literacies within each family and the intersectionality of various social categories such as ethnicity, race, gender, and class in the production process across different racial and cultural groups. It documents the languages/literacies and cultural practices of everyday lives as lived by three racial groups who are a significant part of Buffalo: the Sudanese refugees, the Vietnamese refugees, and white working and/or poor families. It links the analysis of the families' literacy practices to more general ethnographic accounts of cultural beliefs and practices as the families construct certain social relations with other ethnic groups and with the schools and communities in which they reside. Through the "practices that are engaged in by, and simultaneously encircle, men, women, and children on a daily basis" (Weis, 2004, p. 4), this book depicts how these culturally different families contest institutional constraints, resist discrimination, countermand the adversarial context of the inner city, and traverse the narrow path toward success. It also illustrates how the families make sense of their everyday experiences, come to terms with their particular socio-cultural contexts, and craft their identities in relation to a constructed other in those contexts. In this sense, the families' literacy practices and learning experiences are viewed as a social construction and as part of the process of becoming culturally competent members of their community. This theoretical framework is explored in the next section.

Theoretical Understandings of Urban Schooling and Living

Cultural Models of Literacy Learning and Minority Discourses

The everyday literacy and living of the six culturally different families can be understood in relation to the theory of cultural mismatch, often referred to as a lack of alignment between the culture, language and knowledge of minority students' homes and their schools and/or other dominant institutions (Dimitriadis, 2001; Heath, 1983; Li, 2003, 2004; Purcell-Gates, 1996; Rogers, 2003). According to Gee (1989), a learner's social world can be categorized into two overarching domains: the primary discourse of the home and community and the secondary discourses of the public sphere—institutions such as the public schools. Gee (1996, 1999) later defines the two socio-cultural discourses and the different social languages within the discourses as different cultural models of literacy. That is, the different cultural beliefs in school and home discourses can be seen as different cultural models that represent their worldviews as shared within their communities and groups (D'Andrade & Strauss, 1992; Quinn & Holland, 1987). In Gee's words, a cultural model is:

> [U]sually a totally or partially unconscious explanatory theory or "story line" connected to a word—bits and pieces of which are distributed across different people in a social group—that helps to explain why the word has the different situated meanings and possibilities for the specific social and cultural groups of people it does.
>
> (Gee, 1999, p. 44)

Gee (1996, 1999) theorizes that a cultural model not only defines what is normal and to be expected but also sets up what counts as non-normal and threatening in certain contexts. Therefore, cultural models often involve certain viewpoints about what is right and wrong and what can or cannot be done to solve problems in given situations. Such functions of setting up what count as right and normal, as Gee (1996) points out, often result in rendering exclusionary actions and creating and upholding stereotypes.

Research has demonstrated that the dynamics and processes of different cultural models of literacy practices can have a significant impact on minority achievement and school reform (Gallimore & Goldenberg, 2001). Since cultural models carry within them values and perspectives about people and reality, cultural models from different cultures can "conflict in their content, in how they are used, and in values and perspectives they carry" (Gee, 1996, p. 90). For minority students who come from different cultural backgrounds, the models of their own home culture can conflict seriously with those of mainstream culture (Gee, 1996). Studies on immigrant and minority groups' literacy practices suggest that immigrant parents differ significantly in their cultural models of learning and their educated values, beliefs, and actions from their mainstream counterparts (e.g., Gallimore & Goldenberg, 2001; Goldenberg & Gallimore, 1995; Heath, 1983; Li, 2002; Valdes, 1996).

Socio-cultural Construction and Socialization of Literacies and Learning

How do children acquire these different cultural models of literacy practices? Research on language socialization indicates that language and literacy learning is part of a process of socialization through which the learner acquires particular values and relationships in the social context in which learning takes place (Schieffelin & Ochs, 1986). Ochs (1986) posits that children acquire a worldview as they acquire a language. Since the process of acquiring language is deeply affected by the process of becoming a competent member of a community, language and literacy learning is intricately linked to the construction of social roles, cultural affiliations, beliefs, values, and behavioral practices (Schieffelin & Ochs, 1986). For language minority learners who traverse two cultural worlds, the process of acquiring a language(s) and literacies may involve the intersection of multiple/different cultural values and beliefs and multiple social contexts of socialization. For such learners, as Lam (2004) observes, it is important to note that language and literacy practices do not exist in isolation from each other, just as cultures and communities do not exist as discrete entities, but rather interact with each other in various degrees of complementarity or conflict.

The multitude of interactions between different belief systems and social languages define individual learners' social identities and shape what their voice can say (Wertsch, 1991). For example, power struggles between the primary discourse and the secondary discourse may affect individual learners' choices of appropriating or "speaking" a particular social language and becoming a member of that social community. In some cases, learners are capable of repositioning themselves in contesting the official social languages and re/creating their own social languages and identities (Gutiérrez, Rymes, & Larson, 1995). Therefore, literacy learning as a social practice emphasizes the relational interdependency of agent and world, persons-in-activity and situated action; and learners' participation in learning is inherently "situated negotiation and renegotiation of meaning in the world" (Lave & Wenger, 1991, p. 51). Thus, for language minority learners who juggle between two or more languages and cultures, language socialization can be seen as:

> a site of struggle where language practices are governed by and used to produce configurations of power that determine the norms of conduct and where diverse affiliations or socialization experiences of the learner interact with each other to influence how the learner is socially positioned in any specific language learning contexts.
>
> (Lam, 2004, p. 47)

The families' experiences and their intersecting social relationships in the world of home, community, and school can be seen as a dynamic social process in which a learner is an active meaning maker (Vygotsky, 1978; Wells, 1986). This dynamic process involves complex social relationships that a learner forms with other co-constructors of knowledge in their everyday literacy activities and events. These co-constructors are members of the learners' particular socio-cultural contexts—teachers, peers, parents, and community members. Each of these co-constructors represents a voice of learning and knowing, and thus forms a multivoicedness in which multiple layers of values of knowing and learning are embodied (Bakhtin, 1981, p. 272).

Language Socialization, Social Class, and Cultural Capital

When learners are socialized into different belief systems and social languages, they are also socialized into different class-based cultures. Anyon (1980) defines social class as "a complex of social relations that one develops as one grows up—as one acquires and develops certain bodies of knowledge, skills, abilities, and traits, and as one has contact and opportunity in the world" (p. 71). These different bodies of knowledge and skills are subtle mechanisms that socialize them into different social classes and thus reproduce the class structures.

In her ethnographic study on social class and school knowledge in five different elementary schools, Anyon (1980, 1981) concludes that, even if there is a standardized curriculum, school knowledge in different SES schools is highly stratified and there are profound differences in the curriculum-in-use between schools for working-class, middle-class, and affluent groups. In the two working-class schools studied by Anyonh, the emphasis in curricula and in classrooms was on mechanical behaviors (such as carrying out procedures), simple facts, and basic skills as opposed to higher-level skills such as sustained conception. This type of school knowledge encourages the kind of cultural capital that is reproductive of the children's blue-collar working-class community. Compared with that of the working-class schools, knowledge in the middle-class school was highly commodified, in that it emphasized skills such as accumulating facts and information and generalization—skills necessary for the middle-class jobs, which are becoming increasingly industrial and clerical. In contrast, school knowledge in the affluent professional school (which had a parent population at a higher income level, who were predominantly upper-middle-class professionals) and the executive elite school (most of the fathers were top executives, e.g., presidents and vice-presidents, in major US-based multinational corporations) was radically different. The school curriculum in the executive elite school promoted knowledge that is academic, intellectual, and rigorous. The children were taught the history of "ruling groups," and were provided with opportunities to practice manipulating socially prestigious language and concepts in systematic ways. As Anyon (1980) describes, knowledge in this school was derived not from personal activity but from "following the rule of good thought, from rationality and reasoning. In many cases, knowledge involves understanding the internal structure of things" (p. 31).

Bourdieu (1977) and Bourdieu and Passerson (1977) associated these class-specific relations to the concept of "cultural capital," which further explains the school–home discursive mismatch. They argue that children from a higher SES are often socialized into highbrow cultural activities at home (such as opera, classical ballet, and classical literature), and the exposure to this cultural capital will more likely ensure their school success. These cultural "tastes," related to family lifestyles and consumption patterns, are conceptualized as class attitudes, preferences, or "*habitus*." Middle- and upper-middle-class tastes or activities, for example, include regular visits to theaters, concerts, museums, and libraries, interests in literature and art, or access to other cultural resources at home. Through these activities, parents from a higher socio-economic background establish "the intellectual climate for their children's educational aspirations, motivations to achieve, and hence, performance in schools" (Wong, 1998, p. 5). Contrariwise, children from a lower SES would not have access to these "tastes" and activities, and therefore would acquire less advantageous cultural capital and, therefore, be less likely to succeed in school. The discontinuity between school and home cultural capital hinders the educational advancement of lower-SES students in many ways, since school cultures are often based on and legitimize the values and behaviors of the middle and upper middle class.

The complex workings of school sanction and home socialization that lead to class reproduction are further explained in Willis's (1977) explanation about how middle-class kids get middle-class jobs and working-class kids get working-class jobs. Willis illustrates that the working-class lads are socialized into an oppositional identity toward school as "enemy" culture; and their choices and decisions often lead them to take on their fathers' union jobs. He explains that there are also institutional sanctions at work in the meantime in this reproduction: once a working-class boy begins to differentiate himself from school authority there is a powerful cultural charge behind him to complete the process; on the other hand, when students from the middle and upper classes begin to differentiate, there are powerful community pressures for them to abandon the attempt.

Willis's study suggests that human agency can play a significant role in shaping schooling experiences and class locations. Brantlinger (2003) argues that class stratification is not a benign, chance occurrence but the result of people's intentions and informed agency. It comprises experiences, relationships, and ensembles of systematic relationships that not only set particular "choices" and "decisions" at particular times but also give meanings and definitions to these "choices" and "decisions" (Willis, 1977, p. 1). In understanding how classes are lived in isolated residential areas, researchers such as Brantlinger (2003), Lareau (2003), and Walkerdine, Lucey, and Melody (2001) maintain that the intentions and actions of people from different classes (working and middle classes) play an important role in the creation and reproduction of social inequality. In their psychosocial analysis of young women's complex positions in the labor market, Walkerdine, Lucey, and Melody (2001), for example, talked about how young working-class women's self-invention and self-regulation of different class-based signs (their dream of becoming somebody in uncertain times) has become the central way to cope with the contradictory social demands in their lives. In Lareau's (1989, 2003) and Brantlinger's (2003) studies on how parents negotiate class (dis) advantages, they both demonstrate that parental agencies and actions have a significant impact on their children's class formation. Middle-class parents, for example, through efforts of concerted cultivation and relegating others to a lower status in school and in other institutions, manage to negotiate more class privileges for their children and therefore maintain the disparaging epithets of social class distinctions. Working-class and poor parents, however, lack such strategies and power to negotiate similar class advantages for their children's schooling. Instead, they often socialize their children in a cultural logic of childrearing that emphasizes accomplishment of natural growth and this emphasis is out of sync with standards of institutions such as schools (Lareau, 2003). Furthermore, as Willis (1977) demonstrates in his study of working-class "lads", many working-class and poor children often internalize their class locations, and some of them even create counter-school identities and oppositional cultures that further deprive them of class advantages.

In this study, the six culturally diverse families' socio-cultural contexts (school, community, and home) in which they learn about literacies and their meanings, values, and beliefs as ways of learning are explored. I consider not only institutional forces that sustain their continuous engagement with literacies but also socio-cultural and socio-economic factors that facilitate or deter their investment in learning. Viewing the families' literacy practices and learning experiences as social construction and as part of the process of becoming culturally competent members of a community, I connect the analysis of the home literacy practices with more general accounts of cultural beliefs and practices as the families construct/form certain relationships with schools and the communities in which they reside.

Researching Families, Researching Literacies: This Study

Collins and Blot (2003) indicate that the "understanding of literacy requires detailed, in-depth accounts of actual practice in different cultural settings" (p. 64). Since my purpose in this research is to understand the "maps of meaning" in the literacy practices of the six culturally different families, I employed an ethnographic approach that allows me to reconstruct the realities as lived by the families in their socio-cultural worlds (Goetz & LeCompte, 1984; Spindler & Spindler, 1982). In order to provide rich descriptive data about the contexts, activities and beliefs of families, I used a variety of ethnographic methods including semi-structured interviews and participant observations (Creswell, 2005). These methods, highly context dependent, allow researchers to have direct and prolonged engagement with the participants in diverse settings such as school, home and community.

In addition to elucidating the meanings and perceptions underlying the families' everyday realities, I am also interested in discovering "system relations between specific sites" (Carspecken, 1996, p. 206). Instead of simply uncovering culture for culture's sake, I confront the value-free facts and attempt to "describe, analyze and open to scrutiny otherwise hidden agendas, power centers, and assumptions that inhibit, repress, and constrain" the lived experiences of the inner-city families (Thomas, 1993, p. 3). That is, I investigate not only the superficial appearance of culture (the commonsense realities) but also the social entrapment—the various mechanisms for assuring social harmony with and conformity to interactional norms, organizational rules, institutional patterns, and ideological positions. In this sense, this study is also a critical ethnography.

The six families were selected through Rainbow Elementary school. They were part of a larger study on school and home literacy connections of fourth-grade students. Initially, a parent questionnaire was sent home through the school to gain information about the languages spoken at home.

About thirteen parents (out of sixty-five) of the fourth graders returned the questionnaires. These parents were later invited to participate in the study as the focal families. Owing to the frequent changes of addresses and phone numbers of some families, the six families with whom I maintained constant contact became the final focal families for this study.

Like many other researchers, I had help from two of my research assistants—a Japanese doctoral student and a white American doctoral student, Evelyn, who was also a Title I reading teacher in the school. The observational data from the school were collected by the school teacher while my Japanese assistant and I mostly conducted the fieldwork with the families in their home and communities. We also conducted semi-structured interviews with three school teachers outside the school settings in their homes or my office.

To better understand the social context of the families and the schools, I also interviewed two staff members who work closely with minority parents and community members in the city: Nelli, a Hispanic parent liaison, and Marilyn, a white site facilitator for several school initiatives in helping minority children overcome non-academic barriers to improve achievement. I conducted a semi-structured, two-hour interview with each of Nelli and Marilyn in their schools and another two-hour group interview with both of them in my university office. I also interviewed Professor Marshall, a white college professor whose specialty is in teacher preparation for urban schools. He and his wife, a former principal of a Buffalo public school, have been community activists who advocate desegregation in the city schools. The interview also took place in the university and lasted for two hours.

During May 2004 and July 2006, my Japanese research assistant and I visited the families and carried out observations and interviews. Since each family had different schedules and different rapport with us, the number of visits to the families varied. For example, while we visited most families two to three times, we visited the Torkeris and the Tons more than six times. We were also invited to attend church events and cultural activities with these families. Depending on our rapport with the families, the number of our telephone conversations with the six families also varied.

However, all the six families were formally interviewed twice at their houses during the research process. The two interviews were conducted to understand the families' beliefs and values about their children's education and to gain more specific information about the literacy practices in terms of their access to literacy materials and their uses. Each of the interviews lasted approximately two hours. Each interview was audio-taped and subsequently transcribed. At times, on account of language barriers, we occasionally asked the children to translate some of the questions and answers. In addition to these interviews, observations and casual conversations with the participants were also recorded in field notes.

Data analysis in this study was ongoing throughout the data collection period. Content and thematic analysis was used to examine field notes and transcripts whereby themes relating to the research questions were identified and illustrated by using verbatim comments from formal and informal interviews (Creswell, 2005). A coding system was created to identify patterns from the participant responses. Based on the identified patterns, a table of contents that contain bigger themes was created to visualize the data in a categorical organization. To better demonstrate the "true value of the original multiple realities" (Lincoln & Guba, 1985, p. 296), direct quotes from the formal and informal interviews were used to give voice to the participants.

Although our presence as researchers may at times change the temporary dynamics of the family routines, our multicultural backgrounds were not seen as abnormal to these families, as they see diversity every day in their neighborhood. Initially, I had doubts whether we, as outsiders to the families and their culture, would be able to cross the cultural boundaries and gain a meaningful understanding of the families. Though we occasionally experienced language barriers (which were often smoothed out by the bilingual children), our positive and pleasant experiences with the families suggest that it is possible for outsiders of a group to study across boundaries, and many other researchers have successfully done so (e.g., Dimitriadis, 2001, 2003; Lareau, 2003; Waters, 1999). I myself have conducted research with members from other cultures such as Filipino (Li, 2000) and white middle-class teachers (Li, 2006). As Lareau (2003) points out, the "groups" at hand are always diverse and there are many ways to cross the divide. In fact, I found that my "foreigner" background constantly served as a bridge between me and the families, as we shared similar experiences of moving to America, learning English, locating useful pragmatic information (such as a cheap phone card to call home), and finding affordable housing. Since I came from the university that they aspired their children to attend in the future, the families, especially the refugee families, often turned to me for information about schools for their children or for themselves and about strategies to help their children learn better. Anne Torkeri, for example, asked me to find information about the English as a second language programs in the school and about a free medication program for her son Fred. Mahdi Myer asked me to find more information about the bachelor degree program in business administration at the university, because he was interested in furthering his studies. Lo Phan and Dao Ton both inquired about how to get into the best high schools, how to diagnose learning problems, and how to support their children's reading at home.

Organization of the Book

Chapter 2: Where the Stories Began: The City and its Schools

This chapter situates the families within the larger socio-historical contexts of the inner-city community and the society where they reside, focusing on the racial, economic, and educational tensions between the minorities and the mainstream society, and between the suburban and urban divide. It illustrates the prevailing racial, economic, and residential segregation and the rising problems of violence, drugs, and the continuing decay that have plagued the city for decades. This chapter also describes how the racial, economic, and residential segregation patterns have significantly influenced the making of the school systems in the city. It explains how various socio-economic and socio-political factors have resulted in the declining quality of, and the fragility of public confidence in, the city's public schools.

This chapter also details the West Side schools the children attend. It describes the transient nature of the community and the levels of stress experienced by the schools' ESL programs and curricula, as well as the degree of teacher preparedness demanded by the large immigrant and refugee influx into schools such as Rainbow Elementary. It shows that the programs are insufficient for meeting the needs of the students; and the curricula in the schools are highly scripted and lack multicultural substance. Teaching in a multicultural school without multicultural substance, most teachers push students toward fast assimilation and transition into the mainstream language and culture. The chapter also examines the teachers' and staff's perspectives on minority students, and of parents' involvement in their children's schooling. Their narratives demonstrate that the teachers and staff have conflicted feelings about inner-city parents. On the one hand, they have apathy toward the parents; on the other hand, they believe that there is a widespread "culture of poverty" that has become a barrier to the parents' active involvement in their children's schooling.

Chapter 3: Being Vietnamese, Becoming Somebody

This chapter brings readers into the worlds of two Vietnamese refugee families—the Ton family and the Phan family. Three aspects of Vietnamese culture—appropriate gender roles, strict discipline, and high expectations—are prominent in their everyday life and their educational values. In both families, the girls are raised with the Vietnamese ideal of "the virtuous woman," which calls not only for passive obedience but also for living up to higher behavioral standards than those held for their brothers. Hanh Phan, for example, is not allowed to go out of the house or call her friends on the phone whereas her brother Chinh can go out to play at any time. The parents also hold high expectations for the children's academic achievement. For example, they expect their children to become professionals, such as a doctor or a tennis player. Though the older children are considered successful in school, the younger children in both families have experienced serious difficulties in reading and writing in English. Since the parents are not proficient in English, they rely on their older children to fulfill their everyday needs and to negotiate with the school. Given this, the parents constantly experience difficulties in communicating with the school. To the children, the role-reversal, together with strict cultural values and high (sometimes unrealistic) expectations, has resulted in serious psycho-social stress. The two families' experiences demonstrate that cultural beliefs, parents' SES status, and their proficiency in English are factors that shape their children's literacy learning at home, which is distinctly different from their school experiences.

Chapter 4: Being Sudanese, Being Black

This chapter describes the home and school literacy experiences of two Sudanese refugee families—the Torkeri family and the Myer family. I describe the multifaceted factors that influence the two families' adjustment to their lives in America, including their beliefs and values relating to education, expectations for their children, home literacy environments, and interaction with their children's schools. Like many other immigrant families, the two families have experienced multilayered difficulties adjusting to the life in the United States, such as language differences, changes in gender roles and cultural identity, employment, and community socialization patterns (e.g., isolation). Both families assume a very strong Sudanese cultural identity and they differentiate themselves from African Americans. They believe that education should be community oriented and academically challenging and that adults (both teachers and parents) should be the role models for students.

The parents in both families try to enforce Sudanese ways of learning at home while fighting against school practices (e.g., the ESL pullout programs that take their children away from regular class and the school's policy for fast transition to English literacy) that they regard as a hindrance to their children's academic progress. Anne Torkeri, for example, has repeatedly taken the issue up to the officials in city hall, but unfortunately was unsuccessful. Realizing that it was fruitless to work against the schools, the families decide to "work" the system by moving their younger children out of the school. The families' constant struggles against the urban school system mirrors increasing tensions and discords between the school's cultural values and those of the minority families, which in turn results in a further cultural mismatch between their learning experiences at home and in school.

Chapter 5: Being White, Being the Majority in the Minority

In this chapter, I present an account of two white families living in the multicultural neighborhood—the Clayton family and the Sassano family. I also highlight the parents' beliefs and values relating to education, expectations for their children, home literacy environments, and interaction with their children's schools as well as their identity formation as the majority in the minority. In both families, the children's educational experiences are heavily influenced by their mothers' negative school experiences; nonetheless both mothers highly value education and are determined to protect their children from repeating their school experiences. For example, Pauline Clayton, who had a learning disability and dropped out of high school because her teachers did not care, was very sensitive to her daughter Kate's socio-emotional well-being and the teachers' attitudes. When Kate was not treated with respect in early grades, Pauline transferred her to another school and back to Rainbow Elementary a year later when she heard there was a good teacher. Later, in order for their children to be in a better neighborhood, Pauline managed to move to a predominantly white working-class community even though it meant a further difficulty getting around without a car.

In both families, literacy practices emphasize "sustained talk" (Hicks, 2002) among family members, cooperation, and relationship building. Both families believe in the power of open discussion and conversation in transferring knowledge and values. The mothers engage in long talks with the children at the dinner table or in other contexts (e.g., on a bus) about different topics, ranging from school life to sex, drugs, and crimes in the neighborhood. Like the Treaders in Rogers' (2003) study, in these two families, home literacy practices are processes of apprenticeship through which children learn not only the meaning of reading and writing, but also social roles. In the Sassano family, for example, reading is considered a family activity in which every member is involved either by reading on his or her own or reading with each other. In the Clayton family, working together for a reading contest or for a school project is the family norm. These home literacy practices are different from the schooled literacy practices that emphasize individual mastery and decontextualized practices. Such a cultural mismatch places the children in a position of disadvantage when they go to school.

Chapter 6: Multicultural Families and Multiliteracies: Tensions, Conformity, and Resistance to Urban Schooling

This chapter examines the meaning of the six families' inner-city living and literacy practices. It discusses the tensions and the intricate relationships among race, ethnicity, class positions, social life, and urban schooling. The tensions are seen as products of the families' "discursive dual competence" that turns literacy, culture, race, ethnicity, and class into terms of contestation (Baumann, 1996). I argue that the families are dual cultural beings who struggle to construct their own story-lines by both resisting and conforming to the dominant social discourses in literacy, race, class, and gender. These tensions have significant consequences on how the families raise their next generation and negotiate inner-city schooling.

Four forms of tensions are explored. First, I discuss the tensions around the literacy and culture duality—the cultural conflicts around school–home literacy practices, parental involvement, and the politics of difference underlying the mismatches between school and home. I argue that urban schooling is a culturally contested terrain in which the power struggle between school and home is in a constant flux. Second, I discuss the complexities of urban living in relation to the duality of gender politics in the six families. I explain that reconfiguration of gender roles in the inner city is dependent on both culture and context, that is, how the families negotiate "new gendered practices" in the urban context is influenced by their previous cultural and economic experiences. These new gendered practices also shape profoundly how they raise the next generation. Following this, I examine the race and ethnicity duality—the intricate relationships among race, ethnicity, and urban socialization that further alienate the families in their socio-cultural and racial locations. Finally, I examine the duality of class positioning that contributes to the miscommunication and disconnection between school and home. I argue that these members of America's "rainbow underclass" do not ascribe to the "culture of poverty" or choose inadequate schools; rather, it is the "make-believe" school curriculum (one that lacks multicultural substance) as well as the various levels of ideological hegemony that put them at a class disadvantage. By investigating these multiple dualities in their literacy and living, I argue that the tensions and contradictions the six families face are not just isolated, individual issues but closely related to wider social structures and unequal power relationships.

Chapter 7: Culturally Contested Literacies and the
Education of America's "Rainbow Underclass"

This chapter presents the implications and conclusions of this study. I argue that, to overcome the adversities of cultural and contextual barriers in the inner city, minority families and children need to become successful cultural translators who are able to move across diverse physical and social borders and rewrite the hegemonic domination of certain discourses, instead of just reproducing them. To do so, it is not enough to rely on the families' individual empowerment and agency or self-help. We also need concerted efforts from multiple parties in the community including the local government, the schools, the teachers, and the policy makers to help urban teachers, minority parents, and children become successful *cultural translators* and *border-crossers*.

For teachers, I propose a new pedagogical framework, a *culture pedagogy*, to empower educators with the theoretical foundation upon which they can develop new curricula to help students first reconcile diverse cultural differences and consequently become successful cultural translators. It emphasizes not only students' competence (that is, knowledge building) but also their performance (that is, production and action based on the knowledge acquired) in understanding the politics of differences. For parents, I recommend a problem-posing literacy program that focuses on issues and themes brought forward *by* the parents about their own lived realities and ways to transform them. I suggest that this program must use the languages and literacies of the parents and their lived realities as texts, utilize a variety of community resources, and implement/seek actions derived from their thematic investigations with parents and educators being co-actors in the endeavor for change.

2

Where the Stories Began:
The City and its Schools

> Until there is a genuine commitment to address the social context of schooling—to confront the "urban" condition—it will be impossible to bring about significant and sustainable improvement in urban public schools.
>
> **–Pedro Noguera, *City Schools and the American Dream* (2003)**

The City

The year 2005 was a historical year for the city of Buffalo. Two unusual things happened during that year. First, a local politician, Byron Brown, was elected as the city's new mayor. It was unusual because he was the first new mayor in twelve years and he was the first black mayor of the city in its history. Second, the city's public school board conducted a nationwide search, hiring a new African American Superintendent, Dr. James Williams. This was unusual because he was offered an annual salary of over $200,000 and a $100,000 bonus package from the private sector, while the national average for the position was $71,713 and the median household income for the city was $24,536 (Buffalo Geek, 2006). No matter what the price tags were for the hires, the two historical events showed the city's determination to make some serious changes to shake up the power structure, revitalize its declining economy and revive its crumbling school system. Both hires also signified a collective desire for a "new" Buffalo—"a city of hope and opportunities." As many African American residents in the community commented, they really "wanted a change."

The new mayor was elected to tackle some problems that have plagued the city for several decades: the economic slowdown, deteriorating neighborhoods, and the increasing racial divide. Many factors have resulted in the decline of the city with a glorious past. In 1825 the completion of the Erie Canal opened a direct route from Buffalo to Hudson River and to New York City, allowing Buffalo to become one of the most important centers of transshipment. By 1910, Buffalo had become the greatest grain port in the world and the second largest mill port, railway terminus, and steelmaking producer (Dillaway, 2006). The economic growth attracted waves of immigrants both from the American countryside and from Europe. In the city of Buffalo, there appeared different ethnic neighborhoods such as a Jewish North Buffalo neighborhood, an Italian West Side neighborhood, a Polish East Side neighborhood, and the Irish South Buffalo neighborhood. The African Americans from other parts of the country also came. In 1980, African Americans constituted 10 percent of the city's population, and this figure had increased to 37.27 percent by 2005. Though some African American males were allowed to enter manufacturing jobs as overall demand for labor grew, African Americans in general were excluded from those neighborhoods near the mills, which were originally built as company towns to house a workforce of mostly European descent. Consequently, most of the city's African American population lived near downtown in the northeast side of the city, several miles north of the steel mills. Distance alone prevented many African Americans from working in the mills, and those who did were generally excluded from steelworkers' unions. As a result, African Americans were confined to a specific geographic region of the city—a region removed from jobs in the mills to the south (Krieg, 2005). A white resident wrote on his personal blog, "I think the idea is that after the Civil Rights movement Southern Blacks moved up north and then started to work in the factories, which made the white immigrant offspring angry. So they divided the city in half and put each one on its own side. Sadly, they are by no means equal."

Buffalo's strong economic growth lasted until the Great Depression of the 1930s, when the city defaulted on its debts and went bankrupt. Although the two world wars and the Korean War had helped the economic revival, the economic decline worsened with the opening of the Saint Lawrence Seaway in 1959, which allowed ships to move directly from the Midwest to the Atlantic Ocean, bypassing Buffalo. As a result, Buffalo's commercial and shipping industry contracted sharply. In the meantime, however, the labor movement became increasingly militant and a series of strikes or strike threats significantly increased the wages of production workers. This high cost of wages precipitated the flight of manufacturers and corporate headquarters and led to a high unemployment rate among workers. According to a Department of Housing and Urban Development report, Buffalo's manufacturing workforce fell by 70 percent between 1970 and 2000. This high unemployment rate further aggravated the decline of the Buffalo economy (Dillaway, 2006; *Encyclopedia of American History*, 2006).

The declining economy also heightened the racial tensions between the white and black populations and between the city and the suburbs. The gap in income levels between the minorities and their white counterparts continues to widen. According to the 2000 US census data, median household income for local minorities is still only half of white households, and the poverty rate in the metro region is at least four times higher among minority communities than among the suburban whites. For example, in 2000, the median household income was $28,484 for whites and only $19,795 for African Americans, $21,141 for Native Americans, $18,098 for Asians, and $17,536 for Hispanics. In terms of poverty rates, only 8.6 percent of whites were reported to live in poverty, while minorities' poverty rates were up to four times higher: among Hispanics 36.2 percent, African Americans 33.8 percent, American Indians 28.0 percent, and Asians 23.0 percent (US Census Bureau, 2000). John Logan, director of the Lewis Mumford Center for Comparative Urban and Regional Research in Albany, noted, "The disparities are quite sharp . . . and it really hasn't changed much over the past 10 years" (cited in Rey, 2002). Others, like Lumon Ross, president of the Black Chamber of Commerce of Western New York, as cited in Rey (2002), believed that "things appear to be stepping backward."

As mentioned in the previous chapter, the city had witnessed a steady population decline as well as a "white flight" since the 1970s. The demographic shifts had changed the neighborhood characteristics of the city. Today, only a few of the original ethnic neighborhoods (e.g., the Irish Americans in South Buffalo) still exist. The original Polish Americans in the East Side have been largely replaced by African Americans. The Italian Americans originally in the West Side have gradually moved to North Buffalo. Now the West Side has become a melting pot of many ethnicities such as African, African American, Asian, and Middle Eastern, with Latino culture being the strongest influence. In addition to these changes, the "white flight" also resulted in a decrease in tax revenues and resources, which in turn led to a decline in public services for the city. For example, in comparison with the suburbs, the city is known for three things: the snow not getting plowed; police not coming when called; and the garbage not being collected on time.

Despite the rapid demographic changes, the economic and political power had been dominated by a group of elites known as WASPs (white, Anglo-Saxon, Protestant), and their descendents. According to Dillaway (2006), WASPs control the banking industry along with the businesses closely tied to land-based development, such as real estate, insurance, and law. Although various white ethnic groups have been adopted by WASPs over the years, the African American community has historically been excluded from the elite socio-political groups. As Dillaway (2006) describes,

> Politically, the African American community remained outside the patronage systems of the Italian, Irish, and Polish mayors . . . The black community was not on the elite leadership's radar screen, other than in its worries about riots"
>
> (p. 16)

Therefore, while the black professionals, entrepreneurs and workers fend for themselves, the elite, as a social class, is "most concerned with retaining prestige and power" (p. 42).

The power struggles (or imbalance) between the black and white communities were evident in almost every sector of the city's development. For example, to help the whites in the suburbs to commute to offices downtown (in some neighborhoods, suburbanites, not the local residents, get most of the jobs in the city, sometimes as many as 95 percent of the jobs), an expressway was constructed in the mid-1960s. This construction, however, destroyed the East Side's most beautiful tree-lined avenue and cut the black community's most affluent middle-class neighborhood in two (Dillaway, 2006). Several years later in 1978, construction began on a Metro Rail that was intended to be the first line to serve the whole of the city and suburbs. The urban section was completed and opened in 1984, but no funding was available to extend the lines into the suburbs, to the Amherst campus of the University at Buffalo. It has been reported that subsequent efforts to obtain funding for feeder lines have met with little success. The real reason, as many have told me, is "People don't want it to come to the suburbs." Because of its short length, the line is nicknamed the "subway to nowhere."

Efforts to keep African Americans within the city boundaries also went on very subtly in the real estate business, resulting in the inability of many blacks to move into white neighborhoods, especially into the suburbs. Krieg (2005) argues that the classic pattern of "white flight" to suburbs was, to an extent, spurred by a racist housing policy. He points out that the Federal Housing Authority controls real estate markets by issuing credit ratings, which are determined by the demographic composition of the community. Consequently, communities with diverse racial populations are given low credit ratings, thereby driving down home ownership. In this way, white homeowners were directed into the suburbs and African American residents pushed and pulled into the vacated neighborhoods of the East Side by falling real estate values.

In Buffalo, when the blacks start to move into a neighbourhood, the whites begin to move out. A good example is the old Italian neighborhood in the West Side, which is now a multi-ethnic area with African Americans and low-SES immigrants and refugees. Similarly, in the University Heights area at the edge of the city, where many blacks and students live, the real estate value has fallen in contrast to the rises of the previous few decades. My own story of selling my house in a predominantly white community, Williamsville, where I lived for two years prior to moving to Michigan, well illustrates the race relations between the city and the suburbs. My first buyers were a young black couple who were also selling their house in the city. From the first day the couple came to see the house, my agent was suspicious of the couple, warning me to be careful. Eventually, the black couple had proper mortgage papers and we moved on to house inspection. From the mortgage papers, we learned that the wife came from a well-to-do family in New York City, as her parents owned her present home and they were also financing her new home purchase. During the inspection, a white male neighbor on the street—I had never met him and thus he had never been into my house—came over and intervened in the inspection by telling lies about the house. As a result, the black couple left without even completing the inspection and the sale was over. When I went to talk to one of my neighbors about this man's behavior, I learned that racism might underlie his behavior and that the neighborhood had successfully forced out a black resident before.

Buffalo's racial divide is also related to its high crime rate, gang activities, and drug problems. Whereas a suburb such as Amherst has been rated by Morgan Quitno Press as the nation's safest city since 1997, the city of Buffalo has reported a rising number of homicides and other crimes. For example, the city saw a 67 percent increase in its murder rate and a 30 percent increase in its forcible rape rate in 2001. In 2004, the total crime index was 20,668, including 3,938 violent crimes such as murders, rapes, robberies, and aggravated assault and 16,730 property crimes. The average crime rate per 100,000 people in the city was 7,296.2, whereas the national average was 4,627.9 per 100,000 people. These high numbers have earned Buffalo a reputation as one of the highest homicide centers in the country for a population base of its size. The declining infrastructure and subsequent rise of drug- and gang-related violence contributed to the city's serious crime problems. According to a report by the Department of Community Development (2003), "white flight" had left many communities with a proliferation of abandoned houses that would eventually become "drug dens" supporting the storage, trafficking, and marketing of illegal narcotics. The rising number of these drug dens not only brought drugs and gun- and gang-related violence into many Buffalo neighborhoods but also created a downward spiral in the quality of life for residents, paralyzing many in fear. The West Side in particular has become increasingly dangerous nowadays. In fact, on July 14, 2006, the *Buffalo News* reported that Buffalo's West Side has "become a war zone" for gangs (Thomas, 2006). Two violent youth gangs—with members as young as ten years old—were responsible for three killings amid at least a dozen shootings over a six-month period.

The rising number of homicides and continuing decay in the city a year after the election of Byron Brown was disappointing for residents both in the city and in the suburbs. Though Byron Brown gave himself an "A" for his first-year performance, critics have pointed out that he had failed to address the issues that are vital to the quality of life in the city (Meyer, 2006). Apparently, appointing a black mayor was not a magical pill that could cure the persistent urban problems overnight or, in this case, over a period of a year. Instead, it generated what McCarthy, Rodriguez, Meeham, David, Wilson-Brown, Godina, Supryia and Buendia (2005) call "a discourse of suburban resentment and fear of encirclement" by racial diversities and dangers from the depressed inner city. In 2006, the suburban police decided to join force with the city police in several of its drug raids to help eliminate the roots of the drug problem and prevent it from further spreading to the suburbs.

The declining economy and the rising violence and drugs in the city had in turn worsened the racial relations between the blacks and the whites. Whereas the whites blame the blacks for the existing urban problems, the blacks see themselves as the victim of white racism. On the one hand, the economic conditions of poverty and helplessness have clearly made several black neighborhoods a breeding ground for racist ideology (Hiestand & Maloney, 2005). The rising violence and drug problems caused a racial resentment against the blacks among whites. For example, in 2005, African American families in the Seneca–Babcock neighborhood had withstood smashed windows, thrown bricks, racist slurs, and death threats from gangs of white racist youths. KKK graffiti defaced the neighborhood. Finally, in July 2005, when members of an African American family were brutally beaten, the public as well as the media for the first time openly "clarified the serious problems in the community and exposed the urgent need to address them" (Hiestand & Maloney, 2005, p. 1). On the other hand, the blacks perceive that it is racism that is obstructing the progress of the city's revival. As a local college professor, Professor Marshall, an activist against racial segregation in Buffalo, points out, "Whites are still generally perceived as privileged. The [blacks] feel that the power base, to a great extent, is there." In their award-winning action research paper that addresses community revitalization in Buffalo, Taylor and Cole (2001) argue that the failure of the decades-old community revitalization movement in Buffalo inner-city neighborhoods is due to the structural racism and practices that have infused marginal resources into the poor neighborhoods—resources that are below the threshold level and insignificant for making any overall improvement.

The black and white divide was further complicated by two additional racial discourses. One was the "anti-gaming" movement, which was also regarded by the Natives as an anti-Indian racist movement. In 2003, the Seneca Indians proposed setting up a gaming casino in Buffalo's downtown. Even though the political leaders including Governor George Pataki and the then Buffalo Mayor Anthony Masiello supported the proposal, many of the community members were against it. Concerned residents formed Citizens for a Better Buffalo, an anti-casino group, and initiated an anti-gaming and casino movement. When the County Executive, Joel Giambra, turned down the downtown casino proposal, the Seneca Indians proposed to build it in a Buffalo suburb, Cheektowaga. This new proposal, however, led a group of city business leaders to file a lawsuit to halt the plan in the suburb and to locate the casino within the city limits. In the hope that the casino would generate revenue and businesses that would revive the depressed city, the city leaders eventually agreed to build a casino in downtown Buffalo. The Citizens for a Better Buffalo and the Coalition Against Gaming in New York (CAGNY) then also filed a lawsuit in order to keep the casino out of the city. The anti-gaming movement, however, was seen by many as an act of anti-Indian racism. A syndicated columnist and professor of journalism and media studies at Buffalo State College in New York, Michael Niman (2006), argues that the anti-gaming movement is

> the maintenance of a power dynamic that privileges non-Natives at the cost of disempowering Native nations . . . By focusing on Indian gaming and not gaming in general, by joining forces with UCE [Upstate Coalition for Equality] and by admitting leadership that is not opposed to gaming, CAGNY is crossing the line from being an anti-gaming group to an anti-Indian group.

The other racial discourse was related to the national debate on the issues concerning illegal immigrants, especially those of Hispanic backgrounds from the south border. In December 2005, the House of Representatives passed the Border Protection, Antiterrorism, and Illegal Immigration Control Act (HR 4437). The bill emphasizes enforcement efforts, including penalizing employers who hire illegal immigrants and tougher controls at the US–Mexican border. It is believed to reflect the anti-illegal immigration mood in the House, as it proposed strong steps, including building a 700-mile fence along the US–Mexico border and imposing stricter penalties on employers of illegal workers (Pan, 2006). The bill provoked nationwide demonstrations and protests. After much heated debate, the Senate passed the Comprehensive Immigration Reform Act of 2006 in May 2006 to address issues of integrating the millions of illegal immigrants who were already residing in the United States into American life (Pan, 2006). Though the Senate Act grants amnesty and provides a path to citizenship for a majority of the estimated twelve million illegal immigrants in the country, it has created a deeper rift between the Hispanic and white communities across the country. In Buffalo, in one of the on-line discussion forums, a resident compared illegal immigrants to the city's rampant rat problem. In Buffalo's multi-ethnic West Side, where the Hispanic population (e.g., Puerto Ricans) has the strongest influence, the national movement had created an anti-Hispanic sentiment that had made a lot of Hispanic people angry. As Nelli, a Mexican parent liaison in a West Side elementary school, commented,

> A lot of the Hispanic people, they're even upset with the media . . . I think it's definitely going to divide them more than before . . . Right now, the Hispanic community is being targeted. Before, it was "keep anyone who looks Middle Eastern out of here." And now they're switching to "let's put up our borders. Let's stop the Mexicans from coming in"—which makes everybody angry . . . It's divisive, therefore, the Hispanics, they're not doing as well in school. It's like . . . with the African Americans, they're still under . . . the segregation for the longest time, so they're [also] falling under that.

A site facilitator for a West Side school initiative, Marilyn, a white woman who lives in the suburbs, concurred with this view. She observed,

> [On] the micro level, it is going to cause more division between the white race and the Hispanic race, because we all see, "Oh, the White people don't want you." This is from what I've seen on TV, "You white people came over here, you stole our country from us. You came, you took half of Mexico from us. You didn't have a visa. Nobody gave you permission and it was okay. And now you're getting mad at us, because we're in your country." So I think it's going to divide the races.

These racial discourses have formed new racial and social class alliances in the city. As Marilyn noted, "They see themselves in this together." The minorities, though living separately in their own ethnic communities within the city, hold similar attitudes toward the whites. Professor Marshall at a local college shared the same observation: "One thing both groups [African Americans and Hispanics] have in common is they see whites as, if not the enemy, at least an obstacle ... the southeastern Asians here have the same perceptions of whites." Nelli, a Mexican herself, agrees:

> I believe that the Hispanic people think the white people are like the enemy because they are the ones who get it all, have it all, and they're the ones putting the Hispanic people down. I mean, that's a constant event in California, it's like, you know, all the white people don't want Hispanics here. All the white people don't want the Puerto Ricans, don't want the Mexicans ... there's just that fight.

Though there are macro-level racial alliances, at a micro level, racial relations play out very differently as each racial group is also very diverse. According to Professor Marshall, though there is a big white–minority divide, more conflict is actually reflected in the poor whites' relations to other minorities, especially in the West Side. He explains,

> If you are looking at the public schools in particular—the tension is much more between the poor whites and the minority groups. A part of the reason is [they see an] obvious threat to them—the whites are now very much in the minority. What do they do? They can't, they haven't been able to escape, for whatever reasons, but they certainly are threatened. If you go to south Buffalo and look at the few remaining Catholic schools ... you will find a concentration of these poor white kids.

In the city, being called "white" is considered an insult among the minorities such as Hispanics and blacks. Nelli explains,

> One time a little boy who spoke Hispanic and somebody was calling him white, and he was extremely, extremely offended ... It's very much of an insult, because nobody wants to be white, wants to be referred to

as white. So the kids don't see it as a positive thing. As far as the parents, they are—they still feel very intimidated by a white person.

Among the black community, there are tensions between African Americans and Africans. According to Professor Marshall,

Many whites have a very different perspective on an African immigrant than an African American . . . A part of that is the assumption that the immigrants are here by choice and are going to work hard, and that they will be able to achieve, and they haven't had the opportunities that America offers, whereas there is the notion that African Americans have had that and squandered it . . . a fair amount of tension that exists and a part of it still has to do with attitudes toward education . . . Even those who have a little or no education before coming, as the case of some of the African immigrants coming from camps, Kenya or places like that, where they've had very little formal education. Even there, there seems to be an understanding or an expectation that education is a way up and out.

Marilyn's view well represents the different perceptions between the two groups:

The African Americans here don't really pay a lot of attention to the Africans—the immigrants that are coming in . . . I think that the African Americans in this country have so drilled into their heads, "oh, you know, we are Africans . . . we were wrongly brought over here by these mean evil white people, and they don't understand us, they don't understand our culture." Then you get the true modern-day Africans who are coming over, and there are no similarities other than the color of their skin . . . I think they're resentful of that, these are the true Africans, and that it's not anything like what they're trying to tell themselves and everybody else . . . some of the African Americans that are born and raised in this country . . . they don't want to assimilate. They want to stay on the outside; they want to see themselves as being oppressed, and the evil white man . . . look what you've done, you owe me, you owe me, you owe me. Whereas the Africans who come over here are like, "What can we do?" It's like a game; what can we do to play the game, and how can I win it; teach me everything you know, and I am going to win this game.

The Hispanic community had a similar view on African Americans. Nelli explains,

They don't like the African Americans . . . I've talked to the parents and to moms. They don't see them as equals per se, they just kind of see them as there they are. You know, they are kind of there, they're the ones that get all the help, they're the ones who make the most trouble. They're looked upon in a negative way.

Interestingly, even though the Hispanics see the blacks as the problems for drugs and violence in the community, many of them also wish that they were black because "if they were black, they would automatically get welfare . . . because white people are afraid of the black people" (Nelli).

According to Nelli, however, the Hispanics themselves, especially the Puerto Ricans, are seen as having similar attitudes to the African Americans. In general, the Puerto Ricans are "viewed as lazy, like the men are lazy . . . 'cause the men don't like to work. They just want to live off the woman . . . they don't have a strong work ethics." They are also seen as, like the African Americans, not wanting to be assimilated. Marilyn shares her opinion:

> because there's so much transiency among Puerto Ricans—they go back and forth to Puerto Rico, and I don't know that they have put down the roots that maybe African Americans have. So, maybe they see it more as "this is our territory, this is our home, [Buffalo] is where we have been."

The Asians, on the other hand, are often seen through a "model minority" lens and are left out of the major racial discourses. They are often praised for their higher academic achievements than other racial groups. Professor Marshall's view is, for example, very representative among the people interviewed for this study:

> On an annual basis of the students graduating with honors, of the salutatorian and valedictorian of the classes of the schools, it's always interesting to see that Southeastern Asians are represented quite nicely in West Side schools, in Green High School, for instance. The students there aren't a whole lot who are going on to college, but I am quite sure that there's a much higher percentage of the Vietnamese, for instance, who are in that school, who are looking and anticipating going on for higher education than you would find among the Puerto Ricans or the African Americans.

The City and its Schools

The racial, economic, and residential segregation had significantly influenced the making of the school systems in the city. Within the city proper, racial concentrations became the index for school achievement. The whiter the school, the better the academic achievements are. There are two class systems in the city. One is the remaining white middle and upper middle class, who live around the Elmwood Strip, the luxury waterfront condos, and the affluent parts of North Buffalo, and the other is the multi-ethnic working and/or poor class including the poor whites, African Americans, Hispanics (Puerto Ricans),

American Indians, and recent immigrants and refugees who live in the East and West Side, that is, between the Elmwood Strip and the waterfront.

For the whites and/or the few members of the minorities who made it into the middle- and upper-middle-class circle, as Dillaway (2006) describes, "social prestige revolved around the arts and their board of directors—the Buffalo Philharmonic Orchestra, the Albright–Knox Art Gallery—and the Buffalo General Hospital on the city's East Side." Most of the middle- and upper-middle-class children tend to send their children to the private schools, for example the establishment schools such as Nichols School and Canisius High School, and to certain schools in the public system. Many of these families also send their children to some of the eastern boarding schools. In 2003–2004, there were about seventy private elementary and high schools located in the city (City-Data.com, 2007). In these schools, the student–teacher ratio is low (4:1 compared with 13:1 in Buffalo public schools) and the student population is overwhelmingly white. In some schools, the student population is 100 percent white. In Westminster Early Childhood Preschool, for example, there are no minority children at all. Coincidentally, Westminster is one of the city's prominent Protestant churches that most of the WASPs attend (Dillaway, 2006). As one white graduate wrote about his experiences in school,

> In Buffalo, there exists extreme racism to the point of almost absolute segregation. I remember when I moved to South Carolina for College, I thought it was weird that black and white people sat on separate sides of the cafeteria in 1995! Here up North it is no different. The neighborhoods are totally divided. So much so, that in my High School there was only one black person.

In contrast to the private schools, the public schools in Buffalo are crumbling. In 2006, there were seventy public schools in the city, including fifteen charter schools. According to the school board report, the total enrollment for 2005–2006 was 37,000, an 8,000 decrease since 2002. Since 2002, fourteen schools have been closed and the District planned to close two more schools in 2006–2007. Among these students, 83 percent are eligible for the Free or Reduced Price Lunch program. According to the Superintendent, James Williams, and President of the Board of Education, Florence Johnson, several factors, such as a declining birth rate, the growth of charter schools, and families leaving the city, have resulted in the declining enrollment. However, another crucial factor that drives many people out of the city, as many have pointed out, is the declining achievement and test scores in many public schools. Many teachers themselves live in the suburbs and their children go to suburban schools. The few teachers who choose to live in the city (such as Wayne, an ESL teacher in Rainbow Elementary) usually send their children to private schools, not pubic schools. Though Buffalo fared well in comparison with the other Big Five cities—Syracuse, Rochester, Yonkers, and New York City—in the State of New

York, it has fallen "woefully behind its suburban counterparts" (Buffalo Geek, 2006, p. 1). For example, in the 2000 elementary language arts performance (grade 4), only 29 percent of the students met the state standards (levels 3 and 4) in the city of Buffalo, whereas in the suburban school district of Williamsville Central 70 percent of students performed at or above the state standard (State Education Department, 2000). The numbers, however, do not reveal the real differences between city and suburban schools, since what people take more seriously is the quality of curriculum and educational services. Marilyn, who works in a city school and lives in a suburb, notes,

> What does well in the Buffalo school system, and what is really good, isn't going to be real good in the suburbs. I think Small Wood [a suburban school], it's like 97, 98 percent of the kids pass the proficiency test. I think we [the city school where Marilyn works] were like at 78 or 80 or something. So . . . there is a huge difference. But I mean, they still do well, but there is a huge difference. I wouldn't send my kids to a Buffalo city school. I wouldn't do it.

She further explains the differences between schools in the two districts based on her observations of her daughters' experiences:

> [My daughter] is probably a year ahead of herself in the reading department. The curriculum—she has a different special every day. She gets gym twice a week, she gets music twice a week, and she gets art once a week. She goes to the library every single day. We [the West Side school] don't even have a librarian now in the school every single day. The school's library where I work, versus school my daughter goes—you can't even compare. The libraries [in the city] are just so limited . . . [My stepdaughter] is a junior, and she's already working on her senior thesis. How many kids in the Buffalo school system do you think know what a thesis is, let alone would write in their junior year . . . I am going to go in there [city schools], and I am going to help bring them up to any standard as possibly as I can. I mean I love my job and I love doing what I am doing, but I wouldn't send my kids to that school, because the education that they're getting at the school is just . . . you know. I mean, my daughter Betty, she's already had the curve. Why would I want to take her away from that?

Marilyn's sentiment is representative of many of the city's residents. In a poll conducted by Buffalo School Board's Committee on Choice, Buffalo ranked sixteenth in its rate of dissatisfaction among the forty-six cities polled—18.9 percent of the respondents in the city reported that they were dissatisfied with their schools whereas the national average among the cities was 9.6 percent. A local survey commissioned by the former mayor Anthony Masiello indicated that about 25 percent of the parents were dissatisfied or very dissatisfied with their public schools (Council of the Great City Schools, 2000).

There are, however, a few top-quality schools in the public system, such as the Oliver Schools (one elementary and one middle school), Lakeside High (rated as number four high school in the country), and Madison Tech high school. Like the private schools, the majority of the students in these schools are white and middle class. In Lakeside High, for example, whites make up 68 percent of its student population and only 18.6 percent of students are eligible for the Free and Reduced Lunch program (the district average is 85 percent). In the Oliver Schools, 53 percent of the students are white and 41 percent of them are eligible for the Free and Reduced Lunch program. In comparison, in Rainbow Elementary, which many of the children in this study attend, 29 percent of the students are white (including European immigrants), and 89 percent of the students are on the Free and Reduced Lunch program. The economic and racial segregation among the top public city schools also reflects the liberal whites' sentiment of wanting to support public schools but not wanting to send their children to public schools. That is, although some liberal whites feel that they should send their children to public schools to support public education, they do not want to send their children to schools with low performance and meager resources. As a result, their children are concentrated in a few top-performing public schools and thus a stratified school system has been created within public schools. As Professor Marshall comments,

> There is another point I would make about who goes to Lakeside High. There are lots of white middle class liberals who want to be able to place their children in the public schools rather than a private school. It's a personal thing. However, Lakeside High allows them to place their kids in a public school that is not at all like Buffalo public schools, so you avoid problems and you feel good about yourself . . . And at the elementary level, it would be the Oliver.

The fragility of public confidence in the city's public schools is related to many levels of problems. Major factors include (1) historical tensions around budget issues between the school district and the city; (2) a history of conflicts between the district and the teachers' union (Scott & Linsky, 1999); and (3) the leadership and organizational structure of the school system.

First, the Buffalo public school district has been fiscally dependent upon the city, which means that the school district does not have the power to raise revenue or to decide budget priorities. Rather, the city has the power to oversee the overall budget for school operating and maintenance costs. On the other hand, the city has no voice in how the appropriated money is spent, but the school district does. According to Scott and Linsky (1999), this has created serious problems for both the city and the school district, since the state aid to the city has declined but the school budget has been on a continuous rise. The city, however, has been known to have "not ever adequately supported its schools" (Scott & Linsky, 1999, p. 7). For example, the proportion of the school budget covered by the city declined steadily from a high of about 33 percent in the 1980s to 17 percent by the early 1990s. And in 2004–2005, when Erie County's budget was over $140 million in deficit, the school district's budget was also deeply affected—its workforce was reduced by 210 positions between 2004 and 2005 and many city/county-funded resources such as nursing services and libraries were cut. In the meantime, the state aid to the district has also decreased. The Buffalo Public School District was allocated $419.5 million for the district's day-to-day operating needs in the 2006–2007 Executive Budget of the Governor of New York, George E. Pataki. Based on the District's 2005–2006 allocation of $421 million, this represents a net decrease of $1.4 million (Buffalo Public Schools, 2006). The Buffalo Fiscal Stability Authority reports that, even with a balanced 2006–2007 budget, the city and school district have projected significant budget gaps in future years.

Second, the financial tug of war between the city, the state, and the school district has created a strain on the relationship between the school district, especially the board of education, and the teachers' union. Contract negotiations between the school district and the teachers' union have been difficult and have created deep rifts between the union and the school system, leaving teachers caught in the middle. Buffalo has a history of labor strife, with salaries being a constant source of grievance among teachers (Scott & Linsky, 1999). Teachers have gone on strike several times in the past, the latest occurring in September 2000. Though many supported the teachers, others, including the city officials, regarded the strike as a "disservice to the children" or "an unconscionable act" that was "very punitive and damaging to the children and parents" (Anthony Masiello, as cited in Bell, 2000). Today, Buffalo's teachers are ranked the second highest paid in the nation with an average annual salary of $54,039, second only to Grand Rapids (the national median annual salaries of school teachers ranged from $41,400 to $45,920 in May 2004) (Streater, 2005). However, the tension between the union and the school district continued. The new Superintendent, James Williams, who took the position in 2005, believed that the union's contract negotiations were based on an outdated model and those contracts "hinder the development of this community as well as the school district." He laid off some teachers in his first year in 2006 and had gained a reputation for taking a hard line with the teachers' union. In 2006, Buffalo teachers were working under a budget freeze and his negotiations with the union around a new contract in 2007 will no doubt generate more tension in an already depressed city.

A third aspect that had debilitated the city's school system was its "fractured" organizational structure that "tends to stifle progress, rather than stimulate it" (Council of the Great City Schools, 2000). In 2000, all concerned groups, including the city, the school officials, and the teachers' union, charged the Council of the Great City Schools to investigate ways to reform the school district's management structure. The Council, led and charged by the former Superintendent Marion Canedo, reported that the current system is the cumulative result of a wide variety of policy decisions made by past leaders across multiple decades...There are excellent people in the city's school system, but they are poorly organized for the challenges ahead ... For example, the school district struggled heroically for many years to comply with one of the nation's foremost federal court orders to desegregate and to remove the vestiges of past discrimination.

According to the report (Council of the Great City Schools, 2000), the nature of the organizational problem was that:

Its unity of purpose and sense of mission are splintering. Communications are becoming insular. Collaborations are sporadic. Many who work for the system are focused on survival rather than on the goals of the district ... In some cases, the operations actually undermine what the district wants to accomplish. The school district management cannot support the work of the schools in the ways that it should. Consequently, student achievement does not have as high a priority as it should. *The end result is a system that is heavily focused on procedural compliance and centralized control, but that lacks the flexibility, creativity, and incentives necessary to adapt to a changing world, encourage major strides in teaching and learning, or support the city's revitalization.*

(pp. 15–16, emphasis original)

The Council concludes that "*The Buffalo school system is facing a critical choice. It can take the steps necessary to substantially improve student achievement, play a central role in the city's economic revitalization, and increase public confidence in its schools. Or it can keep things pretty much as they are*" (p. 1, emphasis original). It proposed key changes necessary for restoring public confidence in the system, which included: Place first priority on raising the academic achievement of all students; improve and increase professional development opportunities for teachers and staff; decentralize some of the decision-making responsibilities currently vested in the central office of Buffalo schools to principals at the school level; strengthen accountability for results; and provide greater parental access to and choice among public schools and magnet schools. In 2002, the Buffalo Joint Schools Construction Board (JSCB) started a $1 billion, eighty-school modernization project involving renovation and reconstruction of the city's aging schools. In 2005, a new African American Superintendent, James Williams, was hired to implement these changes, especially in increasing its declining test scores. A three-year achievement plan focusing on reading and literacy was in place and the twenty-eight lowest-achieving schools in the district were monitored for their achievements. These changes instilled new signs of hope for the community. As James Williams commented in a public interview, "This is the cultural change I was talking about. We've got to change the way people think about Buffalo and the future of Buffalo."

Zooming in on the West Side Schools

Even though some changes are taking place in the Buffalo school system, for the West Side, the pace is not fast enough. As mentioned before, the West Side has undergone many changes in its demographics over the years. The "white flight" has affected the West Side more than the East Side. As the whites have moved out, a lot of low-income families have moved in. It has become a very transient place where the population is in constant flux. This transient nature has, to some degree, made the West Side a dangerous place to live. As Marilyn explains:

> Once upon a time it was a very nice place to live. And it has gone down-hill. My understanding is [it went] very quickly. I think about 99 percent of the kids that attend my school are considered to be living in poverty. And that's defined by their eligibility for Free or Reduced Lunches. So I think it's about 99 percent. High crime, a lot of gang activity, a lot of drugs, a lot of gun-running, that sort of thing. It comes out of West Side. The kids grow up in this sort of environment . . . My guess is that people have moved out and moved to other places, and then you get the lower-income families that moved in, and the gangs are a big thing as well. A lot of drugs. The corner of our school . . . is supposed to be one of the worst places for drug trafficking.

Almost by default, many refugees and Hispanic immigrants are brought into the West Side upon their arrival because it is a cheap and affordable place to live. These people, especially mothers, often experience a lot of difficulties adjusting to the new inner-city life in such aspects as language, child care, and employment. As Professor Marshall notes:

> With that population, there are number of challenges that they face. It seems to me that men who arrive have a much greater opportunity to get involved with work, and to be exposed to English speakers on a regular basis, and are much more likely to begin to learn the language. And it's an easier adjustment for them, than particularly mothers of young children who are, are in a sense, stuck at home. And with the limited child care available and then within the social service system, the provisions for child care and for recent arrivals would be pretty limited. Particularly to find any kind of home daycare or larger daycare setting where staff are comfortable working with persons from other cultures. And the language issues, of course, if you're going to work with children, and you don't know their language, and they don't know yours, that's quite a challenge, too.

The transient nature of the community and the large influx of refugee and immigrant populations have generated a great deal of stress in the West Side schools, since, as Professor Marshall says, the majority of the teachers have "not been trained or prepared to work with the diverse population that is arriving." Only a couple of schools, such as Rainbow Elementary, can handle the large number of new arrivals by design. The other schools in the district are not equipped to work with large numbers of refugee and immigrant students. As a result, in some schools, the number of immigrant and refugee student numbers is decreasing while in a few other schools it is increasing and students of different racial groups (particularly blacks and Hispanics) are increasingly segregated. In Brown High School, which Owen Torkeri attends, for example, the Hispanic population decreased from 5.7 percent in 1998–1999 to 0.8 percent in 2000–2001 and the whites decreased from 14.6 percent to 10.3 percent while the blacks increased from 78.4 percent to 88.8 percent. The ESL population also decreased by almost half (from eleven students in 1998 to six in 2001). In contrast, in the Green High School, which is known to receive international students, the trend is opposite. Between 1998 and 2001, the ESL population increased from 61.2 percent (433) to 68.2 percent (551).

The population shift among the schools has resulted in schools with different ethnic concentrations. In some schools, the ESL students are predominantly Hispanic or African. The rapid changes in student demographics and the lack of school resources have made it difficult for non-English speakers to receive enough of the ESL services that they need. For example, Rose, an ESL teacher whose time is split between two schools, notes that she has "a harder time to get her students to speak in English at full end [at all times]" in the school with a high Puerto Rican population as "they all speak the same L1 [first language]." In Brown High School, which has only few African refugee students, getting support for these students sometimes can be very hard because the administrators and the teachers are not aware of the importance of ESL instruction. In fact, in Rose's first year at Brown, the administrator "hated" ESL and Rose did not get a room for ESL instruction. She was placed in the library all year without a blackboard or any books. All the content area teachers treated her as a homework helper or a tutor rather than a language teacher. She observes, "There's definitely [a group of teachers], especially among the older teachers but even with some of the younger ones, who don't understand, who'd never taken a class in any sort of ESL, even though there are ESL students [in their classes]." The situation is also worsened by the recent budget cut as there is no funding for even basic instructional materials such as books. Rose has to buy her own books and make her own work sheets, which is getting very expensive for her.

In schools such as Rainbow Elementary, where students come from over thirty countries and speak as many different languages, ESL support is more accepted and welcomed. Over half of the school's population (over 500 per year) are designated as needing ESL support. In the school, transiency is also the norm of the school life. According to a Title I reading teacher, Evelyn,[1] who has been teaching in the school for several years, approximately 300 new students—around 25 percent of the student body—are transferred to the school and the average classroom can suffer a 35 percent change in its make-up over the course of a school year. In the school, since the minorities are the majority, there is a heavy cry among the content area teachers for more ESL support, especially for offering transitional classes for new arrivals. However, the budget cuts have not allowed more ESL teachers. There are only six ESL teachers and six bilingual teachers in the school and the number of Title I teachers continues to go down while the number of ESL students is going up: "at a point of no return," as a teacher puts it. The increasing enrollment in ESL has made teaching very tough. As Nelli, a Hispanic parent liaison who also lives in the suburb, points out, with so many students in one class with so many levels of needs, "Teachers don't have time to sit down and find out what's going on with the students . . . that's a lot to ask for. They do a lot already." Wayne, an ESL teacher at the school, explains,

> Thirty kids in class is too many . . . And half of them are ESL, and maybe four have never been to school before . . . It's too many. They do a better job with twenty. Kids in thirties, so that's a wealth thing, a class thing. As the budgets go down, they are cramming more and more kids in the class, they are dropping more and more extracurricular, they are dropping the nurses.

The number of ESL students has also made scheduling of pull-out and push-in programs very difficult. According to Evelyn, the ESL and bilingual programs are pull-out programs with the ESL teachers having their own teaching space, whereas Title I reading and math are completely push-in programs. Evelyn and another Title I reading teacher together work exclusively inside classrooms in a team effort with classroom teachers. The two of them participate in a push-in program, where they visit twenty-seven separate classrooms. Evelyn herself teaches in fourteen different first, third, and fourth grade rooms, three times (30–45 minutes) a day during a six-day cycle. The constant change of rooms and students makes it hard for her to keep track of students' progress and to really get to know the students. For ESL teachers like Wayne, who has too many students in his classes, it is hard to communicate with classroom teachers about what is going on with individual students. Classroom teachers, on the other hand, find that pulling students out at different times can be disruptive for students' learning, as the students are constantly coming and going, moving the desks and taking their books. A third grade teacher interviewed by Evelyn expressed her frustration:

> Some children are pulled out, some are here, and finding the time to give them the help they need and the lesson, the basis of the lesson, getting used to the curriculum and adjusting it to their needs can be a lot. And when they're pulled out, then it's like, when can I get to this child?

The situation becomes more complicated as the ESL students also come from diverse backgrounds with different levels of schooling. Some children come with previous schooling experiences in their home country in another language, but many come from refugee camps and have never been to school before, nor do they speak any English. Some classes have over twenty ESL students who are at different levels of English proficiency. Teaching increasingly culturally diverse groups of students with different levels of English abilities can be a real challenge. First of all, the school is seriously under-staffed as there are not enough ESL teachers or transitional classes for new students. Many teachers, by default, become ESL teachers. However, they are not prepared to teach ESL students owing to a lack of training in their teacher preparation program and professional development on the job.

For many teachers, diversity is a good thing, but it's also a real challenge as they often "end up with a new problem every minute, every hour." Therefore, teaching is "just being able to survive from day to day with those big problems you have" (a fourth grade teacher interviewed by Evelyn). For example, some students steal things. Some refugee children are not even used to sitting in a school. Wayne says, "They cannot walk down the hall in the beginning . . . Their elbows were all over the place. They are hitting other kids. They might get mad and walk out the classroom." The bigger problem, however, is developing and implementing instruction that addresses their different levels of schooling experiences and language proficiency to engage all these children in learning. A third grade teacher of Hispanic origin interviewed by Evelyn shared her experience:

> Sometimes I don't feel that I can move as fast with a unit that I'm work- ing on, because I have many ESL students who don't understand because of the different environment that they came from. And I move at a slower pace and I have American students who I feel that they could go faster. And my question is, am I holding these students back? I mean, because I'm going a little slower, so that's a concern that I have.

Wayne, who was certified to teach secondary students, is now teaching ESL in Rainbow Elementary. Though he did not have the right certification to teach in elementary, he was transferred to the school because of the budget cuts in his previous school. He teaches about forty ESL students in the third grade. Like many other teachers, he has students from different backgrounds:

> And now at Rainbow Elementary . . . a lot of them are really ESL because half of our school are ESL . . . And, so it's such a broad question because I have all these types of kids. Right now Rainbow Elementary which is different from the other schools again. But at Rainbow Elementary I generally have one class of the kids that just got here. So I got eight kids in that class . . . six to seven never been to school anywhere before. So that creates a totally different situation. These kids are all beginners, they never been to school so of course they are all beginners, but it's a different situation, than, for example, last year I had an Ethiopian

Russian . . . She obviously had very good education in Moscow, and she came knowing no English, and left near grade level in reading. She had been educated in Russia, so a kid like that, they know what the continents are, they don't know what a continent is in English. But these kids coming from the refugee camp, they had no idea of what a continent is. In fact the Africans all think Africa is a country. That's one thing I face . . . if they are from Africa, I want them to know Africa is not a country.

Wayne uses a lot of materials such as a science table, a microscope, and a pond habitat in his teaching and he believes that reading is very important. He tries to "get the kids reading really really quickly, even for . . . those newcomers." His goals for them are that "by the end of third grade they are close to second grade reading level from scratch, from not knowing the letters, because then they can start to teach themselves." His strategy is to "use books as opposed to phonics." He states that he does not believe in the heavy phonics even though he knows that the school system does. In his literacy teaching he tries to build context. He explains how he teaches reading against the school system's push for teaching out of context:

Specifically to teach reading I used Dr. Seuss' books. I teach them letters and I start reading right away. They are half reading and half getting the picture of *Hop On Pop*. That's the first book I use . . . I got a whole sequence, I got a whole system I developed, I teach them letters before they know all the vowels, I start them with *Hop On Pop*. I do it through rhyming words because we don't have any time to lose. We really try to do a lot quickly.

In addition to starting with books in school, he also sends books home with the students in order to get "the parents involved right away, having them going home and have them reading to the parents." He, however, understands that many parents do not read English, but his theory is that "sometimes, they are listening too." So he has the students teach the parents by reading the books to them if the parents cannot read. He also makes an effort to talk to the parents as soon as the parents start to know some English.

Leaving teachers to survive on their own, however, can be a hit-or-miss affair as teachers have different levels of understanding about ESL issues. Wayne points out that, in terms of teacher quality, every school has a mix of good and bad teachers: "You always have a few of them that are very good." He agrees that there are differences among teachers, especially between content teachers and ESL teachers:

There is always a little bit of conflict in the classroom teachers that think they are doing more than anybody else or the others. But part of the problem is that at times it is true that is the classroom teachers are doing more. Some of teachers are out to set duties, the guidance, the ESL,

... some of them are just slapping off... Some of the classroom teachers are doing a good job but they can't slap off because kids are there. Some are not, some are not seeing the kids as much as they should, you know, that occurs, so the teachers and the administrative people figure out pretty quickly who's doing a pretty job, who is working hard, who wasn't.

Regardless of whether they are doing a good job or not, the teachers strive every day to get the students to read as fast as they can. They are also under tremendous pressure to prepare the students for different standardized tests mandated by the state and the city. To follow the federal *No Child Left Behind Act* (NCLB), the State has an accountability system that identifies Schools In Need of Improvement (SINI) every year. Schools that fail two years in a row may be identified as schools in need of Corrective Action, and if no improvement is made the schools will be closed. Students who attend failing Buffalo public schools are entitled to apply for a transfer to non-failing public schools. From 2003 to 2005, Rainbow Elementary was on the failing school list, which created a lot of pressure among the faculty to improve the scores in order for the school to remain open. However, for many teachers, meeting the state mandates was unrealistic, since many of the students are ESL learners with no prior schooling experiences. Wayne decided that he "won't do it. It doesn't make sense." He complained:

[In] first and second grade, there's whole battery of testing—there's Buffalo test, there's state test. The testing is interfering with instruction. Sometimes I just do it quickly so I get instruction ... [On] the standardized test which is not a Terra Nova [an achievement test], if the kid comes over from, say, Somalia, he's been here two weeks and doesn't know a word of English, he's told to do as best he can. So while he's been told to do the best he can, he's losing maybe half an hour of time that could be teaching him how to speak English, that's ridiculous. And there's all the state tests ... Buffalo has tests, the Buffalo literacy profile. That's redundant ... it's supposed to be this great tool so you know exactly what the kids know. I can tell you what the kids know ... But to have a kid from Somalia that has never spoken and told him just to do the best he can, just write "you can't speak English or something", it's just ridiculous. It's counter-intuitive; it's irrational.

To survive day by day without sufficient support, many teachers learn to deal with the instructional challenges in their own ways. As a teacher Evelyn interviewed points out, "We're at a loss as to what to do." Most teachers understand the importance of pairing up new students with older students who speak the same language. In addition, they also understand the importance of starting from the basics. Many teachers use resources such as tapes and basic books as starting points for the students, but it is hard for them to find books that are enjoyable and at the same time appropriate for students' level of understanding. Some teachers discover that using culturally relevant literature to connect students really helps. A third grade social studies teacher Evelyn interviewed testified that when she used a book with stories set in Africa, *Mufaro's Beautiful Daughter,* the children just "came alive, especially the ones that don't necessarily speak out." According to the teacher, who is an African American herself,

> As soon as they find [something culturally relevant]—'cause that's a familiarity with them and then they do [speak out] . . . Today we were talking about Africa and one of my students who doesn't really talk, she just had a lot to say because this was something she was familiar with. So she talked about, we talked about the Nile River and she had seen the Nile River. And it was just really something because they had so much to say! My African students, they had so much to say. And I told them, you know more about it than I do because you're from there.

This kind of curriculum innovation, however, is sporadic and rare. According to Evelyn, the school curriculum is very scripted and all the teachers try to meet the standards, exploring ways to make students get used to sitting in chairs and to reading. Given this, there is little room for adapting the curriculum to make it connected with students' cultural backgrounds. Wayne agrees that "teachers are confined" and under a lot of pressure to help students learn the scripted curriculum. He talks about the pressure from an ESL teacher's perspective: "With that extra program, the people want to see results. The [classroom] teachers too. And the results are mixed, it depends on the teacher. You can have some report results, and then . . . teachers are confined." The writing curriculum, for example, often follows the state's writing prompts and structures which allow little room for students' personal experiences. Evelyn observes that teachers rarely encourage students to connect their writings with home, personal experiences, or their cultural backgrounds. According to her observation, few students deviate from the required tasks and write about their personal experiences or their country of origin. In reading, teachers follow very "neutral" curriculum and instructional strategies that often do not address students' cultural backgrounds (Finn, 1999).

In the school, culture is viewed as a set of customs and traditions, and multicultural activities in the school have been based on this limited notion of culture (El-Haj, 2006; Erickson, 2001). Little effort has been made to help teachers understand the diverse cultures and learn to interact with students in culturally appropriate ways. The school seems to engage in what Gitlin, Buendía, Crosland, and Doumbia (2003) theorize as an inclusionary–exclusionary process in which the school treats all students as the same and welcomes them and at the same time maintains practices that marginalize/unwelcome them. As described above, on the one hand, the teachers and school welcome diversity; one the other hand, they are also concerned with additional burdens or work intensification brought upon them by the diversity.

Another contradictory practice is reflected in the school's concern for preserving multiculturalism. On the one hand, the school believes that asserting one's difference stands in the way of assimilation and therefore must be eliminated (Gitlin *et al.*, 2003); on the other hand, the school takes pride in its multicultural activities. Among the teachers and students, cultural differences are not often talked about. On one of my visits to the school several years prior to this study, the vice-principal at that time told me that, since all children are different, they are treated the same. Discussion about the differences is discouraged among the children. The vice-principal gave an example of a child who asked a Muslim girl about her headscarf and he was sent to the principal's office as no such thing was tolerated in the school. This does not mean, however, that cultures are not celebrated in the school. Every year, the school tries to celebrate the major holidays in students' cultures such as Chinese/Vietnamese New Year, Christmas, Rosh Hashanah, and the Islamic New Year. However, since there are so many cultures in the school, the celebration schedule is often very tight in order to accommodate all the festivals. The Chinese/Vietnamese New Year, for example, is sometimes celebrated in June rather than in January or February. Each year, the school also hosts an International Festival of Cultures in which different music and dances are performed in the school and diverse ethnic foods are served. Though these activities are great in helping teachers understand different cultures and inviting parents to come to the school, they are rarely connected to classroom instruction. As Evelyn observes, "On the whole, teachers do not see it as an opportunity they can take advantage of, as an entrée to further cultural knowledge and understanding in their classrooms." She writes:

> In the classrooms you would fare no better. There are no pictures of scenes from other lands decorating the walls, no special sections in the bookcases for stories about life in other countries, no objects that aren't familiar to most American boys and girls. You would observe the teacher working with a curriculum that is not any different from that taught in almost any other school in the district. In fact, both the school at large and the classrooms as a whole are guilty of what Hoffman (1996) calls "hallway multicultural-ism," in effect, using multicultural trappings without self-awareness, without real substance or depth. Like the school described by Hamilton (1994), *"the cultural self seems to be missing."* (Emphasis original)

For many teachers, another big challenge related to cultural diversity is parental involvement in their children's education among families from different cultural traditions. The teachers tend to believe that the refugee and immigrant parents are hardworking and supportive of their children's education. In some instances, they have parents who are extremely involved. For example, in the school's annual international festival, many parents come to the school and enjoy the foods and cultural performances. But the majority of them rarely come to any other school-related activities such as the parents' night. There is little representation especially among the refugee parents. Wayne explains,

> Though the refugee African kids I had . . . they are really, really highly motivated. The Bantu refugees, the kids have very little absentee rate and they are learning English themselves. I can tell from talking [about] the books that are coming home, they really value education; it's really important that the kids do well at school. There's not the high absentee rate, like for example, with the Spanish the absentee rate is often very high . . . And parents, they really try to come for parents' night, even though they cannot talk English . . . They won't come in otherwise, I think they are intimidated often, I send stuff but I think the school is intimidating to them.

Some teachers understand that many refugee parents work long hours and, for many, transportation and scheduling time off work may be difficult issues to overcome. One parent, for example, did not have transport to come to school, so he sold jewelry and other precious things in order to take a taxi to attend the parents' night at the school. Even though stories like this make teachers understand that some parents are well aware of the importance of education, they hope that more children can be better supported at home. As Wayne comments, "The schools are very undemanding compared with [private schools] . . . the teachers are trying to hang in there like Johnsons [a city high school], but half of the kids are not doing their homework or anything. And if they can't get it from the parents, what can the teachers do? They don't have that home component, their works are not getting done. It's a big problem." The teachers also learn that coming from different cultural and educational backgrounds, the level of parental involvement varies at home. Wayne illustrates:

> The African and Vietnamese will be quite different. The Vietnamese have more education in general. We have some [Vietnamese] kids progress very quickly. They had education, and also the Vietnamese, Cambodian, Laotian parents really, really value education . . . But they are trying to do [their best]. [A Vietnamese parent will] say, "My English is not good, I cannot help them much, so she came home at 3:30, she got a snack, then she has homework hour, then she watch half an hour TV. Then she has another homework half an hour." You know, he has the perfect structure, and the girl is doing really, really well. You got this Bantu Somali with the kids grown up in refugee camps, you can

understand, [school is] quite a new idea. So the whole [school] thing is a lot more foreign to them than the Vietnamese. [The Vietnamese] know what education is. Even though they can't help the kids like this . . . they don't allow them watch a lot of TV, if they are not doing as well as they should. They really support the teacher, very strongly. You find that quite the same in China.

Many teachers noticed that the children are extremely poor. Wayne, for example, sometimes gives his daughters' clothes to some of the children as they come to school in the summer with a winter jacket. Though many teachers and staff are sympathetic about the children's socio-economic situations, there is a widespread belief that there is a "very different culture that goes along with poverty" and this culture is considered to be detrimental to parental involvement and children's school success. According to Marilyn and Nelli, this culture of poverty has several characteristics. First, poor parents move frequently and go from crisis to crisis instead of dealing with it. According to Marilyn, when the families move, they usually leave everything behind, which further worsens their financial situation: "They leave furniture, they leave clothes, they leave toys . . . and just left, just picked up and left, abandoned the home, abandoned a washer, a dryer, a refrigerator, furniture, the whole thing." Nelli describes a typical situation:

And a lot of these families move, I mean every six months they are moving from one apartment to another. It's extremely sad . . . I think when people are in poverty, what happens—even this morning, like I was dealing with this mom who got taken to court because she didn't pay February, March, or April's rent. So instead of paying it, she got mad, took the money and put the deposit for another place. So her reasoning was just the apartment—usually the apartments around here are bad. They are not taken care of properly. Usually people are in crisis situations, it's like, "okay, I need to move in," and the landlord's, "Okay, just give me 50 dollars, move in, don't worry about a deposit or do deposit a payment." Everything is just quickly—so, at first because they're in crisis, they are able to deal with whatever, whatever the situation is in the apartment. But a couple of months later, they start like, "Well, I don't like this, I don't like that. I'm moving."

Since these parents are going from crisis to crisis, Nelli and Marilyn observe that, to the parents, "everything is a quick fix, it's not a long term. So therefore they don't have the patience to see what long-term commitments can bring." They believe that this "quick fix" mentality is also reflected in their commitment to their children's education. Nelli explains, "For example, a high school education's four years, that's a long-term commitment. You know getting your associate's, that's a two-year commitment, and there is no way that they could see how it's going to benefit in the future, because they are dealing with the thing now, and today and tomorrow." Marilyn concurs with Nelli that parents' views of education are of critical importance:

> The most significant way that it impacts is that you have parents who are not educated generally, who do not value education. So they don't instill that in their kids, and they do pass it on to their kids that it's not that important. Um, so many of the kids came in with the mentality of, "oh, I am just gonna quit when I'm 16, anyway. So what difference does it make?" You have parents who, because they are not educated, cannot help their children with their homework . . . But if these people are illiterate, they can't even read what's been sent home, and that's a big problem, too. Um, we've seen it with a lot of the, the immigrants/refugees, they can't speak the language so you send something home with them, it's just going to be ignored because they can't read it. The same thing with somebody that is not educated and they don't even try. So the biggest [problem] is if they are not educated, they are not going to place the value of education with their children.

Nelli and Marilyn also realize that the inner-city environment is closely intertwined with the families' living and schooling. Marilyn argues, "you can roll so much under poverty living in an environment where there are drive-by shootings. There are times that you don't know if somebody is going to come into the house in the middle of the night. There are some families that don't have food from week to week, day to day, month to month. And again that can fall under poverty [together with] lack of education with the parents themselves." The combination of factors, such as parents' educational backgrounds and their inner city environment, influences parents' decision and ability to get involved in their children's education. Marilyn illustrates,

> Suppose you have a single parent, be it a mother or be it a father, trying to cope with working, and raising the kids. And I am not talking about the parents that are on welfare and that don't work. Because to me, they have a lot more time to invest in their, in their—they should theoretically have a lot more time to invest in their kids [but] obviously in drugs, weapons, gangs, violence . . . It's a totally different world.

Marilyn further elaborates how the choices some parents make impact their children's education:

> Some parents just don't care . . . . Sometimes parents are just lazy. That's another big problem and it's very true. I was dealing with a case this morning where there is a mom who lives three blocks from the school and cannot—her children this year alone have been tardy 51 days because she can't bring it—she can't bring herself to get out of bed in the morning and walk her kids to school. The kids are in kindergarten and

second grade, and she can't even get them to walk to school . . . So if the parents are participating in illegal activities, if they are doing drugs, if they are out doing whatever it is that they do at night, they are not going to be monitoring their kids, and the kids are going to be left to their own devices, and they might not necessarily get into bed at a decent time. So they can't get up to go to school the next morning because they are tired. Or even if they do come to school, they might be so exhausted that they can't focus on what's going on. We do have some kids that come to school and they're hungry. They don't eat. The parents don't feed them. Parents palm them off on whoever is around, so they can go out and do whatever they want to do. These are real, honest-to-God problems and happen quite—more frequently than what people might think.

At the other end of the spectrum, some parents do care, but many are single parents who struggle financially. Nelli explains that, in these single-parent families, family life is much less structured than in two-parent families in the suburbs. She believes that it is a huge factor that contributes to the lack of involvement in these families. Marilyn agrees:

> Even if mom is a single parent, and she is working, and she is trying to raise two or three kids, that's an incredible burden—to work all day long and to come home and prepare a meal and to make sure that the kids' homework's done, and kids are in bed in time. That's, that's an incredible, incredible burden. And that's considering that she would work eight to five, or nine to five. Some parents work three to eleven, some work the overnight shift. It's just crazy.

Whatever the circumstances are, however, the parents are not the only ones to blame for being intimidated by the school and not being able to make the right connections with the children's school learning at home. Teachers also play a big part in this situation. Professor Marshall points out that one of the huge problems that the city (as well as many other inner-city public school districts) faces is that "teachers are drawn overwhelmingly from middle-class and white backgrounds." The social class and racial differences between the parents and the teachers can create a "huge conflict" between the two parties. Marilyn explains,

> They're teaching minority kids whose parents probably to a certain extent are resentful because most of these teachers live in the suburbs . . . They come to school, and they are dressed in nice clothes; they drive decent cars; they speak well and, obviously, they are educated. So that's intimidating right there. They don't understand the culture of poverty that these people are living in. And then on top of it, they're teaching kids who may not speak English. Parents may not speak English. They don't believe in education the same way that the teacher believes in education . . . There can be a huge conflict.

Nelli concurs with this view that middle-class and/or white teachers often cannot identify with the children and parents who are poor and going from crisis to crisis. She elaborates,

That's the hardest part, because most of the parents don't want to talk to the teachers. They feel like the teachers are like, they are two separate [worlds]—here are the parents, the teachers are not a team. They feel very intimidated by the teachers . . . [The parents] will say, "Well, I am intimidated when talking to the teacher." We'll be like, "Have you talked to the teacher about your child's problem?" and they will be like, "Well, no. I talked to her once, and she doesn't seem nice, or she's always busy." They have all these excuses, and they're all negative . . . so they see teachers as just like this person that's just gonna make them feel bad or point out their flaws. So it's actually bad, because there is no communication.

Marilyn further elaborates this point:

In the parents' defense, I don't think the teachers look at the parents as being capable of understanding and being able to make the kind of changes that are needed. I would say there are a lot of parents who do fall into that category, but then there are other parents who really are trying, they are overwhelmed, but they want their child to do better, and the teachers don't necessarily make it easy for the parents to approach them. A lot of the time it's, "God, can't you do something for this kid?" or—we've gotten referrals from some teachers: "The kids are—their clothing is dirty, and they wear the same thing three times in a row. Can you talk to the parents?" Or maybe everything that this parent can do is to get food on the table and a roof over this kid's head now, but they are coming to school and their clothes are a little dirty and they wear the same thing. Maybe there is a reason behind it, but to them, it's just like this disgrace, these kind of referrals—"Do something about it" or "Can you talk to the parents about it?" . . . it's just the way that some of the teachers are.

Conclusion

In this chapter, I have described the larger socio-historical context of the city and the community in which the six families reside. I have focused on the racial, economic, and educational tensions between the minorities of color and the mainstream society, around the suburban–urban divide, and within various immigrant/minority communities. I have also described the inner-city schools that several of the six families' children attend. The chapter examines teachers', staff's, and community members' perspectives on literacy and education including their views on the minority students, school practices, policy issues, and parental involvement. As their words demonstrate, teaching in inner-city schools is an increasingly demanding and complex task. Resources are getting more and more scarce, while students are becoming more and more diverse. Teachers not only face multifaceted challenges in instruction and in dealing with daily activities within the school walls, but they are also placed under tremendous social and political pressures that affect/restrict their ability to make better/different decisions about classroom practices and policies. Despite these barriers, many teachers choose to teach in the most challenging schools and they want to be there to make a difference. As their stories reveal, though the curriculum is scripted, their salary may be frozen, and there is not enough ESL support, there are pockets of curricular innovation amidst the chaos. Their stories therefore are not mere stories of survival but signs of hope for the crumbling school system. In the next three chapters, I share the stories of the six families and their children who are, like the teachers, trying to survive on their separate racial, economical, and residential islands in a city they now call home.

3
Being Vietnamese, Becoming Somebody

Sometime I want, [but] they can do nothing I want. Like [I] want [them] to do doctor, lawyer, but I don't think they [can] do.

–Lo Ton (Father), April 2006

In this chapter, I introduce two Vietnamese refugee families, the Phan family and the Ton family, who live in the West Side of Buffalo. Vietnamese refugees are the largest group of refugees/immigrants from Southeast Asian countries. Following the collapse of the South Vietnamese government, there have been three waves of Vietnamese immigration to the US. The first wave occurred between 1975 and 1979 shortly after the fall of Saigon on April 30, 1975, which ended the Vietnam War. The second happened between 1979 and 1983 as a result of the new government's implementation of Communist ideology. The third wave began in the mid-1980s and continued until recently as a result of the US Congress passing the Refugee Act of 1980, which reduced restrictions on entry, and the Vietnamese government establishing the Orderly Departure Program (ODP), which allows people to leave Vietnam legally for humanitarian reasons such as family reunions (Gold, 1999; Povell, 2005). According to the US Census Bureau (2000), Vietnamese refugees make up 8.25 percent of the total Asian population, and 79.9 percent of them are foreign born. Close to 80 percent of the school-age children are 1.5-generation or second-generation immigrant children who are reported to face language, cultural, and social adjustments (AAPIP, 1997; Lam, 2003). The two families described in this chapter came to the US during the third wave of Vietnamese refugees and were among the 2000 Vietnamese residing in the West Side of the city.

It is common knowledge that many Vietnamese immigrants suffered many problems similar to those confronted by other refugees fleeing from poor countries: limited English abilities, limited literacy, and high poverty rates (Chung, 2000; Zhou & Bankston, 1998). Most Vietnamese refugees start in America on the lowest rung of the socio-economic ladder, relying on social welfare (Gold, 1999; Zhou, 2001). Although many Vietnamese parents have experienced tremendous upheaval and changes in their lives, earlier studies have reported them to be "well on their way to 'model minority' status" (Centrie, 2004, p. 84). The first-generation Vietnamese are usually willing to take jobs that Americans do not want, which enables them to forgo public assistance and overcome economic marginalization through hard work (Centrie, 2004). Earlier reports on Vietnamese children's academic achievements also indicated that they perform exceptionally well in schools, especially in science and math, which require less English proficiency. Early in 1987, *Time* magazine even reported that the children of the new "boat people" had become America's "new whiz kids" (Brand, 1987).

In recent years, the "model minority" image has been mainly used to describe the East Asian immigrants (i.e., Chinese, Japanese, and Korean) who have achieved a higher level of education and economic success in a short time period. Whereas the East Asians have been increasingly associated with "an Anglo-Asian overclass" (Wu, 2002, p. 19), the lower-income Southeast Asians including Lao, Cambodian, Hmong, and Vietnamese refugees are gradually more associated with an urban "underclass" image. This is because a rising number of Southeast Asian (including Vietnamese) youths are found to struggle academically in school and face multiple risks such as difficulties in acculturation, identity conflicts, and inconsistent parental supervision and discipline (AAPIP, 1997; Gold & Kibria, 1993; Le & Warren, 2006; Lee, 2005; Li, 2005a). Lee (2005) argues that the messages underlying these differential images imply that middle-class Asian immigrants are seen as Americanizing in "good ways" whereas the poor and working-class Asians are considered as Americanizing in "bad ways." Parallel to these messages, racially, middle-class East Asians have been ideologically assimilated as "honorary whites" whereas Southeast Asians have been ideologically blackened (Lee, 2005; Ong, 1999; Wu, 2002).

The Vietnamese are a distinct group who are placed at a contradictory position in the dominant imagination as Southeast Asians but historically portrayed as a "model minority." In a sense, they are at the periphery of both discourses—neither fully whitened nor fully blackened. This contradictory location, however, along with the social class and achievement gaps within the Vietnamese American population, affords some flexibility in the dominant imagination. Within the Vietnamese subgroups, some, especially members of the first-wave elite (1975–1979), came with the skills and education that permitted their entry into the American middle class. In contrast, others, such as the second-wave (post-1979) "boat people," often lacked job skills and training and had little knowledge of the English language and therefore were often streamed into the urban underclass—in poverty and in sectors of the economy that offer little chance for upward social mobility (Gold & Kibria, 1993). Similarly there are significant gaps in terms of Vietnamese youths' academic achievement. Whereas some studies report high academic achievement among Vietnamese students (Centrie, 2004; Zhou & Bankston,

1998), others have reported high drop-out rates and increasing youth gangs and delinquencies (AAPIP, 1997; Le & Warren, 2006). These within-group variances, therefore, make the projection of the Vietnamese image highly context dependent. That is, like the Hmong students in Lee's (2005) study, Vietnamese refugees can be seen as either "good" or "bad"—either whitened or blackened—depending on their social class, academic achievement, and/or social behavior.

Despite these within-group differences, the Vietnamese, along with other Asian Americans, have taken a unique group position within the dominant black–white racial dichotomy. When compared with other minority groups such as blacks and Latinos, who are often constructed as the "bad" minorities, Asian Americans have been portrayed as "good" minorities (Lee, 2005). Oh-Willeke (1996) suggests that Asians as a whole have been projected as minorities acceptable to and yet different from whites in the racial formations of the society. Asians are often used to serve as an exemplary case of the American dream and to accuse other less motivated racial groups of a lack of proper behaviors and attitudes (e.g., uncomplaining and docile) and work ethic (e.g., hardworking, persistent, diligent, and self-abnegating). In this sense, Asians are triangulated between blacks and whites in a way that pits Asian immigrants and other minorities against one another (Gold, 2004; Kim, 2000). Central to this process, however, is the interest of the white power structure that is being served (Feagin, 2000; Lee, 2005).

In addition to these complex terrains of racial and class politics, research on the Vietnamese refugees has reported the significant role of traditional Vietnamese culture in shaping their acculturation experiences and academic achievement in America. Some researchers, such as Zhou and Bankston (1998) and Caplan, Choy, and Whitmore (1992), argue that Vietnamese cultural values, which emphasize the importance of education, hard work, perseverance, and family pride, have a significant impact on the youths' academic achievement. These cultural values are believed to enable Vietnamese parents to hold high expectations for their children's school achievement in hope for a better future in America and to provide support for their children's education despite their limited social and economic resources (Chuong, 1999; Zhou & Bankston, 1998).

These same cultural values, however, can become a double-edged sword for the second generation, who often walk on a family tightrope but are straddling two different worlds. Researchers have pointed out that the clash of values, behaviors, and standards between home and school culture often produces serious internal struggles for Vietnamese adolescents to balance the two (Lam, 2003; Lee & Wong, 2002; Tran, 2003). For example, Vietnamese culture emphasizes obedience, discipline, and filial piety whereas the mainstream American culture values more autonomy and independence. For Vietnamese adolescents, searching to assimilate and striving for autonomy like their American peers often places them at risk of family conflict and internal disharmony (Centrie, 2004; Lam, 2003). Vietnamese youths, who often learn the language more quickly and become acculturated at a faster rate than their parents, increasingly become family spokespersons, and assume the roles of interpreters and translators because of the social isolation and limited language proficiency of the parents. As these youths progressively adopt more parental roles, parents gradually lose control and the ability to exercise guidance. These changes often lead to intensified parent–child conflicts, role reversal, and ultimately the loss of parental authority (Portes & Rumbaut, 1996; Zhou, 2001). The youths, especially females, are also subject to gender inequality and discrimination historically rooted in the traditional Vietnamese culture. They are more likely to be expected to place domestic issues before school. Many struggle to balance traditional female roles at home with the ideals of gender equality in American society (Centrie, 2004).

How do the two Vietnamese families navigate these muddy terrains of race, class, and gender relations in the inner city of Buffalo? In the following pages, I describe the two families' beliefs and values in relation to education (i.e., their expectations of their sons and daughters), their everyday cultural and literacy practices (i.e., literacy engagement and interactions with schools), and their interpretations and constructions of race and class relations in the inner city. As their stories will demonstrate, both of the families adopted "innovative traditionalism" in their construction of race, class, and gender relations (Zhou & Bankston, 1998). That is, they conform to the traditional Vietnamese values and cultures (e.g., gender roles and importance of education) and internalize the dominant racial and class imaginations (e.g., Asians as model minorities), but at the same time they reinvent new cultural spaces, racial identities, and class relations as creative resistance to the degrading inner-city environment and schools. These dualities of conformity and resistance, however, are played out differently in two families owing to differences in a variety of factors such as family composition, parental strategies, and family socialization experiences.

The Phan Family

The Phan family was originally from South Vietnam. Fleeing from the Vietnamese communist regime, the parents, Dao and Lynne, took different paths to enter America, even though they married in Vietnam. Lynne first went to the Philippines to learn English for six months; she gave birth to their daughter, Hanh, there and then came to Texas as a refugee in 1988. Dao first immigrated to Halifax, Canada, in 1987, and during 1996 he was able to reunite with the rest of the family in Buffalo. They had two children, a sixteen-year-old daughter, Hanh, who was in the eleventh grade, and an eleven-year-old son, Chinh, who was in the fifth grade.

The Phans owned a two-story home in one of the most dangerous and rundown areas in the West Side. The West Side is where many low-income African Americans, African refugees, and Hispanic immigrants live and is known for its high crime rates. Residents in this area often experience problems with housing, employment, and insufficient services. To improve their safety, the Phan family always closed their curtains so that it looked as if no one was at home.

Neither Dao nor Lynne was proficient in English. Dao left Vietnam when he was a second year student in a university, majoring in mechanical engineering. When he was in Canada, he attended an ESL program offered by the government for six months while cleaning parks to make a living. He then worked as a maintenance technician in a nearby school. Lynne graduated from high school in Vietnam. After coming to the US, she had worked many jobs in different factories to support the family. Now, she worked only one job as a nail technician.

Sixteen-year-old Hanh immigrated to the US with her mother when she was two months old. She attended a neighborhood high school with a handful of Vietnamese students. Hanh was the most fluent in English in the family, and was also doing well in school academically. Eleven-year-old Chinh was born in the US, and identified himself as an American. He attended an international school designated for refugees. Though he regarded English (or "American" in Chinh's words) as his first language, he struggled with English reading and writing (and math). He also spoke English with an accent like his parents, and was enrolled in an ESL program at school.

The Phan Parents' Cultural Values and Beliefs on Education

The Phan family's beliefs in education were heavily influenced by Vietnamese culture. Three aspects of Vietnamese culture—appropriate gender roles, strict discipline, and high expectations—were prominent in their everyday life and their educational values.

Dao and Lynne "followed a Vietnamese culture a lot" in raising the two children, especially Hanh. Lynne wanted Hanh to meet the Vietnamese cultural standards of being a virtuous woman. The Vietnamese ideal of "the virtuous woman" urges girls to obey their parents and social norms, requiring higher moral standards than those for men (Kibria, 1993; Routledge, 1992). Hanh was raised to be humble, "[my mom] raised me that way like, 'you didn't know.'" Hanh's parents enforced stricter discipline and social control on her than on her brother. "She let my brother go outside with [his] little friends whatever, but I can't do that because I am a girl. . . . I stay home 24 hours a day unless I'm going to grocery shopping with my mother." Like many other Vietnamese children growing up in America (Zhou & Bankston, 1998), Hanh

Table 3.1 The Phan Family Profile

Name	Age	Occupation	Education	Languages	Others
Dao	NA	Maintenance technician	University studies in engineering, Vietnam (not completed)	Vietnamese, English	Immigrated to Halifax, Canada, in 1987; reunited with family in Buffalo in 1996
Lynne	NA	Nail technician	Graduated from a high school in Vietnam	Vietnamese, English	Stayed in the Philippines for six months; came to Texas in 1988
Hahn	16	Student	Brown High School	Vietnamese, English	Came into the US when two months old; wants to be a medical doctor
Chinh	11	Student	Rainbow Elementary; a semester in a Catholic elementary school	Vietnamese, English	Born in the US; ESL program, also limited in Vietnamese

felt a strong tug pulling her back to her culture of origin. When asked whether she felt more American or Vietnamese, she commented that she felt very much Vietnamese because of the way she was raised: "I was raised by my mother, and she is very careful about how she raises me. I'm not allowed to go outside much . . . I'm not allowed to date, to do lots of things." Though she learned to accept and obey her parents' beliefs and traditions, she did not believe that she was completely isolated: "I'm not in a shell. I know what's going on out there. And I know what I want and I know what people are like . . . I know more than she thinks that I know and she knows I'm smart."

Obedience in Vietnamese culture is also believed to produce achievement and bring honor to the family (Zhou & Bankston, 1998). As part of their filial obligations, children are expected to provide economic resources to parents and other family elders. Kibria (1993) posits that it is in fact partly this strong expectation of future payoff that leads parents to make considerable investment in their children's education. This cultural element, coupled with the folk belief that education is the vehicle for upward social mobility (Li, 2002; Zhou & Bankston, 1998), makes many Vietnamese parents place high expectations on their children's school achievement and their future career directions. Dao and Lynne, for example, hoped that Chinh would become a professional tennis player like Michael Chang (a Chinese American tennis star) and make huge sums of money in America. Since Chinh had a smaller build than athletes from Western countries, who often have advantages in playing basketball, football or hockey, they believed that his physical stature would not be disadvantageous when playing tennis (like Michael Chang, who could also be described as an athlete with a small build). Therefore, they invested a lot of money (about $380.00 a month) in Chinh's tennis lessons by hiring a professional tennis coach. They also required Chinh to practice every week. In fact, Dao invited my research assistant to play a match with them when one of our home visits coincided with their weekly practices, and we came to learn more about their passion for tennis. If Chinh could not make it in tennis, they hoped that he would at least finish high school or go to college, even though they knew that he was not performing well in school at the moment. For Hanh, who was achieving academically, their expectations were much higher. Hanh talked about her mother's goal for her career in the future: "My mom, even though I was little, she was angry if I didn't make up my mind I'm gonna be a doctor. . . . So, there hasn't really that much question what I wanna be. . . . It's already been in my head I have to be a doctor."

To make Hanh stay focused on her goals of becoming a medical doctor, Dao and Lynne did everything to make sure that she was not distracted by outside influences. Unlike her American peers who started working in high school, Hanh's parents did not allow her to follow suit: "And I don't work because my parents don't want me to work. They want me to completely be focused on school. [They would say,] But if you started working, you might like go, 'Well, I can live off this' and might start slacking in the school and do the working. That's not good."

Obeying her mother's wishes about her future career goal, however, had caused Hanh to feel emotionally confused. She struggled between what her mother wanted her to be and what she herself aspired to be. Tearfully, she recounted her struggle with her mother's imposition:

> Because you get old enough, you just start wondering why I can't do all this stuff . . . Around eighth grade, I was not happy with it. So my counselor asked me 'What do you wanna be when you grow up?' Like 'I don't know.' And she is like, "How come?" "Because my mom told me I must be a doctor," I said. She goes, "That's what your mom told you. What do you wanna be?" "I don't know." And I started crying out of nowhere because . . . it's bottled up.

Similarly, although Chinh did not enjoy tennis and saw it as a chore, he obeyed his parents' wishes and continued to go, practicing as often as five times a week. According to Hanh, he was indifferent toward tennis and often tried to put it off, asking his parents to cancel his lessons. When he could not get away from those lessons, he often made deals with his parents, bargaining playing tennis for toys afterwards. However, Dao had "very high expectations" and he hoped that Chinh could play well and bring pride and honor to the family. He says, "[When] people usually see, play with Chinh, [they will say,] 'Oh, that kid play like talent . . . could be a tennis player' . . . something like that."

In sum, the Phans had very high expectations for their children due to their cultural beliefs and their immigrant status. Considering that they themselves were not proficient in English, the next question would be how they supported their children's home learning and what their home literacy practices looked like. This seems to be important, since their expectations for their children may not be realized unless the children acquire proficiency in English. In what ways, then, might the literacy practices at home contribute to their children's success or failure in acquiring English literacy? In the next section, detailed accounts of the Phan family's literacy practices are presented.

Home Literacy Practices in the Phan Family

The Phan family's two-story house was spacious, clean and very simple. There was a big 57-inch TV set with a crack in the middle. According to Hanh, this TV was a trade-in with a Vietnamese friend who needed money. There were a set of couches and a coffee table in the middle of their living room. Their walls were decorated with Asian art, and the doors in the living room, kitchen, and bedroom were decorated with Vietnamese calendars and posters. A large bookshelf at one corner of the room was piled with various kinds of books, mostly Chinh's storybooks and textbooks. Next to the entrance door to the living room, there lay a big pile of encyclopedias, which were a little dusty and seem to have been left alone for a long time. This sitting room was where Hanh and Chinh spent a lot of their free time, playing or watching TV while their parents were at work.

"THEY DON'T HAVE TIME . . .": THE PHAN PARENTS'
LITERACY PRACTICES

Since both Dao and Lynne worked long hours, they did not have much time to read at home. Dao worked about seventy hours a week including Saturdays. His work schedule went from 6:00 a.m. to 2:00 p.m. and then 5:00 p.m. to 10:00 p.m., except for Tuesdays, when he worked for only eight hours. During weekdays, after completing his first shift at 2:00 p.m., he went to Chinh's school to pick him up at a quarter to three. Dao then spent an hour or so with Chinh helping him with his homework before he went back to work for his night shift. Sometimes, when Chinh did not have much homework, he taught Chinh math using a workbook he purchased at the well-known Borders bookstore chain. However, it was difficult for Dao to help because both of them had limited English proficiency and Chinh was also not proficient in Vietnamese. As Hanh explained, "[My father] did try, but his English is very poor and he can't help that much. Like he is good at math . . . but when you are trying to explain it to someone, you need to be able to articulate it and neither of them can speak [English] very well, so they can't take a book and help each other."

Sometimes he also tried to read storybooks purchased through a catalogue sent from school with Chinh. Like many immigrant parents who are not confident about their oral English (Li, 2002), he normally did not read to Chinh. He believed that his accent had influenced Chinh's oral language development: "We found when we get book from most English. You know like pronunciation something like that . . . so Chinh learn from English from me, too . . . like really accent, and big accent, something like that. So he pick up from dad and he go school, and when he speak English, the teacher [think] Chinh get problem with English."

On Sundays when Dao had some time off, he usually went to play tennis with Chinh, which he believed was also bad for Chinh's English: "Chinh try to learn the way from me . . . every day, I have to speak English with Chinh because I go play tennis with Chinh, only me and Chinh. I stay home with Chinh. The way I understand [why] Chinh get trouble."

Dao rarely read or had time to read. Occasionally, he read the *Buffalo News*, a local English newspaper, but more often he read a Vietnamese newspaper published in Toronto that they bought from the nearby Vietnamese grocery store. In order to know about tennis and soccer and to help Chinh become a better tennis player, Dao also bought *Sports Illustrated* sometimes. In terms of writing, Dao rarely had opportunities to write at home, except for writing letters and sending money to their extended families in Vietnam. He opened a checking account shortly before we began the study with the family in May 2004, and learned how to write checks from his wife. Since he rarely wrote in English, he had to constantly ask his daughter or wife how to spell the numbers.

Like Dao, Lynne also did not have much time to read or write at home. Her daily routine consists of getting Hanh and Chinh ready in the morning and then driving them to school before going to work at 10:00 a.m. When she returned home from work at 9:30 p.m., she usually read the delivered mail, took care of some bills, and prepared food for the family for the next day. She also read flyers to find coupons for grocery shopping in Tops, a local grocery store, and in a Vietnamese store nearby. Lynne rarely wrote except for occasional letters to her family in Vietnam and jotting down notes on the big calendar in her room to keep track of the children's schedules and appointments. Since she could not see the children much during the daytime, she occasionally left short messages on a white chalk board in their living room, asking the kids not to go out to play after school.

Like many low-SES immigrants, who often experience social isolation (e.g., Li, 2003), the Phans maintained a very limited social circle. They did not have a close connection with other Vietnamese who lived in the area. Most of their acquaintances were their coworkers, with whom they rarely socialized after work. They preferred to keep a distance from them, as Hanh explained: "My father pretty much works most of the time, so he doesn't [socialize]. He picks up a few friends here and there, but my mom mostly brought some friends she has also at work in the same building. She doesn't go out to make friends at all. She doesn't need to ... it's not we don't want to be too close to them. It's just not needed."

Both Dao and Lynne spoke Vietnamese to each other and to Hahn, who could converse in everyday Vietnamese but could not read or write it. However, in order to help Chinh better learn English, they spoke mostly English to him. According to Dao, they wanted to teach Chinh both English and Vietnamese when he was little, but the director from Dao's workplace advised them that it was too early for Chinh to learn Vietnamese and that learning Vietnamese would interfere with his English learning, so they stopped teaching and speaking to Chinh in Vietnamese. As a result, Chinh had not developed fluency or comprehension in Vietnamese as his sister had. Unfortunately, this piece of advice is contradictory to research findings that the development and use of a first language does not impede the acquisition of English; instead, it should be used as a resource for children to learn English (August & Hakuta, 1997; Cummins, 1989; Valdés, 1998). For Chinh, who was not yet proficient in English literacy, building on his knowledge and ability in his first language might have been significant to his mastery of English literacy. Thus, Chinh's underdevelopment in his first language might have contributed to his slow progress in English, rather than expediting it as his parents had believed would occur.

Chinh had not developed English fluency even though he considered English to be his first language. He had difficulties not only in English pronunciation and vocabulary but also in reading comprehension. It was not clear whether he was ever referred to a reading specialist for a diagnosis. I learned from Hanh and Dao that Chinh's struggles with literacy seemed to have been considered an ESL problem rather than a possible learning disability in school, as he had been categorized as an ESL student and exempted from taking part in some of the state examinations. Chinh's family was unable to understand why he failed to learn English and other subjects such as math. Hanh commented that Chinh was very smart, but "does not seem to be able to articulate his words out . . . He can't get it out as clearly as he should." He spoke in his own particular ways, for example, "can we he see" or "he don't like it." At times, Hanh tried to correct him and show a better way to say it. However, Chinh would not listen and often insisted on his own ways of speaking. He rebutted: "So what? I can use my own words for it."

Chinh's favorite subject in school was social studies, in which he learned a lot about history, especially about the American Revolution and wars. His least favorite subjects were language arts and math, which he thought were "hard." After he came home in the afternoon, he usually spent time with his father or sister working on his math or reading homework and then he had to go to his tennis lessons. In his free time, he sometimes watched TV or played video games on the computer. He was quite proud of his ability to play video games: "Naturally go and do like other kids do like want a game and stuff like that." Hanh translated that he meant "he was good at games. That comes naturally." According to Hanh, he spent much time perfecting his game-playing skills: "he will keep playing games and if he dies, he'll try something else."

During the regular school year, Chinh seldom read books outside school requirements. The previous summer, Chinh went to a public library with his sister to borrow books, and he mostly read "army books, more like helicopters, tanks, and guns and stuff . . . not much reading, just a lot of pictures." According to Hanh, Chinh did not enjoy going to the library any more. Since Chinh barely read for pleasure at home, he did not write either, except for homework assignments.

In order to help Chinh learn English, Lynne used sticky notes to write words such as "couch" and "wall" and put them on matching objects. She also asked a Vietnamese teacher from the school to tutor him regularly after school for a while. Yet Chinh had not shown much progress. One year prior to the current study, they heard that there was a tutoring program offered by the school for students who needed help with English under the NCLB Act, so they tried to register Chinh in the program. However, they were told that Chinh was not eligible for the program because their income was above the level specified by the program requirements. The Phans believed it was unfair that Chinh was denied help, because, regardless of their income level, he still needed help. Lynne tried to talk to a Vietnamese bilingual aide about it when she dropped Chinh off at school, but there was some miscommunication between them, which prevented her from talking with the aide again. Hanh shared her parents' opinion: "I guess [the tutoring program] is signed by the government or No Child Left Behind. Unfortunately, Chinh has been left behind because we are not in low income."

One year prior to the interviews, the Phans paid about $3,000 and enrolled Chinh in a Catholic school to see whether he would perform differently. However, according to Dao, it turned out the Catholic school was too demanding for Chinh, as "they read a lot. A lot of homework, a lot of math, [he] work very hard." Lynne and Dao simply thought that, since they both worked a lot and did not have much time for Chinh, if they paid more money for the school, it would do a better job for their son than a public school. However, to their surprise, the Catholic school required more of their involvement at home. As Hanh explained for his father,

> Most kids going to Catholic school come from better-off families. So [the parents] have more time at home to take care of the children, be more involved in the work they do. But we don't have that kind of time. We tried. But my father works very hard, so is my mother. So they don't have a lot of time at home and I have my own school work to take care of too. So we can't always [be there to teach him]. We're happy to want to teach him new things. They should be mostly teachers [to take care of his school work].

Since Chinh's homework was increasing considerably and he was unable to get the necessary help from home, he cried a lot, because he just could not handle it. Eventually, Lynne and Dao withdrew him from the Catholic school and sent him back to Rainbow Elementary School, which he had attended previously. He felt much happier at his previous school because there was much less homework and it was much less demanding. Although the Phans were aware that the public school might not be helpful for Chinh's literacy skills, they were caught in a dilemma—they wanted Chinh to go to a better school to get more help, but better schools required not just money but also more parental involvement, which was precisely what they could not provide. Thus, going back to the international school seemed to be their only option.

MULTIPLE ROLES AND MULTIPLE RESPONSIBILITIES: HANH'S HOME
LITERACY PRACTICES

Hanh lost most of her Vietnamese that she learned when she was little. "I can understand more than I speak," she said. "Actually Vietnamese is my first language and then I started going to school and I stopped speaking Vietnamese. But my mother always speaks Vietnamese to me, so I can understand just about everything, but I can just speak conversation." However, unlike Chinh, Hanh's English was good: she spoke without any accent, had no problem in reading and writing, and was doing well academically. She managed to learn English on her own. As far as she can recall, her parents never read a storybook to her when she was little, as her mother did not know much English nor did she have time. Hanh revealed that she had not been so good at reading until not long ago when she became interested in reading by chance:

> I can always get by, just doing in the middle around the work [when] the teachers teach you to read stuff. I will read it and it'll be okay. But I didn't, I never enjoyed reading. Then one day, I found a particular book that I liked. I read that . . . so I went to find the other books in the series and I just kept reading, and then I really enjoyed reading. So, after I started, I'm getting better and better and even my spellings got better, and my writing got better. My parents never read to me. They didn't do math with me.

During an academic year, Hanh mainly read textbooks, articles, or books required by her teachers. During summer holidays, she enjoyed reading English fiction, especially books that "change your view of the world . . . like a whole different point of view." Informational books were also her favorites. She recalled that she enjoyed reading a big college textbook—their previous Vietnamese tenant left it in the house—with essays on government issues. If necessary, she sometimes used an encyclopedia and dictionary at home to do research for school writing projects. In addition to fiction and informational books, she also liked to check out the horoscopes and astrology in the newspaper.

Hanh identified herself better at drawing than writing. She admitted that, except for papers and essays for class, she did not write. She had a computer and Internet access at home, which she used to complete her school work. Occasionally she wrote e-mails to keep in touch with her great uncle in Texas. However, she did not use e-mails with her friends from school, because she saw them every day and the messages they exchanged were boring to her.

Immigrant youths are believed to make much more contributions to their households and often assume much more responsibilities than their American peers (Orellana, 2001). Being the most proficient in English in the family, Hanh had also taken multiple responsibilities and roles at home: language broker for her parents; helper with various house chores; and, most importantly, teacher and supervisor to her brother. Hanh played such a crucial role in the family that Chinh, who constantly consulted his sister for help, said that "my sister know more things about this place than my mom and dad."

Like many immigrant youths whose parents are not proficient in English, Hanh assisted her parents with language in every single possible way (Orellana, 2003). Whenever her parents had difficulties with the language, she would help them. She read and interpreted school letters and documents for her parents, especially those concerning her little brother. When her parents did not understand what the letters said, Hanh read aloud so that they would be able to understand them. If they did not understand spoken English well, she would translate it into Vietnamese for them. When they bought goods that needed to be set up, she read the instructions for them or set them up for her parents. For example, when they bought a heated mattress one winter, Hanh read the instructions so that Lynne could assemble it. It was always Hanh who filled in applications or other kinds of forms. When they bought expensive items with mail-in rebates such as a computer or a calculator for school, Hanh filled in the forms, barcodes, and the appropriate addresses and all her mother needed to do was to put it into a mailbox. She also took care of tax forms for the family and helped her mother pay bills. If her mother needed to call a bank or a credit card company or order something from a restaurant, Hanh would make the call.

In addition, Hanh also helped with some household chores such as grocery shopping, preparing food, and sometimes cleaning. Her only outing after school was to accompany her mother to Tops supermarket for general groceries and to a Vietnamese store for special Asian ingredients such as fresh fish and vegetables on Sundays. Hanh helped her mother when she could not read the product names or did not know what the products were. Sometimes when their heating or cooling systems were broken, Hanh checked the yellow pages to find repair information.

Besides assisting her parents with language and house chores, Hanh's biggest responsibility was to help her brother improve academically: "Who's gonna help with his homework? Dad? He is not gonna do it by himself and I will be stuck with doing homework with Chinh." She further explained, "I'm the only one in the house that can speak English fluently or other stuff you know. So, in reading and stuff, I'm the person in the house to be teaching him. And math, I mean my father is good at math but he is limited in his vocabulary, so they can't communicate as clearly as I could communicate with him. So I do have a big hand of teaching him."

Dao acknowledged that when it came to his son's school work, Hanh "can know the most." Hanh's daily routine in the afternoon after school was to help Chinh with his homework. "If there are notes from the teacher, I will read them, and I'll do for him what he needs to be done. I won't sit down to translate it to him. I will say to him, 'This is what you need to do. Now work, I'll work with you while you are doing it.'" After Chinh finished his homework, Hanh checked it to make sure it was done correctly.

Hanh tried to help Chinh learn English whenever she had time. In order to teach him correct pronunciation, Hanh taught Chinh how to sound out a word if he had trouble pronouncing it. For example, she helped him sound out words such as "fat [fæt]" by spelling out the word and asking him to repeat after her. Hanh used to read storybooks with Chinh, but the experiences were often negative, so she did not do it any more. She explained, "Because he's reading and he'll get some words wrong and I have to sit and look over his shoulder. It's kind of straining for me. I'll look over his shoulder and say, 'No, it's this word. I'll help you say it.' Sooner or later, I just get lazy, just fall asleep. . . . I sometimes ask questions like, 'What's happening?' But it's boring, I'll nod off and fall asleep. And he'll call my name, 'Hanh, Hanh,' and he sees I'm not awake, so he won't wake me up, and he'll put the book down and go do something else."

Previous research on immigrant youths' contribution to household work seems to have focused mainly on the socio-cognitive benefits, seeing the contribution as volunteerism and opportunities for learning (Orellana, 2001). Few researchers have attended to the negative effects such work might have on the youths. Centrie (2004), for example, observes that, though the Vietnamese females continue to take up the traditional division of labor at home without resentment, they tend to have less time to think about higher education due to the additional domestic work. Further, they have to negotiate a larger burden than their male counterparts in terms of identity formation, balancing traditional expectations with more liberating American values and options. The cultural clashes between school and home often lead to various psycho-social as well as emotional problems. In learning about Hanh's responsibilities, it seems that she had made more sacrifices and has been under serious psycho-social stress. In order to have more time to help Chinh, Hanh had to give up opportunities to join school clubs or attend after-school activities. She explained, "I'm not too concerned with joining clubs right now. I have to be home to take care of my brother and stuff. I just can't stay after school whenever I feel like it, or whenever they need me to stay in school. I have more responsibility for home." Though she was willing to help, she felt that her responsibility of teaching her brother reading and math was overwhelming. She sometimes wished that her parents could do more to help, like taking time off to speak with the teachers about his learning problems or to sign him up for counseling, but she knew that it was hard for her parents to do so, given their financial pressures: "I wish they'll take time off for him, because he seems like he needs it. But I wouldn't ask them to do that. So, I'm really accepting of them not spending too much time or to take time off. So I accept that." Knowing that her parents could not help, she had high hopes that the school could take more responsibilities in educating Chinh. She believed that if Chinh went to school, where he was supposed to learn from teachers, they should not assign work for the family to teach him. The teachers should be the ones to teach him because that was what he went to school for. However, to her great disappointment, the school often left the responsibility of teaching to the family by always suggesting someone at home help him learn: "They would assign us to teach him . . . [They would say], 'Is there anyone home that can help him? Doesn't he have older sister or something?'" She was frustrated and angry that her brother was left behind by the school and they did not even care: "Teachers, whether or not if he'll fail, they'll still make same amount of money, so if one child is left behind, they just don't really care." She further expressed her frustration with the school:

> They just put him in the ESL class and I think the teacher is Vietnamese. But the thing is, Chinh cannot speak Vietnamese either, nor can he understand a lot of it. So, it just doesn't make any sense [to put him in ESL] . . . And he usually doesn't understand the materials that he learns in school. So, whenever he comes home, and I basically have to teach him the material and it does irritate me because he is going to school for 6 hours but he is not learning anything . . . So, he comes home and expects me to sit there to teach him. It irritates me because I have my own work and I don't mind teaching him if he doesn't understand, but he has to go to school for 6 hours and he is not learning anything and he is coming home and asking me for help. Why don't I get paid to teach him, you know?

Her frustration over her brother's schooling, together with her sociocultural confinement at home, had caused serious psychological stress to Hanh. As described earlier, Hanh could not enjoy the kind of freedom her brother had because her parents enforce very strict Vietnamese cultural traditions on her because she was a girl. Hanh stayed home "24 hours a day" and was "not allowed to date, to do lots of things." However, like many other Vietnamese youths growing up in America, Hanh had found herself straddling two different social worlds (Zhou, 2001). Seeing that her classmates had freedom to do many other things, she had struggled to find answers why her life is different from theirs, "When I was a little . . . like I said, seventh or eighth grade, I started to hate my parents, but I [ask my parents], Why can't I go outside, you know? What the hell are the problems with me going outside, you know? Why can't I go to the movies or something, you know?" To make sense of her unique experiences, Hanh even secretly sought counseling in school. Eventually, she accepted her life as it was, considering her parents' harsh life experiences and her own cultural upbringing: "I accepted it. So I'm okay with it. Like it's the way my mom raised me." She further justified her inner struggle with coming to terms with her situation: "There is not much that more that she can possibly try to shield me from . . . and I'm okay with it and I'm okay being home all the time. Like my mind just says like these are my full roles . . . and I'll have two more years [until I finish high school], I will be out."

Impact of Race and Class Differences and School Attitude

Hanh also reported having experienced racial discrimination. She and other Asian students were treated differently because they looked different and had different names: "And I do see [racial discrimination] affect other Asian kids my age. They'll say, 'oh, your name is kind of weird' and stuff, right? [Asian kids] seem to like keep it in and they'll go quiet and the girls like they walk to the school like their heads down and stuff. They're just feeling like really really shy about it. And I grew to a point like I don't care anymore. I just don't care."

Her painful experiences were not just about their different appearances, but also about how people essentialized all Asians into one group, Chinese. Tearfully, she recounted:

> Because growing up here, and especially when you were little, kids are really ignorant. So, you are different because of your race, and they'll poke fun at you, right? And it would hurt, and at school, I'd cry, but I come home and my parents wouldn't know anything about it, like my mom wouldn't know anything about it. And then, like my little brother, he is still little and he'll come home and say, "They're making fun of me because I'm Asian. They said I'm Chinese. I'm not Chinese," and something like that. They group us all together into one group; and I'll say "I don't want to face it. That happened to me not long ago." [My mom says], "What? You didn't tell me that. How come he's coming home crying and you didn't?"

The treatment she received from others (including her mother's attitudes) had significantly influenced her self-esteem and self-perception. She internalized the negative perceptions and blamed herself for everything. For a period of time, she struggled to understand why: "I didn't understand what was wrong with me because my parents couldn't say, 'you are Asian, so they don't like you.' They couldn't do that. The teachers didn't wanna deal with it. So I didn't know what was wrong with me. I thought I had some internal problems like . . . you know."

Hanh did not receive positive treatment from her school counselors either: "my school counselors . . . they just tell you 'just deal with it,' you know, 'Grow up, deal with it,' right?" In her opinion, the school counselors should at least have the time for immigrant children like her and her brother and were supposed to take care of them. They also needed to be proactive in connecting with the students, as students were too young to make appointments with the counselors and seek help. However, she (or her brother) had not received such care from school personnel. Without the school's support, she had eventually grown to accept it and became more aware of her own power to counteract the negative receptions from peers like the way she dealt with other differences in her life:

> I didn't realize the impression that I used to walk with my head down, and my friends were looking at me like "No." There's just this one boy, he comes to me and he would say, "Why are you looking at your feet when you are walking? Why are you looking down?" and I realized, yes, I was looking down . . . because like you were just trying to hide. But since sophomore year and junior year, I walk with my head up and I'm not scared of anything. I'm not embarrassed about anything. If someone has a problem, they can talk to me about it, you know. If they want to talk behind my back about it, that's them . . . they can't bring it to my face, so . . .

In addition to dealing with racial differences, Hanh also struggled with understanding social class differences. Though her family was now above the poverty line because both her parents worked, she understood the profound differences between those middle-class white people living in the suburbs and immigrant and minority families like hers who lived in the inner-city neighborhoods. She was very agitated by the prejudice that whites had toward them and the ignorance they had about their lives. She was appalled at how little the whites understood the hardship of their life in the inner city:

> There's this one boy, right? I grew up in a kind of bad neighborhood. . . . I had a friend who lived next door, and her friend came over and her mom lives somewhere out in the suburbs, and she drove her here. And she opened the door, right? She was like "Hurry and close the door, right? Hurry and close the door." She was scared like someone was gonna jump out and shoot her, something out of nowhere. Like some Puerto Rican person is gonna come out to shoot her for no reason. She was so scared [of] just being in this neighborhood, right? To be in my old neighborhood, they're just so scared. And I told this to mom and boy . . . "Because we grew up in Ghetto, it wasn't Ghetto, you know." "But it was bad enough." And we're just like, "we were pretty poor and it was a kind of hard." And he goes, "Oh, shut up, it's not that hard." . . . He is really ignorant. And he has no right to [say that].

Hanh's Coping Strategies

In order to deal with distress and anxiety from the cultural conflicts and the negative perceptions of others, Hanh had developed several strategies to cope with her situations. One strategy was to suppress her feelings, to bottle them up, so that neither she nor her parents would notice. She illustrated her coping strategies: "When you don't think about it, just it doesn't hurt you. It's like in my head now I've suppressed it. . . . I think 'How could somebody suppress their memory like how could you forget, right?' and then, as I got older, I realized, 'That did happen. Why did I forget about that?' I think I suppressed my memories sometimes. If I don't think about it, I won't cry about it. I'm very happy here."

Another strategy involved having a detached attitude toward the world around her. She tried to remain distant from people in order to control her emotions and feel safe: "Like my mom says I'm naturally cold-hearted, which is probably why I don't get so [emotional] about things, like I don't come home and cry about them . . . I'm not cold-hearted. It's just a little more aloof than others, you know."

Hanh also appeared to have developed a pessimistic and pragmatic view of people and the world. Like many Vietnamese youths, she tended to withdraw within her family circle and does not like to be connected with people. She explained, "I think I'm smart enough to realize that anything that happens is just temporary and the only thing I can do is be happy with who I am and continue on because people are temporary, like I told you already, our family doesn't connect with people. We don't write letters, we don't have an address book . . . If I'm not benefiting from it, I don't need it. So, I just cut it like loose enough, continue on with me and my family. That's all I need."

Because of her closed social circle, she felt that she could not handle close friendships and chose to be on her own:

> I think it takes a special person to be my friend, too. I can't take people who cling on to me. I don't need that weight on me. So people who need like, social or spiritual or psychological support, I can't handle that, you know . . . if I'm benefiting from you, you benefiting from me, that's fine like I will enjoy that, right? I don't need people to be all close to me all the time, if I don't see you for a couple of weeks, we talk to each other, that's fine you know. You'll know we are friends, but we don't need to be connected that hip-hop-time. I don't need that.

The Ton Family

The Ton family came to the United States in 1993. Like many other Vietnamese refugees, Lo and Cam Ton first went to the Philippines to study English for seven months before arriving in America. Their first child, Mien, was born in

Vietnam and was seven months old when they were in the Philippines. After they immigrated to America, they studied English for three months through a local Catholic church and were hired to do embroidery work in a hat factory in the city. Since then Lo and Cam had had two more children, their daughter Nyen, who was 12, and their son Dan, who was 8 in 2006. They had been working in the same factory since then, but with different schedules, which enabled them to be home with their children at different times.

Lo and Cam both finished grade 11 in high school in Vietnam. Lo could speak conversational English with a heavy accent and Cam only minimum English such as general greetings. They both spoke Vietnamese at home to their children and they socialized mostly with their Vietnamese friends in the neighborhood. Cam's mother, who was a devout Buddhist, also lived with them. She spoke only Vietnamese as well. Grandma helped with cooking and some household chores, and spent a lot of time in a Buddhist temple. The family had lived in an apartment for four years and bought their two-story house in 1998. Even though Lo wanted to live in the suburbs, where there were better schools, he decided to settle in the West Side of Buffalo because it was a relatively affordable place to live and there was a thriving Vietnamese community.

The three children all attended Rainbow Elementary, which is located within walking distance from their house. Lo and Cam liked the school because there are Vietnamese teachers in the school with whom they could communicate. All three children could speak fluent Vietnamese but, like the Phan children, they could not read or write it. Mien was almost two when he came to America with his parents. From first to sixth grade, he had been on the honor roll in school, but slumped slightly in the last two years in the elementary school. To his parents' relief, in 2006, Mien was accepted by the Madison Tech high school, a good high school in the city.

Nyen was born in the United States and identified herself as both Vietnamese and American. She had attended the ESL program for three years and left the program when she was in the fourth grade. She liked to read and draw and had been doing well in school as well.

Dan was also born in America and was "the baby" of the family. He was raised by grandma before going to school and did not attend preschool or kindergarten. In the first grade at Rainbow Elementary, he had a hard time learning to read and write English and doing math. His teachers described him as "slow" and he received two hours per day of special support by a Vietnamese teacher in the second grade.

Dealing with Inner City Living: Gender and Culture
The Tons bought their house in 1998. At that time the neighborhood was still good. However, in the past several years, especially since 2000, the neighborhood had seriously deteriorated. When Lo returned from work at

Table 3.2 The Ton Family Profile

Name	Age	Occupation	Education	Languages	Others
Lo	NA	Factory worker	Finished eleventh grade in high school in Vietnam	Vietnamese, English	Stayed for seven months in the Philippines; came into US in 1993
Cam	NA	Factory worker	Finished eleventh grade in high school in Vietnam	Vietnamese, minimal English	Stayed for seven months in the Philippines; came into US in 1993
Mien	14	Student	Rainbow Elementary; Madison Tech	Vietnamese, English	Born in Vietnam; expected to be a medical doctor
Nyen	12	Student	Rainbow Elementary	Vietnamese, English	Born in US; likes reading and drawing; attended ESL until third grade
Dan	8	Student	Rainbow Elementary	Vietnamese, English	Born in US; "slow" in learning at school

around midnight, he always heard loud music and, in the summer, roaring motorcycles. According to Lo, a lot of people in the neighborhood lived on welfare and did not have to work, and their lifestyle consisted of having parties at night and sleeping during the day. Lo and Ton were also aware of the problems with drugs and gangs, which made them very disappointed. Lo noted, "Before I bought our house here . . . in this neighborhood, I like this very fine. That's why I send my kids at that school. But after a couple of year later, I heard a lot of people say about, not about school, but about neighbor . . . a lot drugs. And then, shooting, something like that . . . I worry about that."

Lo liked the Rainbow Elementary School very much because they had Vietnamese teachers there. However, to his disappointment, he also heard about the neighborhood problems in school. He learned that students were taking drugs such as cocaine and marijuana and "it's not [just] black children, and Hispanic and Asians too." According to a Vietnamese teacher, there were four or five Asians in the school that were like a gang. Lo was advised to keep an eye on Mien. In order to prevent Mien from getting involved in the gangs and to keep him safe from random shootings in the neighborhood, Lo had started to pick up Mien from the school and from friends' houses where he hangs out. Lo explains, "If he want to go somewhere, I take him go you know. I take him, brought him. Then, he want to go home, he call me. I tell him a lot." Sometimes, he did not want Mien to play with some bad friends as "they scare him." However, Mien did not always listen to him: "It's up to [what] they do, you can't [make] them. Like Mien, he have a friend, like bad friend. But if he didn't want to, it's okay. I talk to him a lot about that."

Even though Lo had heard a lot of horror stories about shootings and drug problems in school, he still believed that the school was good, but "just the students were bad." Most of his Vietnamese friends told him to move to a better place, but he had no choice but to stay until the kids completed high school. He explained, "I don't know yet . . . a lot of people say Rainbow Elementary School is bad too. But I have no choice. Mien get one more year. He go to the high school . . . Here, the [living] cheap right now, and couple of years, Nyen go to high school too." He learned that "if you have money, you go to Williamsville [a suburb of Buffalo]. In America, if you have money, you don't want live downtown, but live outside." Lo wanted to "go outside Buffalo," but for now, he had decided that they were going to stay in the city and save enough money for that.

Living in this kind of environment, Lo and Cam found it hard to raise their children according to "the Vietnamese way." In their view, American culture is too open and gives too much freedom to children, which makes them disobedient to parents and elders. Lo noted, "In Vietnam, they listen to us more. They scare . . . Like I said, in America, it's . . . more open." As a result, when Lo talked to Mien about safety in the neighborhood and about going to the best high school, conflicts often arose as Mien would not listen sometimes. Since corporal punishment is not allowed in America, Lo was frustrated that he was not able to discipline Mien: "For example, Mien [did] wrong to me, I just *talk* to him [emphasis his]. But like he make me mad . . . I can do nothing. If he in Vietnam, I beat him something like that . . . But here, I cannot. I worry about that. That's like . . . do nothing. That scare me too . . . He know that. That's why he don't worry because sometimes he mad me, I just *talk* louder [emphasis his]."

Another concern for Lo was raising their daughter in America. Lo commented, "We had a worry about girl in Vietnam [but] not like in America." He believed that, because of frequent exposure to TV, girls in America "experience a lot" more than those in Vietnam. Since it is so open, parents can "say nothing." He noted, "That's why a girl experience a lot too, like Nyen. She grow up, I scare what she don't know. I want her grow up, but I scare when she grow up." Lo preferred that "they follow the Vietnamese way" and that the Vietnamese community would play an important role for that in America: "that's why . . . a lot of people [live] with Vietnamese here. Girl. They're too. The boy too. I know [they're] bad. I'm worry about that." Since there were many things that were out of their control in America, Lo was not confident that he could raise his daughter in the Vietnamese way: "I wonder right now. I don't know how . . . [In] a couple of year, I don't know." Despite these concerns, Lo and Cam would like the children to remain in America even though they themselves wanted to return to Vietnamese someday to live. They acknowledged that "In America, education is good, better than Vietnam . . . When the kids work . . . I don't want them to go back to Vietnam because here is better for them."

Interpreting Race Relations and Class in the City

The Ton family socialized mostly within their Vietnamese community. Lo and Cam's principle about the non-Vietnamese community was keeping a distance. Cam stated, "I don't touch them, they don't touch me." However, in their workplace, they had to interact with people from other ethnic backgrounds. They had coworkers who came from all kinds of cultural backgrounds, white, black, Laos, Korean, Thai, and Chinese. In the community, their neighbors consisted of people who were black, white, Mid-eastern, Puerto Rican, and mixed race. In general, Lo mostly talked to whites or other Asians, occasionally interacting with the blacks for pragmatic reasons. For example, he and his two sons often went to a black neighbor's house for a cheap haircut. All in all, Lo had four black acquaintances in the neighborhood. According to Cam, "We usually don't talk to black people too much . . . I go home and I cooking, clean house, and take care of my children. I don't wanna go to outside."

Lo and Cam's perception of race was very much in line with the popular stereotypes: Asians are smart and hardworking, blacks are trouble-makers, whites (or "American" in Lo's terms) are good people, and the Puerto Ricans are the ones in between. Of Asians, Lo noted in one of our interviews: "A lot of Asian kids, they are smarter than people here . . . . Vietnamese children . . . like they smart more than American people." Realizing that he was generalizing, he corrected himself, "I don't mean smart. I think more probably, they study hard." To give an example, he added, "I work hard . . . my community too. All the Asian people work hard more than American people . . . They smart or not, but [Asian] students, they study so hard more than American people." He further illustrated that Americans (whites) had very different attitudes toward work: "American people [say] 'I've gotta go. Got ten [dollars per hour].' They told me they didn't need to work hard, you know, work like 10 dollar, 4 dollar hours, [and that's] Okay. I don't want that. I want more—15, 19 [dollars per hour] . . . That's why, I work hard more [than] them."

In Lo's view, another attribute of Asians was that they did not complain or make trouble. He explained this at length: "Lao people, Chinese people, Vietnamese people, Thailand, Korea, work very hard. One thing is they [are what the] company want—they not much complain than American people . . . That's why [Asians] still work, work, work, just keep working on something. American people like, they need a thing, they want to complain . . . they complain. They want more money and they [don't] want to work very hard. That's why, they can [take a] leave once a month. But Asian people they don't care, they keep working." Since they worked so hard, Lo believed that it was unfair for many of the neighborhood people to just collect welfare and get all the benefits.

Lo believed that, in each race, there were good and bad people, regardless of skin color: "I say how you report, black and white, some good, some bad. I don't say white good, black bad." Based on the blacks he knew, Lo concluded that "some blacks are good . . . some good, some bad. About three or four people I know very good . . . they don't make trouble." However, he also attributed some of the social problems in the neighborhood to the blacks: "The big problem is shooting, kill people. It's big problem. That's why we think, it's only, it's black, cocaine like that." In general, he regarded the blacks as troublemakers: "Black make trouble, I saw on street. But the people I know is good." When asked about the whites, Lo commented, "White? I know them always good. They don't make trouble." He further commented, "I heard [blacks] always something like trouble. More than the white people. More than the Puerto Rican people . . . It's always make trouble; they act like that. Black more than white, yeah." Lo and Cam considered "being loud" as a sign of trouble-making as well. To them, "talk make trouble . . . Talk too much is have trouble. No talk no trouble." In their view, blacks were "loud" and whites "not so loud." Of the

Puerto Ricans, Lo noticed that they are loud sometimes as "they don't leave, like ride motorcycle."

On the other hand, he seemed to concur with the popular perception that blacks are good at sports whereas whites are smarter than the former. Judging by what he learned from sports on TV, he noted that some blacks were richer than the whites because "black . . . play sports. That's why all athletes are black. That's why. It's more rich, white people like Microsoft—it's white people, they rich because they smart."

Even though Lo considered whites were always nice people, he was also aware that racism exists in the society: "Sometime[s], they [Americans] don't want Vietnamese . . . the boss . . . they don't like Vietnamese people." Lo went on to say, "Sometimes American people and Vietnamese people . . . American people have more chance . . . I'm not [getting] my pay more, but I don't know how to go [to the boss], how to explain, I don't know . . . [so] work for Vietnamese harder. I know it's Vietnamese in America, American hated Vietnamese people little bit." Lo believed that it had to do with Vietnamese people's language skills: "I think that American people, they born here. They speak very well . . . But we are Vietnamese, we just come here, not know much. So we, like me, I don't know how to speak very well; [I] speak little. That's why, a little bit harder . . . Sometime, they [Americans] make trouble, I can't complain them. I don't know how to speak. That's why, that's not fair."

The Ton parents' interpretation of racial relationships was also reflected in the children's socializations in school and at home. Mien seldom hung out with kids outside the Vietnamese circle. Dan occasionally went to play at a white neighbor's house. Nyen usually stayed home and had her friend, Mimi, over to play. Nyen and Dan did not like some of the African students in the school. Nyen told me that "some of them are mean. They annoy me a lot at school. Sometimes, they get me in trouble . . . For something I didn't do. They said they'd hit me." Dan added that "Africans kind of make trouble" and sometimes they say "F words." They both favored the Hispanic students in school because "they are nice." Nyen notes that the Hispanics made trouble "only if they are very angry . . . explode! My friends say, 'I'll explode!'" In Dan's words, "'cause they just express their fear, shout out . . . only if you get on their nerves." For this reason, they both wanted to be friends with the Hispanics, not the African students. Nyen also explained that language was a factor for her choice, "Because Africans don't really speak English . . . If you say something, then they would take it the wrong way. Once I said hi, and they thought I was trying to ignore them, because they just moved in, and I was trying to be a good neighbor. But they thought I was trying to ignore them or tell them to get away." They also had a few white children in their classes, and they thought "they were fun . . . and funny." But, to their disappointment, the white kids did not play with them very much. According to Nyen, they had "only a few of my [white] friends, but they ignore me . . . they hate me." As a result, in school, they played mostly with the Hispanic and Vietnamese students. Nyen further clarified that she did not play with bad kids in school: "sometimes there are black kids. If they're good [I play with them]. If they're bad I don't play with them." Nyen's best friends in school included a girl from Cambodia and another girl from Vietnam whom she had known since preschool.

Home Literacy Practices in the Ton Family

Like that of the Phan family, one of the striking features of their living room was a big 57-inch screen TV set. On one side of the TV was a large aquarium and on the other side was a table piled with papers and other things. That seemed to be a corner for materials related to the children's school. On the wall above the table, the children's school achievements (e.g., Mien's honor roll certificates) were displayed. The younger children, Nyen and Dan, spent lot of time in this room watching TV or playing video games. Their brother, Mien, usually did not play with them. He either played video games on the computer in his room or went to other homes to hang out with his friends.

Lo usually returned home from work after midnight, since he worked from 3:30 p.m. to 11:30 p.m. He went to bed about 1:00 or 2:00 a.m. and got up about 9:30 a.m. every day. He stayed home until 3:00 p.m, while the children came home from school at 2:45 p.m. During this 15 minutes, Lo mostly helped Dan do his homework before he left for work at 3:00 p.m. His wife, Cam, went to work at around 7:30 a.m. and came home from work at about 4:00 p.m. She then supervised Dan with his math homework. As Lo described, "She help him like homework because I have to go work. I'm not home. I still help him, I know how to study. I have 15 minutes study with him. When she come home, she teach him homework." He noted that it was not easy for his wife to tutor Dan's homework as she did not speak English well: "Sometimes, she know how to do it, but she don't understand English. He say Vietnamese with her. That's why she know how to do it." If she came across difficult math problems which she could not solve, Cam left notes on the table so that Lo could read them the next day. Since Dan began school, his father Lo had also been creating extra practice problems and purchasing additional workbooks for Dan to use as supplementary materials.

Since Lo and Cam did not know English very well, their readings at home were mostly Vietnamese. The Vietnamese grocery store in the neighborhood was their main source of reading materials as well as keeping their contact with Vietnam. Every week, they went there to get groceries and pick up two Vietnamese newspapers, *Saigon Canada* and *Thoi Bao* [*Vietnamese Weekly*], both of which were published in Canada. In addition to these weekly readings, Lo also read Vietnamese news on the Internet as a means of keeping up to date with what was happening in Vietnam. Lo's parents and extended family are still in Vietnam and he tried to talk to them by telephone once a month. He also wired a certain amount of money to them every month through the Vietnamese grocery store. During their first few years in America when he and his wife were not making much money, he tried to send about $100 to his parents. In the last few years, as their income had increased, he now sent about $300 a month to his parents.

Lo and Cam seldom wrote at home or at work. This was also true for the children except for the completion of homework at home. The children got up about 7:00 a.m. every day and usually watched TV about half an hour before they went to school. In the afternoon, after Lo left for work, they watched more TV or played video games until their mother came home. After supper, before their bedtime, they watched more TV again. They liked programs or channels such as Animal Planet, *Batman*, or the Cartoon Network. Mien usually went to his friend's house to play while Nyen and Dan stayed home. During the first grade, when Dan showed slow progress in school, Lo took away all the video games so that Dan could concentrate more on his studies. Dan told me during an interview, "My dad told us no games until it's summer vacation. My dad said we can't play unless our grades are up and we can pass the grade we are in now."

On the weekends, the Ton family usually got together with some of their close Vietnamese friends in the neighborhood. They took turns hosting these gatherings. They cooked Vietnamese food, hung out, sung Vietnamese karaoke, or watched Vietnamese movies. Nyen wrote about these gatherings, "My mom and dad have very weird friends, but sometimes their funny. They like to make jokes sometimes and when they sing, I just have to burst out with laughter. They sometimes give me money on New Year's, and we go out to hotel's when we want to have fun." Sometimes when the weather was good, they went to amusement parks or to the mall.

On regular weekdays, the three children had very different activities at home. As the eldest son, Mien had a lot of freedom to do whatever he wanted. After school, he usually went to hang out at his Vietnamese friends' house or has them over in his room. They chatted on line with other friends or people from his school, listened to rap music or played video games on the computer. One of his favorite things was playing Yugioh cards with his friends. He usually came home late at night, often returning around midnight on weekends. As his brother, Dan, commented, "He is always going somewhere." He usually only read for homework at home, but he insisted that "when I chat, I read words."

At school, Mien liked many subjects but he found several subjects, such as social studies, science, and reading hard. He did not like "the project system" that the teachers used for these subjects. He confided to me in an interview, "You got to make these cards . . . I don't feel like doing it . . . it just like too much!" For reading, he found that "the tests are hard . . . the definition test and spelling." When he did not know definitions or the spelling of words while he was doing homework, he "just look[s] it up on the computer." When he got stuck with a project or something, he usually did not like to ask for help, since his dad could not read the English words in many cases. He said that he just skipped them or copied from other students.

Nyen and Dan, on the other hand, were allowed to play only at home. Sometimes, when the weather was good, they were allowed to ride bikes in the neighborhood or to play in their backyard. Dan was allowed to go to their neighbors' homes and play with children his age, but Nyen was usually not allowed to go to other homes (not even her cousin's) unless she was accompanied by her parents. Unlike her two brothers, she had to help with household chores such as cleaning the rooms, mopping the floors and washing dishes. Nyen did not think it was fair but she was told by her grandmother that because she was a girl she "was supposed to work like a maid. And the boys aren't supposed to work, only the girls." With her brother, they usually watched TV together. When she was alone, Nyen usually read such books as the Goosebumps series, which she borrowed from her school library. Compared with her brothers, she read much more at home.

Sometimes, she asked her friend Mimi, a Lebanese girl on the block, to come over to her house and play. They drew pictures, watched TV, or listened to popular white singers such as Britney Spears, Jessica Simpson, and Hilary Duff. She noted that she did not like the black singers such as Beyonce. She wrote the following about her friend Mimi: "I like to play with my friend Mimi because me and her are the only girl on the block. We play tag, we listen to music, we dance while we listen to music, I like Mimi because she makes me feel comfortable when I feel shy or scared, I like Mimi because she is very nice to me, she's like my sister but different skin color." As her father noted, "Nyen has different friends."

Unlike her brothers, Nyen liked school a lot, and enjoyed reading because she had found it easy. She was not afraid of tests, often getting perfect scores on spelling bee activities. Her favorite books were *Cat in the Hat* and *Scooby-Doo*. She enjoyed all kinds of school activities such as fieldtrips and bowling, although what she enjoyed most in school was art. She wrote, "What I like about my school is because of art. I like to draw and that's the place where I can draw realistic stuff and I can learn how to draw people realistic[al]ly instead of unrealistic. I would not want to leave the school because it is very fun there[,] I love that school." She was also very proud to be a big helper in school, "My teacher Mrs. Mason is very nice to me. She let me help her grade our homework. I help her clean up the room when it's a mess." However, Nyen admitted that she did not like writing and considered it "not that easy" because she had to "think of something to write."

Since their grandma did not speak any English, with Cam and Lo speaking minimal English, Vietnamese was the main language used at home. Because they were Buddhists, the children had to pray with them (especially grandma) every night in Vietnamese. Occasionally the children spoke English among themselves. Lo considered it very important to maintain Vietnamese at home: "I think we are Vietnamese. I don't want them lose Vietnamese." He believed that their grandma played a major role in maintaining the Vietnamese language at home as he noticed that other Vietnamese kids who did not have grandparents in the home spoke very little Vietnamese. He also understood the importance of English to their children's future in America. For this reason, he wanted them to become literate in both English and Vietnamese, "They speak English. They have to know [English], they go to school. If they don't learn Vietnamese, they lost. That's why, at home, it's grandma, she is really sometimes speak them in Vietnamese or writing. English, I don't teach, but they have to know, they have to go to school. That's why . . . I want both."

In Lo's words, the children "grow up more Vietnamese in America." In terms of Vietnamese language, though Lo was happy that the children could speak it, he really wanted them to be able to read and write it as well: "I hope they write really Vietnamese." Five to six months prior to the beginning of the research project in May 2004, Lo decided to send the children to a Sunday Vietnamese School operated by the Buddhist temple where their grandma was an active member. The children attended a couple of hours of classes every Sunday to learn how to read and write Vietnamese. However, on account of the differences between English and Vietnamese, their progress was very slow. Lo joked, "Now they can read [Vietnamese], but they don't understand too much . . . They can read English, but I don't understand."

Even though the children considered themselves as both Vietnamese and American, they did not like to learn or speak Vietnamese. Nyen, for example, told me that she did not like to speak Vietnamese or learn to read or write it, because "sometimes it's embarrassing . . . as other people [in school] don't speak it." She would like to learn it if more "other people got to learn it." Her desire to have more validated culture and language was reflected in her writing about her Vietnamese friend, Linda: "My Vietnamese friend name is Linda. She is my friend because she understand my language and she don't have to make fun of it, because she is the same culture and have the same tradition as me."

Mien did not enjoy going to the Vietnamese school either. He reasoned, "It's the same thing you learn in Vietnamese school . . . just sit and write down stuff." They were often bored when their grandma tried to teach them to read and write Vietnamese at home as well. Lo was very frustrated about the children's attitude: "But you know, they don't want to read. Or they don't want to write Vietnamese. They just like, they bored with it; they don't want it."

The disparity of language skills between the parents and the children had resulted in communication barriers between the two generations as well as between the school and home. The children often did not talk to Lo and Cam about school, even though they wished they could share more with their parents. Nyen explained, "Because sometimes I can't translate [it] into Vietnamese . . . I just tell them how I did in school, like I did a good job or a bad job." Mien concurred that he did the same. For example, if they were to have a test, they just informed Lo or Cam that they would have a test, without explaining the test in detail. As Lo explains, "Maybe this week they got a test, but I don't know what the test. They will let me know, ok, this week, you got a test, Monday, Tuesday." Not knowing the details sometimes created problems for Lo. In the spring of 2006 when Mien needed to take the IQ test for admission to Madison Tech high school, Lo did not know where to go or what to prepare. They went to the wrong school at the wrong time and missed the test. Lo thought that Mien would forever miss the opportunity to get into the school, but was unable to call the school for more information or to explain the situation. Out of panic, Lo called me for help, almost crying. I immediately got on the Internet, found the location and the phone number of the school, called and explained the situation, and learned that Mien could take the test again the next day. When I provided Lo with all the information he needed and told him that Mien could go take the test the following day, he was very relieved that his son was being given another chance.

Every day, Lo and Cam made sure that the children went to school and checked whether they had homework. However, they were not familiar with what and how the children studied at school. Lo noted, "I know report cards . . . They're at school everyday, if no school, I know. But what they do at school, what they study at school, that thing I don't know." Lo and Cam knew that the children could not miss school because, if they did, the Vietnamese teacher at the school would call to inform them. They were very proud that the children had never missed school even for a day.

Parental Expectations for Children

Like many Asian parents, Lo and Cam had very high academic expectations for their children but, at the same time, they held very different standards for their sons and daughters. Lo stated that he "want my child grow up to good, to study and go to college and good job." He acknowledged that it would all depend on the children: "We can't choose. That's their choice. If they want, yes. If he say no . . . "

Lo and Cam had much higher expectations for Mien, their first son. Mien had been on the honor roll and his grade average was usually in the low 90s. Lo, however, had not been satisfied with his performance, telling him to "get more." Lo explained, "I want them more than that. He knows a lot. I want like 99 [percent]." Two years prior to Mien's graduation from elementary school, Lo had already asked me and his friends about what the best high school was in the city. He learned that Lakeside High was the best so he has been pushing Mien to aim for that school. Mien, on the other hand, did not care that much about what schools he would attend and claimed that he wanted to go to a neighborhood school closer to their home. Yet the school closer to home was known for its low academic performance and violence. Lo told me, "[Mien] said that he go to Johnsons High but I said no . . . I wanna he go far from West Side . . . whatever school . . . but not West Side." Lo was very worried and often talked to Mien about the importance of studying hard to go to a better school. In the seventh grade, Mien's grade average lowered a few points and that really worried Lo. He started to monitor Mien's activities more closely, wanting to know where and what Mien did after school, and not allow him to go out as much. Finally, Mien agreed to go to Madison Tech, another high school in the city that was good but not as good as Lakeside High. Lo, however, still was not happy about that: "But I want he go to Lakeside High. He say he don't wanna. I know it's hard. He want to go to Madison Tech. I don't know. I told him next year, we go to Lakeside High."

The reason that Lo and Cam had been pushing Mien to go to the best high school in the city was that they wanted him to become a medical doctor. Lo explained, "I want him to be a doctor . . . so he can help the family . . . make money too . . . We like that, but I don't think he can get the goal." Mien, on the other hand, wanted to become something quite different—he wanted to become a rapper or rap singer.

Lo also told Nyen about the two best schools, but Nyen said that she wanted to go Fordham High, an ordinary public high school in the city. Lo was disappointed that "she don't want to go Madison Tech. She don't wanna go to Lakeside High." However, he did not insist on it as he did to Mien, nor did he ask for her reasons. Later, Nyen told me in an interview that the reason she wanted to go to Fordham High was because her friends would be attending it. Nyen said that she would like to become a baseball player, but Lo did not take her aspirations seriously or offer her any direction.

Since Dan had not been doing well in school, Lo worried greatly about him. In an interview in 2005, Lo was debating whether to let Dan continue to grade 2 or to stay in grade 1: "I want he go to grade 2 because he's 7 years old already now, if let him stay in 1, you know, it's late. To be 8 years old in grade 1. I talked to the teacher, and he [said] we have him better, better and go to grade 2." Lo had been disappointed at Dan's school performance and realized that his children might not be able to fulfill his expectations of them: "sometime I want, [but] they can do nothing I want. Like [I] want [them] to do doctor, lawyer, but I don't think they do. Dan, he wants to do the police . . . or fireman something like that. I hope he do that."

Helping Dan

Lo and Cam had hoped that Dan would make good progress at the end of his first grade. However, in the middle of his second grade, the Vietnamese teacher told them that Dan was "still slow in everything." As Lo observed, Dan "can speak but he cannot write and read." Moreover, Dan was also slow in math. In the second grade, Dan received two hours of extra help from a Vietnamese teacher. Sometimes, the teacher read storybooks to him. He also attended a summer school in 2005. However, Dan's progress was still slow. Dan admitted himself, "I failed a lot." Lo and Cam were very worried and decided to try their best to help him at home. Lo did not want to go to the school to ask [mainstream] teachers for help. He explained, "Very hard sometimes. I don't speak [English] very well, I don't know how to talk to the teacher. He got another child, you know." They were very frustrated, but could only do the best they could to help Dan. Lo expressed his feelings: "me and my wife just try make them better and better, but I cannot do nothing, because he's slow. I teach them writing, I teach them reading, that's it. You help him better."

Every day when Dan comes home, Lo would check his book bag to see if he had any homework. Usually, the teacher would send home a book for Dan to read. Lo was always surprised by this homework, as he noted that Dan "didn't know nothing about book. He know some words like easy word, like two letters, that's he know, like 'we,' yes he know, he cannot know long word." In order to teach Dan how to read, Lo and Cam first read the letters to Dan. Lo described it: "I still read him the letter, I read first and he follow me. We did it one time he'll tell me that if he don't know, he cannot read alone . . . I let him to read until he can read the book." They also bought some reading toys such as the "Leopard Learning System" so that Dan could see the words and listen to the sounds and read after it. Since Lo was not home at night and Cam could not read much English, there were no bedtime stories for Dan. Instead, he usually watched TV before bedtime. Lo noted, "I not home. If I home, I don't know what story book to read to him."

Lo and Cam also discovered that it was very easy for Dan to forget the reading: "sometimes, he read . . . today, he ok today, he know today, but next week he forget." In order to help Dan commit words to memory, they decided to have him copy each word five times. Each night they selected ten words from his homework book and asked him to copy. Lo believed that copying is a very effective method: "[If] he is not writing, he [did] not remember . . . While I say, write a word he know, he cannot say that, he cannot write, but he see it, he can write."

In terms of math, Lo and Cam noticed that, even though Dan was not good at math, he had very little math homework. Lo only recalled Dan having two math homework assignments. In order to help Dan improve his math skills, he and Cam created some extra math homework for him to practice. Lo admitted that he was not sure how to help his son improve in math and he could not express it to Dan's teachers: "I don't know how to teach math. I try help him. How I want to say to teacher?"

Sometimes, Lo and Cam would ask the older children to help. However, Dan did not like to study with Mien because Mien always wanted Dan "to go fast," whereas Dan could not do so. Mien always ends up being very impatient and mad, sometimes making Dan cry. Dan preferred reading with Nyen, who was more patient. Lo describes it: "he can stay with her . . . She don't get mad. She don't talk loud. But Mien, he want to quit . . . finish it early. That's why Dan don't want it."

When Dan finished second grade in 2006, Lo became more worried, as Rainbow Elementary School would no longer have any Vietnamese teachers. According to Lo, one Vietnamese teacher passed away; one moved away; and the last one, whom Dan really liked, would retire that year. The school would not hire any more Vietnamese teachers because of the budget cuts. Lo was very disappointed: "I don't know how to say about that. I want Vietnamese teacher there because of a lot of Vietnamese kids like Dan . . . We have some parents [who] don't know how to speak English . . . After Mrs. Hon [the Vietnamese teacher], who [will] help?" Even though he wanted to let the school know this fact, he could not get his points across because of his English: "I call them, because sometimes in meeting, we can come there, but we sit down. We listen. But we don't know how to say."

Conclusion

In this chapter, I have described the multifaceted home literacy practices of the two Vietnamese families as they adjust to their lives in an American inner city. Their experiences demonstrate that cultural beliefs, gender, race, and class are factors that shaped the children's home literacy practices. In both families, the parents' occupational status, their busy work schedule, and their limited English language proficiency have shaped not only their own reading, writing, and socialization experiences, but also their abilities to be actively involved in their children's learning, especially their reading, writing, and content area learning (e.g., math). The Phan parents stayed mostly within their own family, creating a private space that separates them from the Vietnamese community. In contrast, the Ton parents were active members of the Vietnamese community, creating continuity between their private space at home and the public space in the community (Centrie, 2004). Therefore, for the Phan children, especially Hanh, home and school were separate spheres that require an either–or position and there was no other outlet or option. For the Ton children, in contrast, even though school and home were separate, their community engagement generated more social capital (Li, 2007) and provided them with spaces of socialization that allowed them to feel comfortable in both spheres.

Whether or not the families interacted with the Vietnamese community, both families tried to practice "the Vietnamese way" in relation to the urban American way. First, Vietnamese culture and language were of paramount importance in the homes. Both parents saw using Vietnamese at home as their identity markers. In terms of culture, both families enforced high expectations, obedience, and appropriate gender roles for their children. In both families, thanks to the parents' own immigrant status in America and their cultural beliefs in education, they had very high expectations of their children's academic studies and their future careers in America. Such high expectations, however, were sometimes unrealistic and in some cases might have caused psychological stress on the children. As noted at the beginning of this chapter, many (Southeastern) Asian children are not "new whiz kids." Instead, many, especially those residing in inner-city communities, are facing multiple risk factors that may impede their academic achievement. In the two families, the older children might fit the "model minority" stereotype; the younger children, however, did not. For example, Chinh Phan and Dan Ton both struggled with learning English and achieving academic success in school and their home literacy experiences were characterized by catching up with school work.

For the older children, especially the girls, in addition to high parental expectations, their experiences were also simultaneously burdened by traditional values and gender roles (Centrie, 2004). Hanh Phan and Mien Ton, for example, were both expected to become medical doctors who would bring not only money, but also prestige and honor to the family; but Hanh, a daughter, was laden with multiple roles and domestic responsibilities (e.g., language broker, teacher, and house chore helper) at home whereas Mien, a son, was exempt from all these responsibilities. Instead, his sister Nyen was expected to take up those domestic roles and responsibilities while he enjoyed the freedom of visiting his friends until late at night. Similarly to the Vietnamese girls in other studies (Kibria, 1993; Zhou, 2001), Hanh and Nyen accepted their domestic roles even though they knew "it is unfair." They were socialized in their traditional gender roles at home while at the same time becoming cognizant of gender inequalities from their experiences at school and the larger society. Thus, they were placed at a contradictory gender location where they had to develop "a double-consciousness." Hanh, as the eldest and the most proficient in English in her family, assumed multiple responsibilities and roles at home. These heavy burdens had increased her frustration with the American school system, which was insensitive to their family needs, and her tension with her parents, which had caused her serious psychosocial stress. Indeed, Hanh had been walking on a "family tightrope" (Kibria, 1993). In contrast, Nyen did not have to shoulder all the responsibilities, as her parents had a support network through her grandmother and other community members. In addition, she had the luxury of breaking her family boundaries and making non-Vietnamese friends who were allowed to come to her home and play with her, even though, like Hanh, she was not allowed to go out. And, unlike Hanh, Nyen did not need to choose to be either American or Vietnamese—she was trying to become "both Vietnamese and American." Moreover, her parents allowed her to have "different friends," and their academic expectation for her is not as high as for her brother. These factors allowed Nyen spaces for accommodating her dual cultural identities and reconciling home and school (and societal) expectations.

In addition to gender, dealing with race and racial relationships was also part of the two families' living and daily literacy practices in the inner-city neighborhood. Just as Asian students were racialized against other racial groups (e.g., those in Lee, 2005), the Vietnamese families also racialized other social and cultural groups while internalizing their racialized selves at the same time (e.g., being the model minority and being the smart, the hardworking, and the non-complaining). The two families were simultaneously superior and inferior in their social positioning. On the one hand, their above-poverty-line income differentiated them from those individuals receiving welfare and the academic success among some of their children afforded them a superior status in the inner city. On the other hand, in both families, they understood America as the white America and viewed the blacks, including African Americans and African immigrants, as the source of the social problems in school and in the larger community. Therefore, just as they were aware of their superiority to the black race, they were also very cognizant of their social subordination to the white dominance and to the existing structural racism. Like the Vietnamese youth in Weis and Centrie (2002), the Vietnamese families "simultaneously experience both social subordination *and* racial and ethnic privilege" (p. 33, emphasis original).

The two families' stories of literacy and living as they move across home, school, and work suggest that home is a place where dynamic intersections occur among structure, culture, and agency—where a creative culture-building takes place within the context of external social and economic forces as well as their own cultural frameworks (Foner, 1997). Through these creative plays or intersections among race, ethnicity, class, and gender, the two families fuse the old cultural values and the new environments to create a new kind of literacy and living. How do these factors play out in the black families who are among "the constructed other"—the troublemakers—in the inner city? In the next chapter, I introduce two Sudanese refugee families and describe the dynamic intersections among structure, race, culture, and agency in their literacy and living.

4

Being Sudanese, Being Black

"We are not African Americans, we are Sudanese American."
—Mahdi Myer (Father), May 2005

This chapter brings you into the worlds of two Sudanese refugee families—the Torkeri family and the Myer family. Each family had six children who attended various schools in Buffalo. Since the early 1990s, the United States has witnessed an influx of African refugees. The most recent estimate indicates that the number of African-born immigrants exceeded one million in 2004, and the number continues to increase (Grieco, 2004). Many of the new African refugees came from Sudan. Sudanese refugees, who were displaced as a result of the outbreak of the civil war that began in 1983 between the northern Sunni Muslims and the southern animists and Christians, are the largest among these new immigrant groups from Africa. Most Sudanese refugees came from southern Sudan, and most of them were Christians. In 2003, it was reported that there were approximately twenty thousand Sudanese refugees who resettled across the United States, with almost four thousand new immigrants arriving yearly, and the number is still growing (Migration News, 2005).

Like the two Vietnamese families in the last chapter, the Sudanese refugee families, who came from different cultural and linguistic backgrounds and resettled in the most impoverished inner-city neighborhoods, also experience various kinds of difficulties and challenges in their acculturation process, such as cultural clashes between the old and new worlds and the impact of gender shift upon resettlement, employment, and education (Hayward, 1994). However, unlike the Vietnamese, who are often at the margin in racially stratified America, Sudanese refugees have to wrestle with different terrains of race and class politics. As members of the black community in America, they are at the bottom of the lowly blacks–lofty whites continuum. They are "the faces at the bottom of the well" (Bell, 1992), who are members of the ultimate "black other" in the dominant racial imagining—an "other" that is stigmatized as being lazy, poor, welfare dependent, untrustworthy, violent, incompetent, and unintelligent (Fordam, 1996; Shipler, 1997; Sigelman & Tuch, 1997; Waters, 1999). Translated into children's schooling, black parents and adults are often painted as uncaring and uninvolved in their children's education (Sampson, 2002). Being white, on the other hand, is associated with "all that is ostensibly good about America and 'being American'" (Lee, 2005, p. 4). That is, whiteness equates to rightness, goodness, self-sufficiency, and independence. In schooling, whiteness becomes what is normalized—the essence of what is labeled knowledge, good behavior, skills, abilities, and credentials necessary for upward social mobility (Fordam, 1996).

The stigmatized images about blacks, deeply rooted in American history, shape whites' attitudes toward various ameliorative social policies targeted at blacks (e.g., the areas of housing, education, and employment described in chapter 2) (Sigelman & Tuch, 1997). Not only that, these images about blacks also affect how immigrant blacks (as well as other minorities such as the Asians in the previous chapter) position themselves in relation to the native-born blacks—the African Americans. As a dark but foreign presence (Bell, 1992), immigrant blacks often see the label "black" as defining an ethnic cultural identity more than skin color. The West Indians in Waters' (1999) study, for example, choose to distance themselves from native-born African Americans by emphasizing the cultural differences. These differences are often constructed around values in education, work ethics, and social behaviors such as drug use and in relation to the "defective" culture of poor African Americans. In this sense, immigrant blacks often position themselves as the "other" of the constructed "black other" in the racial imagining—an "other" that is culturally different and better than the prevalent "black other." Thus, immigrant blacks are placed at a contradictory racial imaginary—they are not white, nor are they truly black in the established racial hierarchy.

Whether or not the immigrant blacks choose to associate with blackness, their dark presence often does not exempt them from personal and structural racism in America (Waters, 1999). To the immigrant blacks such as the West Indians, stigmatized racial imagining is the same inescapable barrier to their upward social mobility (Fordam, 1996). To move up from the bottom of the socio-economic ladder in urban America, the immigrant blacks such as the Sudanese in this study, therefore, must resist the negative claims about the African Americans and at the same time, reinvent/reinforce their immigrant identities that separate them from the native-born blacks.

In the following pages, I describe the tensions the families experience as they straddle between the two cultural norms (those in Sudan and in America's inner city) and reconfigure their racial and class relations in relation to native-born African Americans. As their stories will demonstrate, both families experience conflicts and contradictions between the intrinsically valued ethnic/African identity and the externally stigmatized racial/black identity. Like the middle-class African American parents in Fordam's (1996) analysis, the Sudanese parents, formerly middle-class in their country of origin, intentionally taught their children to conform to established social rules and norms (e.g., being good people/American) as a way to resist society's negative images about blacks. In the meantime, the parents, while conforming to the dominant ideologies about the "black other," also tried to develop their own strategies to capitalize their children's opportunities in America through resisting the school system's sanctions (e.g., in school choices and ESL programs) against refugee children. Each family's daily struggles and contradictory unity of conformity and resistance suggest complex workings of race, ethnicity, and social class factors that both shape and constrain their literacy and living in urban America.

The Torkeri Family

The Torkeri family originally came from a southern city in Sudan called Juba. Before coming to the US in 1999, they had spent three years in Egypt. The mother, forty-one-year-old Anne, was multilingual, speaking Bari (her tribal language in Sudan), Arabic (Sudan's national language), and English, which she learned in school. In Sudan, she was raised in a well-off Christian family which highly valued education. She attended a private missionary high school called Comboni School in Sudan. During her motherhood in Sudan, she took courses in education, clinical psychology, and women's studies, working toward a BA, but did not finish the internship training. After she immigrated to the US, she worked hourly as a family educator at "Even Start" programs organized by the Erie Regional Community Office. She would visit other refugee and/or immigrant families, teaching them English and communication skills. After working for a few months, she was laid off and had since been staying at home to raise her children until 2006, when she found a job as a factory worker.

Anne's husband, Tifa, was forty-three years old. He spoke a Sudanese local language called Natuka. He also spoke Arabic. Following his father's wishes, he studied law in Egypt, although he wanted to become a medical doctor. He left Egypt to immigrate to the US before completing his studies in law. He was currently a welder and often worked long hours. He wanted to become an auto-body mechanic in the future if the opportunity presented itself.

There were six children in the family: Owen (fifteen years of age), Nina (thirteen), Fred (eleven), Irene (six), Jude (three), and Igma (eight months). Owen attended an inner-city high school, and Nina and Fred attended a public school designated for refugee children, Rainbow Elementary. Owen and Nina had also attended a school in Egypt for two years before they immigrated to the US. In Rainbow Elementary, Nina and Fred attended ESL programs. Fred was designated as a special needs student because he had a physical problem with his left arm. He also had an "abnormality in his brain" caused by an expired vaccine when he was three years old. This required him to attend three

Table 4.1 The Torkeri Family Profile

Name	Age	Occupation	Education	Languages	Others
Tifa	43	Welder	Studied law at a university in Egypt (not completed)	Natuka, Arabic, English	Wants to become an auto-body mechanic
Anne	41	Housewife	Graduated a private high school; undergraduate in Sudan (not completed)	Bari, Arabic, English	Left Sudan in 1996 for Egypt; immigrated to the US in 1999
Owen	15	Student	Brown High School; two years of schooling in Egypt	Arabic, English	Born in Sudan; ESL program; interested in engineering
Nina	13	Student	Rainbow Elementary; two years of schooling in Egypt	Arabic, English	Born in Sudan; ESL program; interested in arts
Fred	11	Student	Rainbow Elementary	Arabic, English	Born in Sudan; special education, PT, OT, and ESL
Irene	6	Kindergartener	Hurley Charter School	Arabic, English	Born in the US; likes to read and write
Jude	3	NA	NA	Arabic, English	Born in the US
Igma	8 months	NA	NA	NA	Born in the US

programs during school hours: ESL, physical therapy (PT) and occupational therapy (OT). He must also attend summer school as a result of the therapy sessions. Irene, who was six, was enrolled in a Head Start preschool program at a charter school where all students wear uniforms. All of the children could understand and speak Arabic, but could not read and write it. The eight family members (see the family profile) lived in an upper-level two-bedroom apartment situated in a two-story building located in an inner-city neighborhood known for its high crime rates, drugs, and alcohol problems. In the following pages, the Torkeri family's experiences of adjusting themselves to the urban living and schooling in the US are presented in detail.

The Torkeri Family's Adjustment to a New Life in the US

DEALING WITH EMPLOYMENT AND WORK

Like many other immigrant families, the Torkeri family had experienced multilayered difficulties in adjusting to a new life in the United States, including language differences, changes in gender roles and cultural identity, employment, and community socialization (Hayward, 1994). Although Anne and Tifa learned English while attending school in Sudan and/or Egypt, they never used it there for communication. To learn more English, Anne went to an ESL school run by a local Catholic charity. She was progressing so well that she was hired as a part-time helper by the Even Start program. During that time, Tifa was still in his welder training, so Anne was actually the main breadwinner of the family. After she was laid off, Tifa finished his six-week training and found a job, which allowed Anne to stay home with their children. Anne remembered that it was an extremely difficult time: "I'm too exhausted because whenever I came back, before I change, went to kitchen to do something for the kids and they eat, and wash the dishes, you know. Usually I go to bed like at 12:00, then in the morning, I have to wake like 5:00. Prepare things for the baby and go to work. It's really a problem here, but at home is good because my relatives can come and stay with me, my husband's relative can come and stay with me, they can take care of my kids, they can wash everything for me, the cloth, the dishes, and they can cook even for me. If I'm working, I just go to work and I came back . . . they prepare the food, and they call me "Come and eat!" But here, there is nothing like that, and I can't allow my kids to go and play."

Tifa went to work at 3:00 p.m. and came back home at 12:30 at night. Since his wage was not enough to feed the family of eight (he earned about $11.79 per hour for 40 hours a week), he slept about 4 hours a day, and in the mornings he fixed cars to make extra money. He usually went to look for used parts for cars because he was still learning how to fix cars. Since he knew some dealers, sometimes he went with them to find parts. He usually bought two to four cars a year, fixing and selling them. Since he was always busy and rarely at home, whenever he had time on weekends, he tried to help the children with homework. Although his current job was far from his original dream of becoming a medical doctor or a lawyer, Tifa knew that his training in Sudan would not be recognized in the US, and he had come to accept the fact:

> I got a certificate [from my welding training]. But of course, here they don't consider any certificate you're bringing from outside, so I showed to them, convince them that I can do welding, then I was allowed to do welding . . . I have been preparing myself for 25 years I'll go work as a lawyer, but now I ended as a welder. I don't feel bad because the situation force me to . . . I cannot practice lawyer, . . . first of all, to practice law here, the law here is a business, it needs money; and then my English is not enough good to practice law here . . . I don't think I would be survive here . . . so I'm not thinking of practicing law.

However, Tifa still held his American dream inside. He liked to read books and articles from magazines such as *Quality Black Enterprise*, which often reported stories of successful black people. He reasoned, "I like to associate with the rich people maybe I will be able to get some good ideas from them because everybody is talking one day that you succeed, you are going to have money. So I would like to read about such things about the rich people."

FINDING HOUSING

Anne and Tifa did not like the place where they were living. Anne had been particularly unhappy about the neighborhood: "oh my goodness, these neighbors . . . all out drinking; people coming in and out . . . you can see the women, that there's something going on. I don't want my kids to go out and play." In order to move out of there, they had striven to save money to buy a house in a better neighborhood: "Even now and then, I'm under stress because I'm just thinking if I could just get the place right away, we'll leave." They had a lock on their fridge so that the kids did not have free access to it whenever they wanted. They always looked for coupons to buy things for the kids such as diapers at a cheaper price. One day, for example, Tifa found a one-day-pass coupon for Sam's Club in a magazine, and Anne marked the date and bought some diapers and ground meat. Unfortunately, since they did not have enough money that day, she was not able to buy extra diapers and food. They could not afford the $35 membership fee. They budgeted their living costs every month. Since they came to America, they had been relying on a credit agency to pay their bills, and the agency charged about a dollar for each bill paid. Finally, in October 2004, they opened a savings account and Anne hoped that this would help them save more money. Anne noted, "I keep the receipts always.

We start budgeting all the time because I said we want to know exactly what we use every month. He [her husband] wants to know, so that we may not spend too much on all this. And now, I was telling him, if we can open the saving account . . . if it is like even $25, we have to put it because if we keep on saying that we can't, we can't . . . we are not able to save anything. So, we start opening a saving account the day before yesterday. We open with $50."

Anne especially wanted to move to north Buffalo, because it was a better neighborhood which would provide her children with a better living and learning environment. In addition, Anne thought that the family would need more space in the near future as the children grew older. The current apartment has had many problems such as leaking pipes and an overflowing toilet. The landlord did not want to fix the problems because it was too expensive. Finally, in fall 2005, when the apartment became almost inhabitable, the landlord decided to renovate it. That meant they had to move out of the house very quickly. However, with a family of eight, they could not afford to move to a bigger apartment. Anne discovered that there was a government-subsidized housing program which would provide a three- or four-bedroom apartment at a cheaper price. Unfortunately, it was too late for her to apply and there were no more apartments available at that time. Finally, they found that their next-door neighbor had to move out, so they secured that apartment at a similar rent.

The difficulties in securing an affordable and livable apartment motivated Anne to find ways to get their own house. Recognizing that they would not have enough money to purchase a house through a regular channel, Anne tried to find some alternative ways to obtain an affordable house. Through her Sudanese friends and her church, she found two opportunities which she might apply for: house auction and house donation offered by Habitat for Humanity.

Taking into account some suggestions that her friends gave her, she decided not to apply for a house auction because there was a risk of not getting a house or she might get a house that was in a bad condition and in a bad neighborhood, which would cost a fortune to fix and maintain. Thus, Anne decided that the house donation through Habitat for Humanity was more reliable. She inquired through the church and found that she was eligible and sent an application. In order to obtain a house through this program, Anne and Tifa had to work five hundred hours of community service. After that, they may be able to get a house at approximately $25,000–$30,000 without a mortgage. Anne asked her daughter or friends to babysit to enable her to contribute towards her five-hundred-hour community service commitment. By May 2005, she had already accumulated two hundred hours of community services, and hoped that she could soon get a house.

Being Sudanese, Being Black

Another dimension of their life in America was dealing with their Sudanese identity in relation to "Afro-Americans" (which is what Anne and Tifa call African Americans). In most cases, Anne and Tifa found that others consider them to be "Afro-Americans," even though they clearly differentiated themselves from them. Tifa commented, "the way how we look at things, me and Anne and the kids will be different, the value here and the values in Sudan, the different place." He gave the following example:

> There in Sudan, we have to respect the elder . . . respect all, a lot of things, we have to respect everybody who is older than you . . . That's our [culture], it's very important for us. And . . . the responsibility of bringing up kids is really, the responsibility for the whole society . . . Sometimes like, if I'm going on the street, and I saw someone's son who is behaving very bad there or doing something very bad, I will go to him and said you are not doing this . . . if you continue doing this, I will go and tell you parents. That's home there. But here, you cannot.

Concurring with Tifa, Anne believed that in America everyone was too independent and it was hard to find a safe and responsible community to socialize their kids, as people did not interfere with other people's business: "Here they don't do that . . . [they'd say], 'you're not supposed to talk to my kids like that. Who are you? . . . I don't know you and all.' But at home nobody will say that."

For the children such as Owen and Nina, the differences between them and Afro-Americans were that the latter "do different stuff," "they talk differently," and "they behaved a lot differently." In addition, they also thought that their food and language were different from those of Afro-Americans as well as of other ethnic groups. Anne noted that the differences are historical:

> When we talk to them, they said they don't know their origin, where they came from. They know that they came from Africa, but which is specific country, they don't know. But this is history, you can't deny history. It's there. If you like it or you don't like it, it's there. . . . The difference between us and them, we know where we come from. We know our generation; we know our elder grandpa and all this stuff. But for them is just like, some of them, they like us, some of them, they dislike us. Like one day, I was just talking to one of friends of mine. And he said that you are lucky. First of all, you have a language that you can speak and you know where you come from. Even one day you can decide and go on visit. But for me, I'm just like stuck here.

The families' perspectives on Afro-Americans were heavily influenced by the high crime and welfare rates. In Anne's view, discrimination existed in America, but it also existed in many countries. The more important thing, in her view, is valuing education and struggling for the chance to succeed. This was precisely the difference between Afro-Americans and Sudanese people and that was why she believed that Sudanese people were better in this respect: "There are things like that happening. But still there is chance. Why do you give up that for education? They have a lot of chances here." Anne further elaborated her point,

But they have to struggle. There is nothing that you can find easily like that. Everything you have to struggle for it and then after that, at the end you can succeed. I don't support the system here. That is good that welfare can help, but like if you are helping me, like others, they like to be single mom. If I'm a single mom, I don't think there is a reason that I keep on every year pregnant and getting more children, and no not, I just depend on support, why? . . . Sometimes my heart is just breaking, because . . . there is a time tomorrow, they can become president; they can be, they can serve people like they can be in political places and all these stuff. They are many chances. But if . . . you keep on like [being] a single mom, [having] kids, and be in welfare. My kids tomorrow, they will have kids and they will be at welfare. Why should I keep on doing that?

Tifa also believed that, to fight against the bad images of being black in America, the black have to do good things. His philosophy was that "you cannot force somebody to love you, you have to do something good." He recounted his experience of talking with a white (Polish) policeman who stopped him:

He is an American of course, and he said that . . . [his friends] don't like black people. I told him . . . I'm black, maybe they cannot let black people near. But . . . I think that black body, if you look at that color, they are brown. But they said, I'm very black . . . we should accept that there are so many things bad. If you accept them, we will be able to look for a change. So if they head here, not because of the color of the skin, but because of what they are doing . . . so when I told him that you cannot force somebody to love you, you do something good, then people love you despite the color of your skin, you are black, you are white, they don't care about the skin.

Tifa and Anne tried their best to instill this outlook into their children. Tifa reasoned that it all depends on how you would act and interact with people: "It depend on the way how you are dealing with people. Like me now, I am a big guy, sometimes if I'm going on the street, and they will stop like this way, they are afraid of me . . . then they will run away from me, but if I smile to people, people will instead come close to me. You know, like that." He himself had been stopped by police officers several times, but each time he was respectful, so he never got into trouble with them. These positive experiences made him believe that being respectful and doing good things was the key to changing people's perceptions of black people: "It is because of the way how I was talking to him. If I started cursing the police . . . sure I will be given a ticket, but he is a human being—we talked very nicely; sure, he will treat you the same way." He hoped that his children would also learn these lessons: "I'm always telling them that . . . because . . . we as black people in the US, we notice so many bad habit coming from us, so mostly if you are dealing with some people who are not black like you, they will be hesitant. Sometimes, the person will come to their mind with bad things, but you have to prove to them that not all black people are like that by doing good things."

Even though they were aware that being black was associated with negative images, the family had a very strong Sudanese identity. When asked about who they were, Anne and Tifa firmly identified themselves with a Sudanese identity. Similarly, Owen stated without hesitation that he was a Sudanese because he likes to play soccer whereas Americans like football and basketball. He also believed that his preference for Sudanese food made him Sudanese. Nina also regarded herself as a Sudanese. She explains, "My sister [Irene] is an American because she was born here, so I was born in Sudan. My friends just call me African American."

For Anne and Tifa, a significant part of being Sudanese was educating their children through Sudanese ways. Owen, for example, was not required to do many household chores or to take care of the babies whereas Nina was, because in Sudan "men are not allowed to do anything." However, since Anne believed that children should adopt some American ways, she occasionally asked Owen to wash dishes. However, as the eldest child, Owen was expected to be a good role model for the younger children by behaving and being responsible. Owen, who was under tremendous pressure to be the role model, remarked that, "Mom doesn't want me to do things that are bad so they don't follow." Because they lived in a bad neighborhood known for drugs, alcohol, and crime, Anne and Tifa had to enforce much stricter discipline on their children:

> If they go to school, I don't know what they are doing there, like if they have friends, I want to know who are they . . . who are their parents and how do they behave, all these stuff. I'm more concerned about that because my elder son, he got a friend from Philippine, and most of the time, sometimes he stay with his friend . . . I told him I'm not happy . . . to be very strict with you or like telling you not go with friends and all this stuff. But you're still very young that I want to know whom do you go with. Is he staying with his parents or staying lonely, all this stuff, I mean. One day, I said I want to go and meet, [the friend's mother] and he said okay. The following day, he came with the mother of the boy . . . So I said it's good, and one day I took my son and I want to see . . . the house of his friend to make sure that he was in the good place.

To prevent Owen from joining gangs in school, Tifa and Anne did not allow him to play on the basketball team at his school, but they permitted him to join a church basketball team. Compared with Owen, Nina was responsible for more household chores—she helped Anne take care of the babies whenever she needed to go shopping, run errands, or do community service. Nina also helped with cooking and cleaning up. Though it was easy to enforce Sudanese traditions at home, Anne and Tifa found it much more difficult to implement outside of the home, especially for girls. Anne reasoned, "This is more difficult to me . . . The custom in this country is not like ours. There I can trust anybody, and I can let her go. But here, I can't trust anybody. [Nina] got friends like, sometimes she want to go, I said, 'No, no, no. Don't go to anybody's home. Don't enter the home completely. You can play at the porch outside. But don't enter the home.' Because if something happen to you, the first thing the police will ask me, why did you let your son or your daughter go there? And you are not there, even if she tell me the story, if I relate the same story to the police, they will not believe me because you are not there."

In order to inculcate the children with Sudanese culture, Anne often told them stories about her life in Sudan—how she grew up there, the schools she attended, and how she listened to her parents. She hoped that they would learn to listen to her and appreciate the advice:

> I always like to tell them the story about our country, how we have been . . . I said, we are now in a different country, with different cultures. But it will be good if you could keep like, you can go somewhere else, you can learn the positive things, not the negative things . . . If you learn the positive things, it will be good for the future. But if you learn the negative things, it will destroy you . . . But now, you have been hearing that a lot of stories that kids, they are misbehaving, they don't listen to their parents, they call police for their parents, and all this. So, this is not our culture. I said . . . You should listen. Don't say that "Oh because we are in America, and free, I can do whatever." Because there is too much freedom here for the kids. When I was in school, if I ask my parents, "I want to go like for basketball court," if they said . . . "No, no, no . . . Study instead of going there, and waste your time playing. You can get things later." So, I always listen to what [my parents] said. That's why I reach up to this country. If I don't listen to my parents, I will not even finish my school at that time.

Anne was pleased that the children were interested in the stories and wanted to visit Sudan and see their grandparents and relatives some day. Fred, for example, even asked her about Sudan for a school project about his family tree.

Even though Anne and Tifa did not like to be categorized as Afro-Americans, they were proud of their children's English ability: "they are like American now and his friends mistaken his accent as Afro-American from here." They also wanted their children to maintain Arabic (and Bari), their first languages. Since Anne spoke Bari as her mother tongue and Tifa's mother tongue was Natuka, which she could not understand, they mostly spoke Arabic at home, which enabled the children to maintain their primary language. They believed that keeping their first language was important for them to communicate with their relatives from Sudan in the future.

The Torkeri Family's Adjustment to US Schooling

PARENTAL EXPECTATIONS AND HOPES FOR CHILDREN

For the Torkeri family, the biggest challenge in their adjustment to US schools was language. Upon their arrival, the children were "thrown" into schools, which required rapid language acquisition and cultural adjustment (McBrien, 2005). For Owen and Nina, who were schooled in Egypt in Arabic, the adjustment was very difficult at the beginning. Anne remembered that she worried a lot:

> It's really very difficult with my kids, because shifting from one language to another, it's very difficult for the kids ... I worry a lot when we came, I said, 'Let them start from zero. I don't want them to be put according to their ages to the class.' But they said 'No.' This is the system here. They can't put them with like younger kids, and they put elder kids with them ... so that's why, I was worrying at the beginning, but they just picked up like that, not like us.

Having traveled a long way from Sudan to Egypt and then to the US, Anne and Tifa were very excited about the new opportunities they would have in the United States. Like many other immigrant parents who come to the US seeking better opportunities for their children, Anne stressed the importance of the "chances" that her children could get in the US. She compared what they had in Sudan with what was available for their children in the US and believed that their children should make use of the opportunities available. She expected them to become responsible citizens and be successful in the future. She expressed her hopes for them: "I want them ... go to college, go to university. If they want to do further study, that's good, because there are chances here. Don't miss the chances, since you are here. In my country, there is no a lot of chance[s] like that. For me, when I came here, I was thinking, 'Oh, my God. If I came when I was young, I will do so many things.' But for me, I consider myself now like a late comer ... The most important, I want [for] my kids. Then after that, I can look for myself."

Tifa, who also expected the children to go to university, had more specific goals for them: "Irene is always studying because she wants to be a doctor. One day she will be a doctor ... Owen like fixing things, so when I ask him, he said he want to be an engineer. Nina is always talking about, I think, she like to be a teacher, but she didn't say that, you can tell from how she always act. I don't know . . . Fred want to be a policeman, but . . ." Doing his best to support them, Tifa felt very proud that his children were working hard to achieve what he could not in the US, "because what I didn't achieve . . . if they did it, that will be good for me, . . . I'm doing [work] like this to help them to achieve what they are dreaming. I try my best."

However, being African refugees, they also realized that there was discrimination against blacks in American society and that their children had to work even harder to succeed. This realization made them stress even more the importance of education: "You know, education plays a big role. Although I know that sometimes there is discrimination like here, because there are some places that black people leave their work and you find just white people, and some places you can find out they are mixed up, multicultural group working at the same place . . . But still there is a chance. Why do you give up for education? . . . Like us, we came, we try our best . . . There are chances that you can do."

Anne and Tifa had also made a lot of personal sacrifices for their children. Anne wanted to take the opportunities available for her in America to update her own knowledge and skills. However, her priority had been her children. For example, she wanted to take a computer lesson once a week for an hour that was offered by the government, but she decided not to go because it would affect the study time of her eldest daughter, Nina. Her family's financial situation did not allow Anne to send her children to a daycare center. If Anne had gone to a computer class, she would have had to ask Nina to take care of her younger brother and sisters during her absence. Moreover, all the children returned home at different times, and she wanted to be there when they arrived, allowing her time to talk to the children about school or anything and provide homework help if necessary. She believed that always being available to her children would create a better home environment and build more trust between the children and her. She hoped that her personal sacrifice would instill a strong motivation for her children to achieve: "It's [taking care of her six children] a full job although without pay. I was telling them, . . . although now I feel too exhausted . . . only thing I'll be happy if one day, I could see you graduate, you are in good process, you are capable for yourself, you are responsible for yourself. That will be the time that I get my pay."

DIFFERENCES IN SCHOOLING

Because Anne and Tifa valued education highly, they paid close attention to the differences between schools in America and in Sudan. The biggest concern for them was the safety issue in school. They were shocked to learn that "even in the primary schools here, they have a lot of crimes." Anne commented, "This is more advanced country. But still there is a lot of crime because there are other crimes that I have never seen in my country. So when it happened here, I'm not happy. When they are at school and just playing, let them come back safely. And I can't keep on taking them to school, [wondering whether they will come back home] and all this stuff, because I have a lot to do."

Tifa attributed the crime to the lack of discipline in American schools:

In the country I came from, the way how they discipline kids is different from here. Here they allow kids even to say bad words about their teachers. One of the schools I know here . . . a girl beat the teacher, and he was bleeding. Anne saw it in the TV . . . and the end, she was suspended for sometime, then they brought her back to the school. If it happened in the country where I came, of course, first it will never happen, for the Sudan teachers, he is our high respect . . . Because of the system here, sometimes it happens . . . In the class, students sometimes when the teacher is teaching, and students are talking, doing different things than paying attention to the teacher . . .

According to Tifa, another factor was that American schools fail to promote the benefits of education for the children. Tifa explained at length:

They learn less in primary. For example, the kids there don't know what is education, so we have to force them face—we teach the children at certain age . . . then they will learn what is education otherwise they won't be able to. Because he knows already if I did good one day . . . like my son or my daughter . . . he would be like Professor Li . . . live . . . in a better good house, she drive a very good car, and people like her; then she will say, "ok, I want to be a doctor like Professor Li. So like one day I would be driving the same car or live in a house like Professor Li's house." This they will learn . . . they would understand what is education, but like my daughter here, she don't know what is education, so at least we have to . . . I don't know what to say, but sometimes schools have to [teach her that] . . . she may not know [she] want to go to school, but maybe we have to [educate her] go to school.

In terms of curriculum and instruction, they believed that, although American schools had more material resources, they were less rigorous than those in their native country. Comparing with her own schooling experiences, Anne believed that the school her children attended in America was "too loose" because there were not enough tests and there was not much homework, especially during weekends: "Today is Friday and they came [home] without any homework . . . that means [they] have Friday, Saturday, and Sunday [off]. Sometimes, they don't want to do anything." In addition to sharing Anne's concern about the quantity of homework, Tifa also emphasized the difference in disciplining students who had not done their homework. In his view, those students should be punished, and teachers should pay attention to it. He explained, "You will be punished . . . if you don't do your homework. But here if the parents didn't pay attention, after some time the teacher will stop paying attention too . . . They don't care."

Anne and Tifa also found that the subjects taught in American schools were different and felt that American schools lack adequate instruction in what they called "general knowledge" which included math, geography, and history. Anne explained:

> Like when before I came here, I know all about . . . geographical . . . the Great Lakes and . . . all these stuff. I get it in school. So it's not new [to me] like, River Niagara is the longest and the big river in this country, but others [here] they don't know, even if you ask the American family . . . I think they don't teach. We call this is . . . "general knowledge." They don't have general knowledge. And it is very important . . . I am new in this country and their system is different from ours, and there're subjects that they don't even teach, because [we] taught history, and geography, and it's not like that [here] . . . even sometimes I watch the TV like *Sesame Street* . . . they ask simple [math] question and [students] couldn't answer, I said "Oh, my goodness." That means you have a limit [in teaching general knowledge].

Tifa thought that some subjects such as "mathematics are poor" because of the schools' emphasis on the use of calculators: "Sometimes I'll try to demand the kids to go and learn more . . . what we called it, formula. . . . When I was at school, we had them. But mostly they don't do that thing here."

In addition to differences in curriculum, Anne also noticed differences in teaching styles. In terms of language instruction, for example, Anne discovered that there was not enough reading aloud in class: "When I was in school, they encourage me like we have a reading at class, turn by turn, everybody must stand up and read loudly with colleagues. But I don't think they do that here." However, the biggest difference the family had experienced was the ESL program in the schools, which was a totally new concept for them. In the next section, the family's struggle with the ESL programs is discussed.

STRUGGLE AGAINST THE ESL PROGRAMS

In contrast to the popular belief that ESL programs are beneficial for immigrant and refugee children's acquisition of the English language, Anne and Tifa saw the ESL programs as an obstacle for their children's academic progress. According to Anne, their two sons, Owen and Fred, were the most disadvantaged by the ESL programs. By New York State regulations, ESL students are to be assessed, and then participate in a program which requires that they be pulled out from regular classes for small-group English instruction. Anne believed that such pullout programs were detrimental to

ESL students like her children. She reasoned, "Most of the time, they got pull out from the classroom, like if they have history in class, and then they come and pull my kid out and while the others are getting the subjects. So, he is going to miss the subject. They pull him out and he will go and get that ESL and when he came back, he will find his colleagues, they got their homework, their lecture was over. And they will not lecture for him anymore, so this is really a big problem."

Anne was particularly worried about Owen, who was in the eleventh grade and needed good grades to go to college. She observed that the process of pulling Owen out of the mainstream classes had caused problems in his performance in major content areas. His teacher did not provide any opportunities for him to make up what he missed while participating in the ESL pullout sessions; however, he was held accountable for the same material, and graded by the same standards as the other students. At times he was unaware of the assignments he missed while in the ESL classes, resulting in lower grades. Anne believed that such a situation was unfair to Owen. She complained, "And now he's not taking Spanish, and he's losing the marks for that. That's why sometimes his average is not very high. That's what he is complaining. And he said he want to attend the Spanish class so that he may get the mark for that. But he don't attend that. He get zero for that, which I think is there is no logic here."

Anne's complaint seemed to show a lack of understanding of the high school requirements and miscommunication between the home and the school. According to Owen's ESL teacher, Owen only needed one foreign language credit for his graduation and this was explained to him:

He just did not take Spanish 1 last year which isn't that big of a deal. I mean considering he's learning English almost fluently at this point, and our course 1, course 2, course 3 in Spanish is not terribly difficult, so, and I told him like "You do not need Spanish 2 or Spanish 1 to graduate. In order to get your Regents diploma, you need one credit of a foreign language." So he's getting that this quarter, and I told him that I can help him out with Spanish if he feels that he's not learning it well, because as I have minor in Spanish, but that shouldn't be a big problem for him.

In 2006, Owen was not taking geometry, a subject Anne regarded as one of the core courses. She was very frustrated: "Even now, now I have a problem with my son. I have to go to school and talk to the teacher about it . . . They say that he is not going to take geometry because of ESL. So, I worry much. I think why? Geometry is most important even. He need it. Yeah. He is going to miss that because of ESL. He just miss it. . . . How comes like that? I'm really mad about that, you know. I talk to him before two days because I got a letter at the mail. And it's saying that he should take at least 39 hours for ESL."

Again, there seemed to be miscommunication between the school and the home. According to the English teacher, Owen would take geometry in the summer. Because of his ESL schedule and the magnet school requirements, he was unable to take the class at the same time as the other students. Instead, he would be required to make it up in the summer at another school. Several other students would have to do the same and they all have different schedules depending on their magnet requirements. The ESL teacher assured Anne that "he's not failing math. He's not gonna get zero at the end of year. And it's not gonna drag down the grade towards graduation." She tried to explain it to Anne when she went to the school to talk with her. After she learned about Anne's concerns, she realized that she "must not have communicated that well."

When asked about the ESL programs, Owen himself stated that the ESL programs were helpful, especially in the first two years when he could not speak English, but he did not think he needed them now. He did not like being pulled out, because he missed "being there" with his regular classmates. Furthermore, he did not like the heavy writing requirements in ESL classes "because in every chapter like she [the ESL teacher] gives us paper and ask us questions and let us write about it after we read it . . . in the regular class that's the same thing, but they only ask questions about the chapter."

Fred, who was in Rainbow Elementary, had a similar experience. As mentioned earlier, he was pulled out of mainstream classes for the three programs that he had to attend during the school hours: ESL, physical therapy (PT), and occupational therapy (OT). Despite being absent from many of the mainstream classes, he had being doing well academically. Anne thought that, if he had attended the mainstream classes instead of being pulled out for the ESL class, he would have done much better. However, regardless of how well he performed in content areas, he still could not be exempted from the ESL class; moreover, he had to attend summer school as a result of his therapy sessions. According to Anne, the common conception among students was that the summer school was for kids who did not do well in their studies. The mandatory requirement that Fred attend the summer school program may affect how he feels about himself and how others see him. Anne told us that Fred worried that other students might think he was not doing well in the school and would distance themselves from him. Anne described the situation:

> Now, Fred too having the same issue in school. Three times he is out of the class. All this OT, PT and ESL . . . This is a lot. Like sometimes he came home, I said you don't have homework? And he said I don't have homework. What about the other kids? Do they have homework? He said, "Yes. When I left for the ESL class, they gave them homework when I was not there. And when I came in, I don't have my homework." And then, one day, I went to school and I talked to the teachers. And he said no . . . even if he is out, they will put his paper, because he has like a bag behind his chair. They put his homework there. Maybe he is the

one who didn't check and pick the homework. And I said, "okay. If like math, they have to explain it. And then, you have to do sometimes like class work . . . If he miss that part of his explanation even if you give him the homework, he will not be able to do it." . . . And he say, "well . . . what should I do? I can do nothing for that because . . . he has to attend the ESL. It's very important for him. And he has to go for his PT and OT." . . . I raised that problem before like two years or three years, there was a meeting in Rainbow Elementary and I raised that problem. And we say, ten day, find solution for that ESL, then they insist that our kids should take the ESL. *Why don't they do it after like after school program?* [Anne's emphasis]

According to Anne, her family was not the only one that disapproved of the ESL programs. Many other refugee and immigrant families they know also voiced similar concerns. Anne and other parents went to discuss their concerns with the schools, but they were told that that was how the ESL program was going to be and nothing would be changed. She expressed her frustration:

We discussed it before at school like at the PTO meeting and all this stuff. But they said it's according to the system, they can't change anything. It depend on the government, because this is not the first time that they are doing this, and this is not their fault. If the government could pay for that because we say, "why don't they teach the ESL like, they select some days, at the evening instead of pulling the kids out from the class, and then leaving the others going on with the lecture?" But they said, "No." They can't do that. They said, it needs like a special budget for that and all this . . . They said "What should we do? It is the system."

Realizing that they had to fight the "system," Anne actively sought ways to work the system. In the next section, I describe Anne's efforts to work "the system" through choosing schools for her children.

WORKING THE SYSTEM THROUGH SCHOOL CHOICES

Anne learned from another Sudanese family that, if an ESL teacher writes a letter of recommendation, then the student can go to City Hall and ask to be removed from the ESL list. So she contacted the ESL teacher in Owen's school for a letter of recommendation in order to petition for a waiver allowing him to be exempt from ESL classes. However, shortly after she contacted the teacher, she received Owen's report card, which indicated that he was not doing well in his English class. Therefore, she inferred that she would not receive a strong recommendation letter from the teacher. Nonetheless, she was not ready to give it up and decided to go to the City Hall and petition without a letter.

Anne's frustration with the ESL programs in her kids' schools made her realize the importance of school choice for them. However, she did not know the differences among different kinds of public schools such as "government schools" (for refugees), magnet schools, and charter schools. She learned from her Sudanese friends that "The magnet school, usually, you go to the City Hall, and then they do it through lottery. If you fill the paper and . . . if they pick one of your kids, then if they are siblings, they can go through."

It was apparent that Anne did not know that Owen was already in a magnet school because she actually applied for Owen to go to another magnet school, but was rejected. After a couple of attempts to change schools for her children, Anne learned that Owen, Nina, and Fred, who were not born in the United States, had no choice but to go to the schools designated for refugee children. She decided that the younger children who either grew up or were born in the United States would not attend those schools even though there were good aspects about the schools (e.g., she liked the administration style in Owen's high school and the multicultural aspects in Nina and Fred's school). Since Irene did not have any prior schooling experiences in Sudan or Egypt, she decided to send her to a different school:

> I would like to apply for my daughter, but I don't want her to go to Rainbow Elementary . . . because she starts here. That means, she don't have any problem with the language . . . My idea is I want her either go to the charter school, or either to go to the magnet schools. And they said, magnet school, they will not allow her to go there unless you have to apply at the City Hall also. That's the same obstacles. So, but the charter school . . . sent me a letter and I took all the paper they needed, document that they needed, and now she got the acceptance.

Anne was very satisfied with the Head Start program in the charter school that Irene attended. The school gave Irene different reading activities in class and ample homework every day. Anne described the differences she had observed:

> Today, they [Owen, Fred, and Nina] don't have homework. Although today is Friday, Irene will have homework. Usually there is one that she gets it on Monday or Tuesday. And then, she has to submit it today. And then she will get another homework for next Friday. Like a week she has to do it either with me, or sometimes her sister. And she has to read books in the library and she has to write the names of the books and their writers and all. And she has to turn in. And then they have something called 'Open Circle.' They always discuss.

Anne noted that, because of the diversity in homework assignments, Irene was becoming a good reader and writer. She described Irene with pride: "She can write the alphabets very beautiful. That's why I'm very happy about her. Maybe because of the system that they insist the homework every day, every night, she has to do. And reading, too. She has books, she has to read when she came from there from school, because every day she has a new book."

To encourage Irene to read more, she sometimes asked Nina to take Irene to the public library to borrow more books. She was also happy that the school taught children "applied technology," which was another difference between Irene's and the other children's schooling experiences. For example, when Irene came home from school, she often went to the computer to play a math-related game, whereas the other children would just watch TV. In addition to these benefits Anne saw about the charter school, she was also happy that she could keep more frequent contact with Irene's teachers through writing notes and participating in school fieldtrips; this is in contrast to the difficulties she experienced in communicating with the teachers at Owen, Nina, and Fred's schools.

Anne and Tifa also learned that Nina had different options for middle school. Nina did not want to become a teacher, contrary to Tifa's observation. She wanted to become an artist, and her school counselor advised her to go to an art academy. Anne and Tifa consulted several people who attended the same church and were advised that they could choose a school that was more academic for Nina. Since they really wanted Nina to go to a university, they decided she should apply for a more academically oriented school, even though they were forcing her to do something she did not like (just as Tifa's father did to him) and she might not do well in the school. Although getting information about the school and sending in their application was difficult and worrisome—they even missed the first orientation—Nina was eventually accepted. Anne and Tifa were very pleased, proud, and hopeful. Knowing that there were differences in schools and programs, Anne said that she would continue to struggle for her children, "But you have to struggle for yourself. If you didn't struggle, you are not able to [get ahead] from where you start."

The Torkeri Family's Home Literacy Practices and Parental Involvement

Anne and Tifa's recognition of school differences made them more vigilant about their children's studies at home. Since Tifa worked most of the time, Anne took most of the responsibility for checking the children's homework. With limited English and limited understanding of the American school system, it was a tremendously difficult task for her:

> Although I know that there are some subjects, they have difficulties. But I try my best to help them. If there is something that I could help, then, I will help. But if there is something that is very difficult, I cannot. Sometimes I called the teachers and I said, if there is an example, so that I may follow the example. Maybe I can help them. Like math, it's very difficult. And I had difficulty with math when I was in school, too.

Every day when the children returned from school, Anne asked them about their day at school and checked their backpacks to see what homework was required for that evening. The children usually watched TV or played on their old computer while she prepared supper. Owen usually went to a nearby after-school program where he tutored young children for a couple of hours to make some extra money. After supper, Anne asked everyone to clean up the dining table and their coffee table to make space for their homework. When they were studying, no eating or drinking was allowed because it might ruin their books and notebooks. Anne believed that it was important to "do one thing at a time."

Irene seemed to receive a lot of attention from Anne. Her homework required Anne's involvement. Anne usually read with her first. Their routine was that Irene read the book and, if she got stuck with an unknown word, Anne helped her figure it out by referring to a dictionary. After reading, Anne asked Irene to copy the words. If she did not write neatly, she made her redo it. Anne also helped Irene practice her spelling. She often tested her by asking, "Can you spell this word?" Sometimes, she sounded out the words to help her spell or pronounce a word. She modeled the pronunciation and asked Irene to repeat after her. At times, she also used pictures to help Irene understand difficult words.

In addition to reading and writing, Anne also played card games with Irene to teach her numbers, colors, animals, and fruits. She also played Scrabble, a word game, with her to increase her vocabulary. Sometimes, she and Irene invented new games to play. For example, one day Irene pretended that her mother was not there and she had to take care of all her young siblings. Anne wrote down Irene's story about her taking care of her brothers and sisters, and they read it together.

Anne tried to do the same thing with Fred, who was required to read twenty minutes a day for his school assignment, but it was very difficult to get him to read. Because of his disability, Fred "easily gets mad." Most of the time, Anne just let him copy the words and then she corrected it: "I'll let him know which one is right, which one is wrong. After that, the wrong one, he has to write it like three times so that he may remember the mistaken word." Fred sometimes just wanted to complete his work fast and go out to play. Anne usually did not allow that and tried to teach him the importance of good penmanship. She told him, "No. This is not the reason. You should be neat. Because now you said, 'I'm grown-up and I can do. I don't need any help.' And I said, 'No. You need help because this is not the way that you write. You need your copy book to be neat at school, so that you may get, even that neatness, you get marks for it.'"

In addition to writing, Anne also helped Fred with math: "But the only thing I'm very poor is with the math. I can't help them with math. Only this one [Fred]. I help him with the multiplication. I wrote the multiplication up to 12. And then, every day I have to test him for . . . multiplication of 2, and then the following day, 3, and then, so all until he finish with it."

For Owen and Nina, who were older, Anne just "let them do it by themselves" first and then checked later "if they are doing it right or wrong." As for Nina,

Anne noted that she often forgot to hand in her homework, even though she had completed it. Sometimes Nina and Fred forgot to bring their homework to school, and Anne had to "run to the school to take it to them." She questioned them, "You miss mark that you are not supposed to miss if you did your homework. Why don't you submit the homework?" Anne again believed that the pullout ESL program should be blamed, "Because . . . sometimes they are not in class when they go to ESL, automatically, they will forget anything. They will not submit it, like if they go there and the teacher came in and maybe she will ask, check the homework and they are not there."

Although most of the time Anne enlisted Owen's help with difficult words or math problems, she tried her best to be actively involved with his homework as well. She was not happy that he did not pay attention to his handwriting and spent too much time playing basketball. She knew that she could not keep him home studying all the time, but she had to remind him that he should not "put basketball like the major thing." She tried to review his major assignments before he handed them in. When reviewing some of his essays, she taught him that the way he wrote should be different from the way in which he spoke; and she also pointed out some spelling errors, asking him to check the dictionary.

Her active involvement had at times saved Owen from unfair penalties from school. One day, Owen's teacher called her and said that Owen did not submit his essay assignment. Anne reviewed the essay the night before and corrected it for him. She believed that the teacher must have misplaced it. She described the occasion:

> The teacher has to call me and . . . she ask me, 'Your son was having an essay and he was supposed to submit it. And now he said he submitted it. Do you remember that he was having an essay?' And at that time, I remember the name of the title of the text. I said 'Yes, I review it. And then I give it to him. I make some correction. I said let him correct it.' And she said it's okay. She was just asking about that. That's why he get the mark. Otherwise, she is not going to give him the mark.

This incident reinforced her belief that it was very important for her to participate in the completion of their homework. When the children had a test, Anne usually helped them prepare for it. She had them study first and then she tested them: "first of all, you study by yourself and then, if you know yourself that you learn them all by heart and you come and then, I will do the test for you." Her children joked, "Mom, you are pretending that you are a teacher." Sometimes, the older children helped their younger siblings: "they play that role sometimes, Irene and her sister [helping each other]. And his sister, his brother [helping each other]."

The Myer Family

The Myer family came from a southern Sudanese city called Wāw, not far from Juba, where the Torkeri family came from. They came to the United States as refugees in 2000. Compared with the Torkeri family, the Myer family experienced much more hardship before coming to the United States. The father, Mahdi, was an accountant in Sudan. Because of the civil war, they lost six of their family members. In 1995, when it became unsafe to stay home any more, he and his family had to flee the country. He joined the twenty thousand Christians in southern Sudan who walked on bare feet from Sudan to Kenya without regular food for three months. He was one of the final four thousand survivors known as the "Lost Boys of Sudan" who finally made it to the Kenyan refugee camp. For a long time, he did not know where his wife and two children were; finally, he learned that his wife and children were in Egypt. After many more hardships, in 1998 he was reunited with his family in Egypt, where they gave birth to a twin boy and girl in 1999. In 2000 they came to the US and in 2001 they had another twin boy and girl in Buffalo.

Mahdi and Gloria did not know any English before they came to the United States. After they arrived, they attended ESL classes offered by Catholic charities for a few months where they learned basic survival English. As Gloria points out, the brief English classes taught them only how to speak some simple sentences, but they did not learn how to read or write English. Like Tifa, Mahdi participated in a six-week training program and got a job in a meat factory. Gloria stayed home for a few months before she got a job in a food factory about an hour away from their house. Their hard work eventually allowed them to purchase a two-story house in 2004.

Their oldest son, Rahman, was fourteen and was in the eighth grade. He had been in the ESL program since he started school in the United States five years ago. According to Mahdi, he was "not good with English and he is behind in all subjects" and he also had been involved in fighting with other children in the school. Their eldest daughter, Abok, was performing better in the school and had no problem with English. She came to the US when she was five and received only three years of ESL support. Mading, who was repeating grade 1 was not doing well in English, but his twin sister, Achan, was doing well and had moved on to grade 2. The youngest twins, Sadiq and Sattina, were attending preschool in a charter school and were doing well so far.

The Myer Family's Adjustment to Life in the US

Like the Torkeri family, the Myer family was also very grateful for the opportunities that they had in America. However, they had also experienced many difficulties adjusting to new life in America. As Rahman put it succinctly, "Everything is different." One of the biggest challenges was that

Table 4.2 The Myer Family Profile

Name	Age	Occupation	Education	Languages	Others
Mahdi	50	Meat slicer	High school in Sudan; community college in US	Dinka, Arabic, English	Was an accountant in Sudan
Gloria	40s	Food factory worker	Undergraduate in Arabic in Sudan	Dinka, Arabic, English	Was an Arabic teacher in Sudan
Rahman	14	Student	Green Middle School	Dinka, English	Born in Sudan
Abok	11	Student	Rainbow Elementary; one year schooling in Egypt	Dinka, English	Born in Sudan
Mading	7	Student	Rainbow Elementary	Dinka, English	Born in Egypt
Achan	7	Student	Rainbow Elementary	Dinka, English	Born in Egypt
Sadiq	4	Preschool	Hurley Charter School	Dinka, English	Born in the US
Sattina	4	Preschool	Hurley Charter School	Dinka, English	Born in the US

"language is difficult" (Abok). For Rahman and Abok, the first two years had been especially difficult as they could not follow or understand many of the classroom activities. Rahman, for example, relied on his Sudanese classmates to translate for him in class. Though Gloria and Mahdi studied English, their short training was not enough for their daily lives, especially when they wanted to be more involved in their children's homework. For the children, language became a barrier to doing well in school. Mahdi described the children's struggles: "When we came here, don't know anything about English to assimilate, so even they doesn't know how to greet people that day. My elder son was just came when he was 10 years, and when we came, he was just couldn't communicate full without knowing ABC . . . And he don't how to count one, two, three."

Although both Gloria and Mahdi had jobs and were homeowners, their jobs here were very different from those they used to have in Sudan. For Mahdi, the most important thing was to have a job that enabled him to pay for the house and to support the children. He went to work from 4:00 p.m. and returned home around 2:30 a.m. except Saturday night. He slept about two to three hours when he came home from work, then he had to get up at around 5:00 a.m. to drive Gloria to work. After he came back from Gloria's workplace, he then drove the children to school. After that, he attended classes at the community college where he took courses in business administration. When his classes finished at 2:00 p.m., he went to a computer lab to do his homework before he went to work. Sometimes he went home to check the children's homework or to take a quick nap before going to work. On Saturdays, he shopped for the family groceries in the morning, and took the children to a laundromat in the afternoon, and on Sundays he took the whole family to church in the morning. In the afternoon, he had a couple of hours to run errands or catch up with his school work before going to work. Though work (and life) was hard, Mahdi knew that this was what he had to do in America: "Now I know a little bit English. So, I want to go ahead. For instance, my major is now business administration because I was working as an accountant in my country. I like my job that time. But here like, can I do that? Here, I have to do, start from the beginning, so that I can get my degree or my certificate so that I can work . . . you don't want [this meat slicing] work in my country. I don't do that. I was sitting at the office and doing the calculation thing."

For Gloria, the change had been even greater. In Sudan, her job as an Arabic teacher was neither stressful nor physically demanding. At home, she had relatives to help with house chores and she did not have to do anything. Now, she had to get up at 4:00 a.m. every day to get the children's meals ready before going to work at the food factory. In the afternoon, she took the bus home, and was often so exhausted that she could barely move, but still she must make sure that the children complete their homework and prepare dinners for them.

For outsiders, Mahdi and Gloria had achieved the so-called American dream—they had their own house, both were employed and they had a car.

But Gloria had never felt happy here; she really missed her life in Sudan and would return at any time if possible. "Here I have to do everything. I'm all alone here. I am not alone back home. I have a lot of people." For her, being in America was like being "a guest in another person's house." However, she knew that she would not be able to return because her family had fled to different places all over the world as a result of the war, leaving no one in her immediate family in Sudan.

In addition to being uprooted from her family and community, Gloria also missed the vast safe and open spaces they used to enjoy back home in Sudan. She noted, "Back home, you know everyone, you have a lot of place for kids to go out and play. Here you don't know your neighbors, and houses are so close to each other, no yard. No place for kids to play. It's driving them crazy." To her, the only solace was that she could get together with a few other Sudanese families on weekends once in a while.

The Myers also had a strong Sudanese identity. Mahdi states, "We are not African Americans, we are Sudanese American." Gloria also commented that, even though African Americans and Sudanese have the same skin color, they "behave differently." Mahdi explained the difference at length:

Africa is composed of many countries, more than 40 countries, and people say that I'm African American because they don't know their origin from Africa. This is Sudanese, Nigerian, Egyptian, Ethiopian . . . you don't know . . . you don't know where you came from, but to me, or my kids, they know that origin where they came from. I know my country, I know my hometown. I know my village, I know my parents like that. Even my kids, I have to tell them, that twins, they were born in Buffalo. I used to tell them. Now Sudanese, their hometown is Wāw, that village, something like that and also there were cultures, you, everybody . . . has to learn, to know, to teach them from his father [to] grand, grand, grandfather . . . They supposed to know that.

For the children, being Sudanese meant being respectful to others whereas African Americans tended not to be; in their view, African Americans did not like to listen to elders or parents. Their children mostly socialized with Sudanese friends at school, because "you can talk to them normally" (Abok). They were also very sensitive to how others treated them as blacks. Abok, for example, noticed that a white bus guard treated black students differently from the whites: "If a black student chew gum on the bus, he'll say it's not good, but when white students chew gum, it's okay."

In order for the children to keep up with their home culture, Mahdi and Gloria bought a satellite dish in order to receive TV programs from Sudan. However, the programs were mostly in Arabic, which their children did not understand since they spoke only Dinka at home. To them, bringing up children in a different culture was quite difficult because the basic ideas of childrearing were different. Mahdi elaborated: "Because in my country we have the concept that the children [are] the property of that family issue, property of the nation ... you should take [care] of that child ... If I don't know how to brought up my kids, somebody must interfere ... come and talk to the kids and children how to behave ... Like when you bring them up here ... the concept is the opposite. Like your business is always your business, nobody else's."

Despite the hardship they were going through, Mahdi and Gloria wanted their children to "get the opportunities" in America. Mahdi, for example, wanted the children to "go ahead with education." He did not want for them to choose which career they would have in the future, but he told them, "I don't want any one of you to do the hard job I'm doing now." He and Gloria wanted the children to finish school, and attend college. They did not have any specific expectations for the children, except for their youngest daughter, Sattina: "This one going to be a doctor ... because I will be very old when she becomes a doctor," said Gloria.

Involvement in Homework

The Myer family's expectations for the children were clearly aligned with their performance in school. Since two of their children constantly had problems at school, Mahdi and Gloria really wanted them to do better in school, utilizing all kinds of methods to help them overcome the language barrier. They understood the importance of mastering English: "English is an international language. If you know English, you going to survive; you work with a lot of people."

In order to help his children learn English during the first few months after their arrival, Mahdi borrowed video cassettes from a school teacher to help them: "They can saw pictures and they learn how to pronounce it and how to exercise ... they learn how to pronounce A and B, how to read letters." But he soon realized that his limited English was not enough to help the children successfully complete their school work, which made him decide to go to school himself. He said, "I want to go to a high school if there's a chance." Eventually, he attended an adult ESL program for nine months, where he received a certificate: "I started to learn English so that I can help my kids." After he gained enough English, he decided to attend a local community college with the assistance of a government subsidy. His original intention was to show his children, especially Rahman, in a direct way that one can learn at any age: "Education, that is not age [issue], don't standardize because you are refugee."

Juggling between his work and the college, Mahdi had even less time to be with the children. He joked that he did not have much time to read with the children or help them with their homework because "I need somebody help me work." Since he was so busy, Gloria took up the daily charge of checking the children's homework. Since she did not know how to read English, she could only supervise the completion of the children's homework. After she came back from work, she told the children to "come and sit there, and everyone have to open his book . . . even if you don't have homework, you have to read. No play." Since Gloria couldn't help, the children usually helped one another, especially with math and English. The younger children spoke better English, so they sometimes helped Rahman with pronunciation. Abok, as the eldest daughter, took on the responsibility of checking everyone's homework, ensuring that it had been done correctly. Sometimes, she helped the younger ones with spelling or math problems and volunteers to read to them. After finishing homework, the children usually watched TV for one to two hours before they had supper at about 8:30 p.m.

Perception of Differences in Schooling

Mahdi and Gloria were happy that the children had the opportunity to go to school and learn English "with more materials and facilities" than in Sudan: "[There are] more students in Sudan and the teacher only has one book. They have to copy the book. Some books on the blackboard. Everything is here better, much better facilities." However, they also saw some significant differences between the school systems in the two countries. For example, Mahdi learned that the curriculum in the US is not centralized: "I don't have experience about how education is working in this country, and I don't have other kids in different schools and I don't know, I don't contrast . . . What I know in this country, each school has its own program. But in our country . . . Ministry of Education . . . decide the curriculum." Mahdi likes the centralized curriculum. He reasoned,

> It's probably better because some school, if they don't have qualified teachers, but they don't work, they are not going to produce a good program because of the teachers . . . and that may be going to affect the children. But if . . . Department of Education in the state design the program, and set up school as a uniform to every public school. It's supposed to do the same program or same teachers for education because I'm going to seek the same across a nation and how you can accept as a nation without your knowing the program?

As a parent, he also felt that schools here placed much more responsibility on parents: "Actually in Sudan . . . it is responsibility . . . from both school and parent . . . and here sometimes parent have to take three quarters of responsibility of education of children." Both Mahdi and Gloria felt that it was very difficult for them to take the responsibility as parents in the US because physical punishment was not allowed: "if you hit your child, they call police. What can you do?" Mahdi further explained,

In Sudan, by law, teacher can beat the child. But here, no. And even talking bad word is forbidden in our country. If the teacher . . . is going to punish that child by his hand, and [parents] also have to punish your child by doing so . . . You have to punish him because . . . the child believe if in the school, teacher is going to beat him and then when they come back home, the parents are going to beat them, so there is no initials . . . you have to accept what the teacher, you have to accept what a parent. But here . . . I have to accept that, I know also this country . . . I don't want to value, they may call police and police may take my child away from me.

Since they could not discipline the children in the same way as in Sudan, they now tried to "talk to them." Mahdi also wanted to educate the children by being a role model for them: "If I have time, I have to go with [them to] everything [in] my car, [to] workers, so that they can see from how I can behave with others." However, despite his efforts at home, the children had learned bad habits while at school and he had been called frequently to the school to meet with teachers. He was disappointed that the school did not make his children behave better: "In my country, children's school, they are supposed to behave better, but here, there's a lot of freedom in school, this is a big problem." He described an incident when he was called to school because of his son, Rahman, "talked in a bad way."

I went there, the teacher told me, 'your son talk a bad way at school; [it] is no good.' I felt sorry but when I come to this country with my child, I was better than my child, my child don't know . . . any single word in the English. I took my child to that school to learn English. I've been [expecting] that he should learn the better, the good language, not the bad language. I don't know where he found that bad language, maybe from the school, not my mistake, that's the school's mistake.

Mahdi was very angry that the teacher blamed him for his son's behavior: "the teacher cannot blame me. He should blame himself and the administration . . . I don't know it was from the teacher or from that school, I don't know. But [it's] from school, not from my house." Again, he was torn between the different ways of disciplining the children:

They said that you should talk to your child. I said OK, we should talk to [him]. But in my country, I have to beat my child, but here, that's the crime . . . All our kids come from this [culture], the same thing must be . . . from home and school. Here they got lot of freedom; if you beat your child that is a crime. I don't know what to do . . . I cannot change it at all. If I don't like here, I have to go back to my country or to keep silent.

Of course, since they could not go back to Sudan, Mahdi decided "to keep silent" even though sometimes he wanted to express his own educational beliefs. However, he was still concerned that "in this country, there is no control in the school. Children used to play bad things in the school." His "big fear" was that his children may be involved in drugs and alcohol and the teachers do not care:

> In America, it's a country of freedom, teacher is free to do anything, like I see accident [fights] from here sometimes between teachers and students . . . The teacher should respect themselves, respect that job, because respect got us to respect them . . . That's why my child learn the bad way, to talk in bad way . . . That's why drug use in school is very common. Because teachers are not care enough . . . [when] I went [to school], sometimes they smoking inside school, [kids] learn with somebody, they get the children [learn] that . . . Sometimes I see [the students] sitting on the table, his teacher's table. Look, unless you [are] a teacher, you sit down, no problem, not to sit down on teacher's desk.

Realizing that he could not rely on the school, he resorted to his strategy of being a role model for the kids at home: "I don't want my child to see that you're doing bad and you prevent me from that." He reasoned,

> I try to show him that . . . I was a smoker, I smoke 20 years. And I don't like them now, I discover that smoking is not good. Now because it's no good, I'm going to stop smoking in front you, I promise you, I am not going to smoke again. The point [is], you don't smoke, you don't do bad, something bad . . . I can quit. That is no good. From cigarette and others, don't do that, because it's not good . . . At home we don't drink beer something like that . . . I don't drink, my wife, don't drink, so we don't buy any beer for our guests. That is I don't like any alcohol, it's not good.

In addition to these issues, Mahdi was also puzzled by the fact that American teachers taught all the subject areas in the lower grades. He explained the difference: "Teachers [in Sudan] used to go from class to class . . . For instance, the school start at 8:30. From 8:30 to 9:00 . . . [math] teacher come and teach math. After 9:00, math teacher need to go a different class, grade 6. English teacher may come after him and teach that class. " Mahdi believed that the American system was not an efficient way in teaching the children: "here [teachers] almost won't share one class. That is to me, it's not good . . . if teacher cannot find several himself doing a big gap." For example, one of the twins, Mading, had troubles because "he did not like the homeroom teacher" and the teacher did not like him, either. Since the teacher taught all the subjects, Mading got stuck with the teacher for a whole year. In Mahdi's opinion, this might have affected his attitude toward learning.

Fighting Against the ESL Programs

Mahdi was extremely unhappy about the ESL program—its placement policy and structure. He believed that his children, especially Rahman and Mading, were behind academically because of the schools system. Rahman came to the US at the age of ten and was placed in grade 4, "simply because of his age." Mahdi considered this inappropriate placement as the primary reason why he was not doing well: "Because he did not know how to write a word . . . how to do . . . so when he was in school, there is no difference between him and this table. Because he don't understand, he don't listen, he don't know what the teacher is talking about. And they give him psychological effect, because [he] don't understand, he got himself behind in schooling, he was not happy . . . from that day on."

In order to make a case for Rahman, Mahdi went to the school to talk to the teachers, but what he heard was "that is our system. We work that way." He did not think that age should be the sole basis for placement. Rather, what mattered is a student's proficiency level, "because you don't know how to write, so you have to study from the beginning, not your age from the beginning, you have to study how to learn." He recounted what he told the teachers:

> I told them . . . I know it's the system in your country, but if possible, try to start him with the beginning from ABC. Now he's in grade 4. But give him, how to write A. He don't know how to write it, maybe alone. He don't know how to, to listen, how to make calculations in math, he don't know anything about science . . . They just go ahead and . . . they push on him with no base. But the sister start from first grade, they are good now, because even although she don't know English by then, but she start from ABC.

When Mahdi learned that Rahman was being pulled out of regular classes to study ESL, he became even more upset: "That is sad to me, I think it's not good because some time they can get a problem because they pulled him to go to that class meanwhile that colleagues are being taught a different subject. Sometimes, they give them test without his presence, and teacher will give him zero. He knows that he's in different class, but in other subject. Giving test without ask where the child is absent from school or is in different class." He described one incident involving Rahman: "Sometimes they call me to come to school and told me, 'your child never turn in homework that day . . . and that month. The score is zero.' So I have to ask my child, 'Why? What happen? Is it difficult?' He told me that 'I was not in there that day. I was attending other class. My teacher [assigned] work to class in my absence, then, he never remind me, he never told me.'"

To his surprise, the teacher did not want to take any responsibility for it. Mahdi retold the teacher's words in anger: "In that case . . . he should not say that, 'I have nothing to do with it, he was not here, and he never did that job.

I have to give him zero. What do you think I have to give it to him?'" Mahdi knew that a zero score was going to affect the child's grades, and he concluded that "They don't care . . . sometimes he missed that lesson, then miss that subject, he cannot get it. Nobody will fit that to him."

He was puzzled by this arrangement. In his view, this was just a matter of rearranging the schedules: "They are supposed . . . to put that subject in the timetable, if . . . he's going to attending ESL class. They can repeat that, they can re-taught, if English [is] after the school it should be good, so that he can attend his all regular classes." He argued that the best way to solve the problem was to get rid of ESL programs: "I think there is no need for something called ESL that you promote other children to go and attend. They shouldn't have [students] out of the class."

Another frustration Mahdi had with the schools was the teachers' lack of knowledge of the children's cultural and linguistic backgrounds. Whenever his children had difficulties in school, the homeroom teachers often referred them to an Arabic teacher so that the teacher could translate for them. However, the homeroom teachers did not understand that his children did not speak Arabic. Instead, the homeroom teachers "who don't know a word in Arabic" assumed that Sudan was an Arab country, and his children must understand Arabic. He was quite frustrated: "They base that because Sudan is an Arab country. That's nonsense . . . [We] have [civil] war between Sudanese themselves. Now, you transfer that war from Sudan to here to Buffalo!" He further expressed his frustration: "Now they used to remove my kids from school to go to attend ESL. They brought this some Arabic guy to come and translate to my child in Arabic way . . . Myself, I know Arabic. But my kids, they don't know Arabic. How can you tell them to that child? That child cannot understand subject in Arabic. My child, nobody understand. They understand English more than Arabic, so that no need for that."

All these frustrations with the schools made Mahdi conclude that American schools pay attention to quantity, not quality: "In my country, they cannot permit you go ahead unless you have to pass all the subjects, but in this country, like my kids, sometimes they don't do well and they pushed them ahead. That is no good." Mading, for example, was not doing well in school, and they tried to pass him to grade 2; therefore, Mahdi went to City Hall to make sure that he repeated grade 1. He explained, "They said that he's going to [grade 2], and let him go ahead and he's going to improve because he's still a child, like to play and laugh. I said no. I want him to know the best . . . and how to write his name, how to read, how to spell the word and know everything, and he need help. If you push him now he don't know anything in grade 1. Automatically he's going [to do] bad."

He himself had experienced similar issues while attending his community college classes when his teacher had asked him to watch a football game to get extra points for his class:

I went to ECC and . . . my teachers uses to give [homework]: if you need extra point . . . see a show . . . go and buy ticket and go attend it, and bring that ticket and I will give you extra point. But . . . simply because I went to watch that football, my teacher to give me extra point? . . . I have 85 point and I went to show, I brought that ticket, he give me 5 point, I pass. That is quality or quantity? . . . I don't want to do that. I want to pass my subject. I don't want the teacher give me the marks without [my] understanding that one, I cannot be happy . . . Marks is a different thing, grade is different things, I want something in my mind. I'm not learning [for an] A or B or C, I learn after learning, you know something.

Conclusion

The two Sudanese families' experiences described in this chapter inform us that, while trying to adjust to the inner-city environment and the American school system, they encountered multiple layers of cultural differences and challenges which are not only social and linguistic but also educational and institutional. Both families conformed to the stigmatized racial imagining against native-born African Americans, while actively resisting society's low expectations for black achievement and the schools' systematic exclusion of their chances in America. They adopted the common strategy of distancing and differentiating themselves from the African Americans by instilling a strong Sudanese cultural identity in their children.

The families' stories also reveal the families' conscious and unconscious resistance to the negative imagining about minority parental involvement. Their stories contradict Lareau's (2003) findings that low-SES families fall short of deliberate cultivation of children's development by sustaining their natural growth. Contrary to these observations, the Sudanese parents valued education highly and tried to provide their children with a better environment and different learning activities. They made personal sacrifices and set themselves as role models. They expected their children to go on to higher education, to be successful, and to have a better quality of life in the future. However, as their stories demonstrate, the families had to overcome multiple barriers to realize their dreams, including the economic pressure, language barriers, cultural differences in childrearing, an unsafe inner-city environment, and the ever more complex identity politics of being black, foreign, and uprooted. In addition, unlike the native-born middle-class families in Lareau's study, their acculturation efforts are consistently thwarted by institutional barriers. In their interaction with the American schools, they encountered a wide range of cultural and structural differences not only in the curriculum and instruction but also in educational values and beliefs, the role of teachers, schools, and community in educating children, and expectations for the children. More significantly, they were limited in their access to knowledge about how the school system works and how to work the system.

Indeed, the parents were actively involved in and gravely concerned about their children's education and development, like the middle-class parents in Lareau's study. They tried to negotiate cultural capital or advantages for their children with the American school system and learn about "the rules of the game" (Lareau, 2003, p. 6). And they did so through their contradictory unity of conformity and resistance—by conforming to the dominant racial hierarchy and resisting school practices (e.g., the ESL pullout programs and fast transition children into English) that they deemed to be systematically putting their children at a disadvantage. The Torkeri family successfully moved their younger children out of the inner-city schools while the Myer family has learned to motivate their children to get ahead by attaining an education and learning good behavior.

Though the parents enjoyed occasional success in negotiating educational advantages, their strenuous efforts and frequent failure in the negotiation suggest that it is difficult for newcomer refugee parents to become advocates for their children's education (Li, 2003; Valdés, 2001). Their stories demonstrate serious unequal power relations between the school authorities and minority parents, especially the immigrant blacks, who also struggled with English language. Like many other minority families, the two families were often excluded from information on how school programs work or "the rules of the game," and thus were powerless to make changes in school programs and marginalized from the decision-making processes concerning their children's schooling (Fine, 1993; Li, 2006). As a result, they often could not successfully negotiate for their children the kind of education they desired. Indeed, their children's success in school was like a lottery draw—relying on good faith and unpredictable chances that might or might not be available to them.

The families' constant struggles and resistance against the urban schooling system mirror the increasing tensions and discords between the school and minority families caused by the differences in cultural values, and race and class positioning. This in turn resulted in a further mismatch between children's learning experiences in school and at home. The barriers to the children's school adjustment and the schools' failure to listen to their voice suggest that they are examples of refugee and immigrant children who are "overlooked and underserved" in American school systems (Ruiz-de-Velasco & Fix, 2001). Will their working-class and poor white peers have similar experiences? In the next chapter, I present an account of two white families' experiences of living in the multicultural neighborhood and interacting with schools—the Clayton family and the Sassano family.

Being White, Being the Majority in the Minority

Africans are the majority, so the minority is now reversed . . . it used to be the other way around, and now the people who are the minority have to fit in, and the minority is the white in this area.
—**Loraine Sassano (Mother), May 2006**

In the last two chapters, you met the Vietnamese and Sudanese families. In this chapter, I introduce two white families and describe their experiences in the inner-city environment. Through my interviews with the teachers and community members, I learned that Buffalo has two "class systems"— the "overclass" (the middle and upper middle class), who tend to send their children to the private schools or the best schools in the public system, and the "underclass" (the working class, poor, and/or minorities), who can only afford to send their children to neighborhood public schools. The two white families we will see here, being white but not middle class, belonged to the "underclass" system. Their children attended the declining inner-city schools with Africans, African Americans, and Puerto Ricans in Buffalo's impoverished West Side.

Their experiences as "white" but working-class and/or poor families have complicated the meaning of being white. Historically, whiteness has been associated with middle class and/or maleness and has often implied a privileged position in the power hierarchy and dominance (Bettie, 1995; Fine & Weis, 1998; Weis, 2004). The presence of the "unmarked categories of whiteness" (Bettie, 1995, p. 126)—the working and/or poor whites in the most disadvantaged neighborhood— has added a nuanced layer to the meaning of whiteness. That is, whiteness, though still a racial privilege, is no longer inherently a class privilege. This new dimension of whiteness has influenced how the working and/or poor whites relate themselves to the other poor working-class minorities and vice versa. For the working and/or poor whites, as Professor Marshall commented, "it was something hard for them to swallow and let go." They want to feel privileged but they cannot. At the same time, the immigrants and minorities, who have been historically placed opposite to the ideal of whiteness and signified what whiteness is not (Lee, 2005), cannot do away with their hostility toward the whites even though there are different shades of whiteness (middle class or poor alike) (Perry, 2002). The inherent tension between the whites and the non-whites, therefore, goes on unchanged despite their alliances in terms of social class. As a result, the white poor and working classes, though they do not possess the same economic power as their middle- or upper-middle-class peers in the suburbs, continue to be separated from the other minorities and become a distinct social group detached from the multicultural and multi-ethnic fabric of the West Side.

Many studies on whiteness have centered on the traditional aspects of whiteness and maleness and few studies (e.g., Weis, 2004) have included white working-class women. In this chapter, I focus on the white women's perspectives. In contrast to the conventional white male-dominated families, these women are considered to be the heads of the household. In both families, the women, not the men, are more involved in their children's education at home and in school. In a sense, these women increasingly assume more power in the home sphere, and can be regarded as the white working males' counterparts in their discourse of privilege loss at home, in the neighborhood, and in the deindustrialized economy (see Fine & Weis, 1998).

According to Marilyn and Nelli, two parent liaisons in a local school, there are two categories among the poor and working-class white women—those who make it out of West Side and those who can't. The first group includes the resilient ones who understand the current situations in the West Side and work hard to improve their conditions, seeking ways to escape to the suburbs eventually. The other group consists of those who get stuck in the city and cannot get out. They are often stereotyped in the community as "having mental problems" for their lack of mobility. The common belief is that most of the poor whites in the local area have a supporting network of other family members who can help them move out to the suburbs if they so desired. Therefore, not being able to make it out means something is wrong with them or they are "hopeless." The parent liaisons point out that this group tends to be single white mothers with several children, who often have different fathers.

The two families introduced in this chapter somewhat fit within the stereotypes of these two groups. When this study began in 2004, both families were living in the West Side. However, after two years, their situations became quite different. The Sassano family, through the hard work of the mother, eventually joined the white exodus and now lives in the suburbs. The Clayton family, though they tried to join the exodus, could not make it far from the inner city. As of 2005 I have since lost contact with them as a result of their frequent moves around the West Side community. In researching these two families, many questions surfaced such as: Does being poor decrease the perceived advantages of being white? Do the white parents have different ways of interacting with the children from the other minority families such as the blacks and the Asians? Are the white home literacy practices closer to school norms than those of the immigrant families? In the following pages, I give a detailed account of the two families' experiences at home, in the school, and in the community as they make sense of their race and class relations in relation to the other ethnic groups.

The Sassano Family: The Minority in the West Side

The Sassano family was local to Buffalo. Loraine Sassano grew up in a military home and moved around a bit when she was a child. Her family currently resides in Florida while she remains in Buffalo. After she and her husband married fifteen years ago, they settled down in the upper West Side of Buffalo where her husband grew up. The area was predominantly an Italian neighborhood whose residents moved up from the lower West Side after World War II. By then, the area, though declining, was still a desirable place for many working-class whites who wanted to remain in the city but could not afford to live in the affluent neighborhoods just blocks away. They have two sons. In 2004 Scott was thirteen and in seventh grade and Rod was ten and in fourth grade.

Scott and Rod both attended Rainbow Elementary, where the children from the Sudanese and the Vietnamese families were enrolled. In Rainbow Elementary, they were among the few American-born white students in the school and considered to be minorities in the school. Scott had been on the merit roll in the school and was admitted to Madison Tech, a good high school, in 2005, but was having a hard time catching up academically in the high school; his first report card showed only a 72 percent grade average. The school, according to Professor Marshall, has a strong emphasis on the technical side (math and science) and therefore attracts more of the working-class and/ or minority students. Also, it does not have such high language requirements as the other top high schools such as Lakeside High, which emphasizes a liberal arts curriculum and admits mostly middle-class white students from the city. Rod had been on the honor roll in the international school with a 90 percent grade average, but, according to Loraine, he started to "regress" like his brother between 2004 and 2006, because of a lack of motivated peers who wanted to succeed and being picked on by other African and Hispanic children in the school.

Work, Study and the Welfare System

In 2004, when I first began interviewing the family for the research project, Loraine was attending a community college, studying for a registered nurse degree. In order to help support the family financially while pursuing her degree she stepped down from a managerial full-time position as a butcher to work part-time in the meat department at Tops, a large grocery store chain.

Table 5.1 The Sassano Family Profile (as of 2006)

Name	Age	Occupation	Education	Languages	Others
Stanley	40s	Local jeweler	Graduated a high school	English	Grew up in the West Side
Loraine	40s	Part-time butcher in 2005 then became a nursing aide in 2006	Graduated from a community college in 2006	English	Highly values education; wants the kids to learn independence
Scott	15	Student	Graduated from Rainbow Elementary; enrolled in a high school first in the city and then in the suburb	English	Wants to be a technologist
Rod	12	Student	Enrolled in Rainbow Elementary, then one in the suburb	English	Getting good grades; loves to read

Even when she was working full time at the managerial position, Loraine was making only $6 an hour and could barely make ends meet: "I worked five, six days a week, hard, for nothing. I was bringing home maybe $200 a week." In addition to the lower wages, she did not like the male-dominated work environment where her manager, "a white, white Irish alcoholic," hated her because he "didn't like women in the meat department." Loraine realized that "it was a dead end job that goes nowhere" and she needed to make some changes in her life. So she decided to go back to school to pursue what she always wanted to do—becoming a nurse.

Loraine's going back to school caused a financial burden on the family. Stanley, a Class C jeweler, was bringing home only $400 a week before taxes (about $330 after taxes) to support the family, which was not enough to pay the household expenses and Loraine's tuition. Loraine went down to the Social Services office to ask for food stamps and, to her surprise, she was told they couldn't get any help. She recounts her experience:

> I went down to get food stamps; and they told me that because of my husband's income, we make too much money . . . And I talked to the woman, I said, "I'm in school full-time." I said, "I need help." And she said to me, "Well, maybe you should quit school and go back to work, then." . . . It was rude. It was very . . . I was so upset when I walked out of there, and you walk through Social Service waiting room, and there's people draped in furs and gold, on their cell phone saying "Yeah, I can't believe I have to sit here this long to get my money," and another one sitting there ordering pizza to be delivered to Social Services waiting room. I can't get Food Stamps 'cause I'm trying to better my family and never have to depend on the system again. I was livid, livid when I got out of there.

Like many who hold negative stereotypes about the "black other," Loraine apparently saw the welfare system as the blacks' system. She believed that the welfare system was extremely unfair and possibly racist against the whites. Though she did not spell it out explicitly, she suspected that she was refused food stamps because she was white. She noted being so upset after she was told, "If you can't afford it, you should quit school and go back to work full-time." She interpreted her experience solely based on race and skin color and she was angry that there seemed to be a double standard because she was white. She remembered that she almost walked back in to ask the woman, "Do I need to put shoe polish on my face so that I can get some help?" But she did not go back there to fight the system, since she knew she could not win. Instead, she walked out: "I bit my tongue, and I came home and I vented."

To her relief, the family was able to get some help from the government. For example, the Heating and Energy Assistance Program (HEAP) helped them to pay energy bills, and they got Medicaid insurance for the family. It was not easy for Loraine to get this help: "I had to go downtown and sit for six hours, but it was worth it. I got $700 off my gas bill." She accepted the assistance they received from the government but was disappointed, since "many people take advantage" of the welfare system and, because of this, "the system's definitely broken." Even though she knew "many people who take advantage of it," she chose not to turn them in: "What good does it do? It doesn't help me, so I don't care!"

Even though they were refused food stamps, unlike the Sudanese and the Vietnamese families, who did not have a kinship network in America, the Sassano family was able to "amass a small 'nest egg'" from their extended families (Fine & Weis, 1998, p. 5). Stanley's mother, for example, chipped in when Loraine was in school and helped them get through the difficult time. His brother Gary, a successful businessman in the city, paid for their vacations to Florida every year and other bigger family travels so that they could relax and have fun during the stressful time.

Valuing Education: "Do Well in School and You Can Have Whatever You Want"

Loraine's tenacity, her "willingness to move on from [her] unfortunate situation . . . rather than languish" (Weis, 2004, p. 144), clearly shows the value she placed on education in changing her life circumstances. During our interviews, she stressed again and again that "education is the most important thing," not only to her, but more so to her children, Scott and Rod. She expected them to take advantage of what education could do for them: "I want them to do well in school. And in our life, the better you're doing in your school, the better job you'll get. That's right. I'm better if both of [them] get a better education . . . do well in school, go to college, get a better job." Since Loraine did not go to college right after high school, she asked Scott and Rod not to follow suit. Using herself as an example, she emphasized the importance of focusing on education: "Go to school, do well in school, and you never end up like we are." She told Scott and Rod, "Don't wait like I did . . . working at Tops, a dead-end job. Get a good job early, and you can earn some money, and you can do the things you want to do in life . . . if you don't get a good education, what are you gonna do? You are gonna work at Tops. You're gonna work at the gas station, or whatever."

Since Loraine and Stanley talked about the importance of education with Scott and Rod all the time, their views of education had been instilled in them. Both Scott and Rod stated that they were "going to college right after high school" (Rod) and "finish right away and get a good job right away" (Scott). Scott, whose dream was to become a technologist, concurred with Loraine: "Mom, like you say, you get a car you want, and other people will be sitting there, probably working in the gas station and pumping the gas."

Loraine also believed that the children had to make many decisions and choices in life, especially living in an inner-city context where there are many opportunities to encounter the issues of sex, drugs, alcohol, and violence. According to her, education is so incredibly important because it can also help her children make the correct choices and decisions, not the wrong ones. She explained, "My husband and I both firmly believe that if you educate your children, they're gonna make their decisions anyway. But if they have education behind them and know, then they're gonna make a better decision I think. And that's all you can hope for. I can't watch over them all the time."

In addition to using Loraine's experiences as an example to educate Rod and Scott, Loraine and Stanley also enlisted the help of Gary, Stanley's brother, to instill the importance of education, especially when Scott sometimes slacked off in school. Gary, who finished only high school, owned his own production company and was very wealthy. Loraine described Gary with admiration, noting that "he drives a BMW" and "gets whatever he wants." Scott was very enamored of Gary and believed that "he is the best thing in the entire world" and, of course, he did not want to disappoint Gary. Loraine and Stanley often encouraged Scott to look up to Uncle Gary, telling him that "You can do it, too. Go to school, get a good job and make some money, and you can do whatever you want to also." This way, Scott had something to work toward. They found that having Gary as a role model was extremely helpful: "[Gary is a] very good role model, and he is so good because when we have problems with Scott, all we have to do is say something to Gary and Gary looks at him and says, 'What are you doing? What's up, Nephew?' And Scott just, you can see him shrink, like 'Oh, my God, I'm disappointing him.'"

In 2006, Scott was having a difficult time adjusting to the high school, and his report card showed grades in the low 70s average range. Loraine was worried that, if he continued to have a 72 percent average in school, he was going to end up at a community college. She asked Gary to speak with him. Gary took Scott out to lunch and "set him straight." Loraine recounted their lunch talk to me: "[Gary] tells Scott, he said 'I got lucky. You won't get lucky, 'cause it doesn't happen to everybody. You need to do well in school and go to college.' He said 'I got lucky. But don't count on getting lucky yourself.' That's what he tells them. 'Do well in school. You can have anything you want too.'"

Besides having good role models, Loraine also believes that family stability is important for keeping children out of trouble. This was why she had not moved for thirteen years while the children were growing up, even though she knew that there were problems in the West Side. Living in the West Side, she had observed a lot of troubled kids from broken families. She explained, "And a lot of them are living in a house with just Mom, who's overwhelmed, trying to raise a family and work at a low-paying job, so you work a lot of hours to make no money. And you know what? You don't have time to raise your children and do what's right, because you are too busy trying to survive."

Home (and School) Literacy Practices: "We Read All the Time"

Loraine and Stanley's views on education were well reflected in their home literacy practices and their involvement in their school and homework. In their household, Stanley was the "hands-on" person who was in charge of fixing and building things. He did not read or write much at home except for reading newspapers and writing some notes to Loraine or grocery lists. Loraine described Stanley, a high school graduate, as "more of a laborer than he is a mind man." She, on the other hand, was an avid reader. She did not like horror, fiction, or romance novels, but read a lot of medical mysteries. There were books and materials everywhere in their house at the West Side. She expressed her love of reading: "I love to read. I could spend all day in a book." Besides writing emails and letters to family and friends, when she was a full-time student, Loraine had to read her class textbooks and do homework, writing reports and research papers in the evenings, and thus "was on the computer all the time." When she had some free time, she did planning and writing for the Boy Scouts group with which her family had been heavily involved throughout the years.

Loraine hoped that her love of reading and writing would "rub off" on the children: "I want them [the children] to learn it that way." She always bought them new books or took them to the public library to borrow books. Loraine emphasized in our interviews that "whenever they ask for a book, I never say no." If the kids needed some books, no matter how tight their budget was, they would take them to the bookstore and buy the books they wanted or needed. She bought them all the Harry Potter series and thought that they would love them, but to her surprise, the kids did not like them and had not read them yet. Both of the kids had book shelves in their rooms, full of books. When the kids were little, she used to read with them. They took turns to read and, if the kids seemed to be confused about meaning, they would go back and read it again. When they ran into a new word, they sounded it out first, and if they could not figure out the meaning, they would look it up in the dictionary. Loraine always tried to have the kids do as much as possible independently as she believed it was the only way the kids were going to learn. When they were older, they wanted to read on their own. She understood that "it's no fun having a mom read with them. Now they just curl up at the corner on a couch and just grab a book and read!"

Rod, a fourth grader when the project began, was also an avid reader. Like his mother, he enjoyed reading mystery books. He loved to read for fun but hated to read for duty. He loved chapter books such as *Fudge*, a popular book in the Judy Blume series. He had read every single book in the series. Each month when he received the Scholastic book order forms from school, he always asked his parents, "Can I get the books?" When he went to the public library close to their house and saw some new books he was interested in (e.g., an animal book that he had never seen before), Loraine always encouraged him to take it home, read, and see. She told him, "If you don't like it, you don't have to read it." This unfortunately changed in 2006 when the library closed on account of a lack of funding from the city. Now they did not have free access to books and had to rely mostly on their own purchases.

Sometimes when Loraine was reading a good book, Rod would also want to read it. She joked that sometimes they competed for good books. One of their favorite times was sitting out on the front porch and reading together. Rod sometimes liked to read for school. He had to write reports based on reading and answer text-based questions. He mostly liked to work on school projects. Rod, however, equated writing with printing. He stated that he "[liked] to write essays because it helped his handwriting [get] better." He sometimes made greeting cards for holiday occasions. But mostly he did not write much except for homework.

Scott, in contrast, did not like to read. Loraine described it that "he hates to read, hates with a passion." Understanding this, Loraine constantly made an effort to push him to read. He managed to finish the Goosebumps series. When they used to go to the library, Scott took some books home, but he did not really read them. Every month he had to complete a book report for school, and Loraine was forced to make him to read. The day before the book report was due, there was always a big fight to get Scott to finish the book so he would write the report. Loraine reasoned that two factors had probably affected Scott's attitude toward reading. One was the motivational factor, as "Scott doesn't have a choice on what he reads for book reports. There's a list of books that he has to read, and he hates it. He hates the fact that he has to read these certain books." The other factor was his problem with vocabulary, as he had problems with verbs and his vocabulary was limited. Scott himself admitted that too many new words were the reason why he did not like to read or write. He explained, "Because you have to try to figure out what this word is and stuff, but you don't know what word it is." He also admitted that sometimes he did not know how to spell the words "because you kind of sometimes mess up." He realized that school was getting increasingly tough because there were more exams. They used to have just spelling tests, but now they had "exams, math assessment, science assessment, reading assessment, stuff like that."

Besides reading, the boys' other home literacy activities included listening to music, watching TV, and playing computer games. For music, both Scott and Rod were into new rock, such as Nicole Becham, Linkin Park, and Trapped. To Loraine's relief, they did not like rap, as she disliked rap. In addition to new pop rock, the family pretty much listened to the same music, especially rock songs from the late '60s and early '70s. While they rode in the car, they all listened to the oldies station and sang along because they knew most of the lyrics. With TV, Rod was a cartoon addict. Every day when he came home from school, he did his homework first and then watched cartoons for about half an hour. Scott liked to watch programs such as *American Choppers* and *Myth Busters* on the Discovery channel. Both of them also enjoyed watching MTV and some of the comedy shows such as *Pimp My Ride*. At night, Scott and Rod sometimes joined Loraine and Stanley to watch some of the regular TV series that they all loved, such as *House*, *Law & Order*, *Close to Home*, and *Without a Trace*. Rod loved *CSI*, but had to miss it because it was on at 10:00 p.m., which was his bedtime. As a family, they also rented a lot of movies from Blockbuster Video. They enjoyed family movies such as *Four Brothers*, *Yours, Mine, and Ours*, and *The Wild*. Though Scott and Rod loved computer games, they did not play often. Scott had a TV and computer in his room to play video games, but his parents took these away in 2006 because of his declining grade point average.

The family engaged in a wide array of fun activities together. Compared with the children in the Sudanese and Vietnamese families, who were often stuck at home during summer and winter vacations, the Sassano children were constantly involved in different kinds of fun family activities, especially in the summer. Loraine believed that a good home life was important to a child's school achievement; she observed, "You can see parents who care about their kids by the grades that they get. The kids [who] are doing poorly in school, are the ones that have no home life." Therefore, the family tried "to do a lot of outdoor activity, bike riding, running around, playing ball, that kind of thing. In the evenings, usually we try to a lot of family games. Keep active." Sometimes, in the summer, the family also went fishing together. On Sunday evenings, they often went bowling for a couple of games. On weekends, they were active in Boy Scouts activities such as water skiing, camping, fundraising, silent auctions, or community service. Scott was only nine months away from becoming an Eagle Scout in 2006. Loraine and Stanley highly valued these Boy Scouts activities. They believed these activities could teach them to respect others, as Boy Scouts was very different from the school, where "everybody kind of hangs in their own group, and they don't mix with the other people." Loraine explained, "In Boy Scouts when the kids are there, everybody acts the same. Everybody is the same. It doesn't matter what color, ethnicity, none of it. It doesn't matter. It's so weird. It's so different than school. They're all working towards a certain goal . . . So it doesn't matter what color you are or anything, it's just you're all there, you're all scouts. You are all together."

Besides Boy Scout activities, sometimes they got together with Gary's children in the suburbs. Unlike the Sudanese and Vietnamese families, who rarely took vacations, the Sassano family would take the children to Pennsylvania to spend a weekend at Splash Lagoon, a water park, twice a year. Since their budget was tight, they chose to go on Sunday and Monday when it costs only $150 for a family of four, saving $300 per trip. The parents usually pulled the kids out of school during the week days. Loraine noted that she was not worried if the boys missed a few school days as they were doing well in school (even though she indicated earlier that she was concerned about Scott's grade average). She stressed that the boys brought their homework with them on the trip. For example, in March 2006, the whole family went to Florida for a week of vacation (paid by Stanley's bother, Gary). Scott and Rod were pulled out of school for the week. Loraine described, "So we let the teachers know they were gonna be out of school, and they gave them what they needed to do, and they did homework sitting by the pool."

Dealing with a Declining Neighborhood and Dinner Table Conversations

Another unique dimension of the Sassano's home literacy practices was their family dinner conversations. Loraine and Stanley made sure that family members all had dinner together and talked about issues that they thought were important. Loraine explained, "We always talk about something at dinner time . . . We talk about drugs. We talk about sex. We talk about everything at the dinner table. Everything is flat out open." Loraine and Stanley believed this kind of open conversation was critical to the children's survival in the West Side. Loraine further explains, "We are [in the] West Side of Buffalo. It is not a good neighborhood. They are gonna be exposed to all of these [things]. I am sure they've been exposed to drugs already . . . They won't tell me, but I'm sure they have had cigarettes and I know for the fact, because I heard kids talking about sex."

Scott and Rod often talked about things that they saw in school and on the street. Rod, for example, came home one day and told them that somebody was smoking marijuana in the bathroom in the school. Another day when the city had a big drug bust, it happened just around the corner from the Sassano's house. The children watched police pull three black men out of their car and found huge bricks of a white drug in their car. As Lorraine said, it was like "watching a movie, except it's happening right outside their house in my neighborhood. My kids are SITTING RIGHT THERE!" The children were also aware of sex and the consequences of having sex because they often heard about nine- or ten-year-old girls getting pregnant. This kind of exposure could potentially influence Scott, who then had a girlfriend in high school and spent a lot of time with her. Even though Scott and his girlfriend were seldom alone, Loraine and Stanley believed that it was important to educate them and help them make better decisions. When Scott asked questions about the relationship, Stanley gave Scott three condoms and told him that that was "not permission by any means, but if he was going to do something, don't be stupid." Loraine and Stanley firmly believed that if the boys were aware enough to ask questions about sex, they should have open and honest discussions about being sexually active. Loraine was very adamant about this early education in this kind of neighborhood: "Exposing early . . . Teach them the right way and the wrong way how the things are done, and you hope to God, when they are all by themselves on the street they make the right choice. But they are informed and they know what the right choice is. You just have to hope that they're smart enough to make it. That's all. I cannot be with them all the time. I just have to make sure I teach them."

Parental Involvement

Parental involvement includes involvement both at home and in school. Loraine was a firm believer in parental involvement. In her words, "The more parents are involved, the better the school, the better the schooling is for the children." She was actively involved at home as her schedule did not allow her to be in her children's schools. At home, she closely monitored Rod and Scott's homework, making sure they completed their homework. When Rod and Scott came home from school, Loraine always asked what homework must be completed. She established a very strict homework-first policy, so they understood "they have to do homework immediately, that's automatic." She explained, "After school, it's always homework first. When they walk in the door, homework has to be done, so that they can do anything. Then it depends on the day. If it's a miserable day, no kids around, they either jump on a computer and play a game on the computer or grab a book and read, or just play Yugioh cards or something like that."

In addition to making sure the children did their homework, Loraine also checked all their homework. Her principle was that she did not change anything they wrote, even if it was wrong. She, however, did point out that there were errors and asked them to locate and correct them. She believed that they needed to learn from their own mistakes: "Something like that, making them go back and see if they actually figure it out. I don't hand anything to them. No, that makes life too easy and that's not real." She also paid attention to their handwriting and if it was unintelligible she would ask them to rewrite their work.

When Loraine was attending classes at the community college, she usually studied and did her homework together with the boys. Later, when she started to work as a nurse's aide, some nights when she was on her shift she could not do that any more. But at nights when she was free she continued to study for work while Scott and Rod did their homework. Every day, Rod spent about an hour and a half on his homework, writing book reports and other school projects in science, language arts, math, and social studies. Scott's homework, on the other hand, varied, with some days or weeks having very little and others having much more. This situation continued even after he entered high school. Feeling surprised, Loraine asked Scott about this, and was told that he did it in school as they had some free time. Unconvinced, she went to the school to ask his teachers about it. She found that sometimes this was true, and sometimes Scott had "stuff missing that he's never turned in." She realized that Scott, now a teenager, was "playing games" with her. In order to change his attitude toward homework, she sometimes took his TV or computer out of his room as a punishment.

In addition to being involved in her children's homework, Loraine was also actively supporting Rod's school's reading programs such as "Parents as Reading Partners." The program required parents to read with their child for twenty minutes every night for five days a week. Even though Loraine knew many parents just signed off on it without really doing it, she made an effort to complete the program with Rod as required. She did not want to teach her children that it was ok to just sign off on something when they do not actually do it. She sat with Rod, listening to him read for twenty minutes, five nights a week, for several weeks. Occasionally, she asked some comprehension questions to help him read. After they completed the program, they attended a breakfast party at the school where Rod received a book and a certificate and a medal for his home reading. Both Loraine and Rod were very proud of the awards.

Loraine and Stanley tried to participate in the children's school activities as much as possible. They attended most of the PTO meetings and were involved in some school activities such as the annual international festival and school plays. If Rod or Scott took part in these activities, Loraine and Stanley always made an attempt to attend. When Rod and Scott were in preschool and kindergarten, she used to be in the school to help all the time, but now that they were getting older she wanted them to have their own independence as "they don't need mom sitting there watching them." She now made a point of knowing what was going on, but she did not "want to be on their shoulder watching what they're doing." She went to the school as often as her schedule allowed. Sometimes, she just "popped in" and visited the teachers to see how things were going with the children in school. Since they seldom received notes about the children from school, she believed this kind of "actual, verbal communication" was critical to keep her informed about the children's school performance. To the teachers, she made it known that she was available if they needed her. She stated, "I work my schedule around my kids."

Loraine's communication style with the school appeared to have changed over the two years of this study. In 2004, when discussing the school's responsibility for Scott's (and Rod's) low writing ability and his missing homework, Lorraine seemed to be very passive toward the school's responsibilities. Even though she believed that the school could do better to teach the children "the way it's supposed to be done or write a paper the way it should be done instead of getting through it," she had not said anything to the school about it. She stated, "They do things their way and that's the way it's gonna be. You know what I mean. We are not gonna change the school system. At least, it's not me! Not by one person. It won't happen." Instead, she believed that, as a parent, she should do more at home: "I push my kids. I do it at home. I tell them, 'It's one thing to do your work and get it done; it's another thing to do your work and do a good job at it, and you are proud of what you've done.' And one thing that I push really strongly in this house is all about 'do one thing and do it right,' because it takes less time to do it right the first time than to do it right the second time when I make you redo it."

When Scott entered high school in 2005, he continued to miss homework assignments. The situation became worse and his grade point average continued to decline, falling to a C average. In fact, his report card showed that every single teacher commented that he had missing assignments. Loraine realized that Scott's declining grade point average was a result of his missing homework. She made a point of saving his homework on her computer so that she could keep track of what he had completed. Doing this also helped her better communicate with his teachers about what he had or had not finished. In addition to continuing to push him to do more at home, Loraine also pushed the teachers to take more responsibilities.

Scott's bio-lab teacher, for example, often lost Scott's (as well as many others') lab reports and Loraine decided to insist that he had completed the assignment because she had those lab reports on her computer and she was sure that Scott had turned them in. She first called the teacher who informed her that he did not have Scott's lab reports and thus Scott could not take the biology final. Loraine told him that she had all the reports on her computer and she would ask Scott to reprint and hand them in the next day. Three days later, the lab teacher called and said that he did not have them. Loraine decided to call the principal and report the problem. The principal arranged for the lab reports to be handed in to the vice-principal. Since there was no guarantee that the school was losing them, Loraine now demanded a receipt from the vice-principal. Since then, no lab reports have been missing. However, Loraine's fight did not stop there. After she learned that many other students also had similar problems, she suspected that the teacher had "some kind of power trip" going on because, if the lab reports were not in, students could not take the biology finals and they might have to repeat the ninth grade. Since they needed proof that the teacher/school lost their lab reports, she asked Scott to tell all of his classmates that they should turn everything in to their guidance counselor or vice-principal and have them sign off and get a receipt from them. She hoped that this would encourage the school to recognize that a problem existed and they must find a solution.

Rod and Scott's School Experiences

Though Rod was very punctual in handing in his homework assignments and he was earning good grades in school, his school experience became more and more negative as the neighborhood deteriorated over the last several years. Rod and Scott, as well as their parents, agreed that Rainbow Elementary School was "an excellent school and they've got a good education so far for a city school." They particularly liked the multicultural environment in the school. Each year, Rod and Scott were active in the school's annual international festival. As Loraine noted, "It's incredible. My kids know the difference between different Asian people, and different black people because they don't look at them as black, they look at them as African, or Egyptian or just some other things, and they can see the differences, which I think is fabulous."

In 2004, when asked about the implication of diversity issues for the children, Loraine pointed out that the children were exposed to different cultures, which was "a great way to stop prejudice." When they discussed different cultures at home, they did not "ever talk in racial terms at all." When asked their experience of being a racial minority in school, Loraine believed that it was "a good thing" and "a good taste" for the children as they learned what being a minority felt like. Rod thought that he did not learn much from students from other cultures as they did not know much about America. However, he enjoyed being exposed to them and learning a bit about other cultures. At times, he enjoyed helping them and teaching them English. In school, however, Rod (and Scott) mostly socialized with Asian children, not the Africans, who were the majority.

In 2005, Rod had a good peer group in his class who wanted to succeed, and they had a friendly competition which enabled them to increase their achievement. However, things started to change as more and more whites began to leave the school. The academic environment that Rod once enjoyed seemed to have disappeared. According to Rod, in 2006, no more than five people in his class of thirty-seven students wanted to get good grades, and among the five students he was the only white student. He did not like it, because "if you stand out, you sort of freaking [them] out." Most of the students did not want to be in school and often made excuses not to come to school. Rod noticed that "people like to miss school" to stay home and the school also did not take care of them or want those people to be there either. Loraine pointed out that, since the parents were out working, "they [the kids] had the day for themselves to do everything they want to." This "subtractive" school culture had caused a problem for students like Rod who wanted to excel, as the teachers often had to repeat the lessons for those students who had missed the class. Rod often became bored, because "they don't really teach much there. It's all kind of review." Sometimes, it took several days for the class to finish reading one simple book. Since his teachers (such as the social studies teacher) often taught the same content over again, Rod found that school was "kind of easy." As Scott summarized for Rod, "they don't challenge him."

The lack of academic challenge in Rainbow Elementary might have also contributed to Scott's academic difficulty in high school. Scott, now in a better high school, compared his experiences in the new school and Rainbow Elementary. He concurred with Rod that Rainbow was "not very organized" academically and lacked discipline for students. Now facing a much more rigorous curriculum and a stricter school environment, Scott realized that his old school did not prepare him well for high school academically or socially. In his words, "they did not prepare us well at all."

As the only white student in his class, Rod's situation was getting worse in 2006. He was constantly picked on by other students, especially by the black students. Loraine explained, "He is the only kid in this class that's smart. And he is overweight. So he gets picked on, 'cause he is heavy. He gets picked on 'cause he's smart, and he gets picked on 'cause he is white." Rod believed that he got picked on because the black students hated him for his being white and for disagreeing with their behavior in school. He confided to me, "They pick on me because of my teeth [which needed braces] and because I am not black." They called him "a Nigger" or sometimes "Chinese" and hit him. "They don't care. They call everyone whatever . . . they call white people whatever that bad word, they just call everyone that . . . they don't even understand what a Negro is. He swears at people 'cause he just learned from someone else." He noted, "A lot of students in my class are racists . . . They don't really pick on black people. They pick on white people and Puerto Ricans." Among the blacks, as Rod observed, mostly African Americans liked to pick on people. Even though the Africans had different attitudes, they were being influenced by the African Americans. Scott, who had similar experiences, explained that Africans "are becoming just as bad . . . just [going] downhill. Just trying to fit in, that's the problem . . . try to fit in with the African Americans."

When talking about this, Rod expressed a sense of despair, "People don't care in my school any more. No respect at all . . . I used to care, but I don't care anymore . . . I just do my work in school and leave." He also noticed that the situation had gotten worse, and picking on people and fighting became the school culture: "It used to be better and now it got worse." Rod, for example, could not believe that in his class, when one student's father died, other students made fun of it. He believed that all this was happening because of a general lack of caring and respect in the community. He further explained, "People have just been worse; people just don't care any more . . . They just are bad . . . Fight, scream . . . People just punch people. They don't care. They don't really care. Teachers are just as bad . . . Shout the kids down."

The family noticed that disrespect was everywhere in the city. As Loraine observed, "it's that way in the city, though. It really is that [way] in the city. You see it when you walk down in the street; you see it sitting on the front porch; you see it in the schools; and you see it in the neighborhoods." The epidemic of disrespect has affected the whites who were the racial minority in the community. Scott commented that it used to be the problem of one race (by which he meant the African Americans and the Puerto Ricans), and now it was everybody and everywhere as everyone was trying to fit in this culture. Rod agreed, "[It used to be just] Puerto Rican and black. They used to get into fights. They don't care. And now whites, a lot of white people don't even care now. Just trying to act in advance so they don't get picked down, anything like that . . . they wear the same clothes. They talk like the blacks. They walk like them. They act like them."

In order to help their children fight this conforming culture, Loraine and Stanley tried to help their children recognize what was going on and make right decisions about their own behavior. They repeatedly stressed to the children, "You don't change to conform; you don't change to make friends; you stay who you are, and stand by what you believe in." Scott and Rod tried to follow this in school; for example, unlike everyone else, they did not wear baggy pants and huge T-shirts. Scott tried to "do his own thing, doesn't conform to anyone." Since he was a free agent, a non-conformist, many students in the school did not like him. Loraine assured him that he was maintaining the right attitude and he should continue because, no matter where he went, he should be himself. Even though Scott was trying, he was very pessimistic about the city schools, including his own high school, which was one of the better schools. He commented, "All the city schools are going down . . . 'coz everyone disrespects everything."

Rod, who loved the school two years ago, also became very pessimistic. In 2006, during the interview, he stated that he did not like the school at all. He expressed his disappointment at the school: "I have been here since pre-K, eight years . . . It kept going down and down in terms of behavior. The [teachers] are trying their best to teach, but people are bad. They can't teach because people actually have to hear and learn." He described that learning was becoming increasingly hard in the classroom where students were very disruptive: "We have someone who just sits there during teaching, and just sits there, doing nothing, drawing. Someone slapped someone across the face, gave them a bruise like here, and her glasses flew off. People don't care. They just hit people, pick on them." He understood that teachers were under a lot of pressure as well:

> They try their best, and sometimes lately, my teacher's been, if they're bad enough, then they, she sends them to a different class because we have a teacher, a sixth-grade teacher that is really strict. And if they are bad, they don't know how to control themselves, they send them to her for the day. And she has this thing that, it's like a chart, for like pizza parties and field trips. If you are bad enough, you get an X, and if you get three Xs, you can't go on this field trip. So, a couple of people couldn't go . . . My teacher doesn't like to reward people that don't do their work.

Other times, he found that teachers were not doing much to address people's misbehavior and just allowed students to do whatever they wanted. He observed that "when people don't do their work . . . [they] just sit there, doing nothing, drawing . . . People don't care. They're just happy." However, he felt lucky that sometimes his class was a little better than others, "Because my teacher doesn't give out many tests or stuff like that . . . Like [in] a couple of classes you can't . . . they don't talk, you have to do your work by yourself. My teacher put us into groups. So you can work with the groups and talk and work with each other and everything."

Loraine believed that the widespread problem in the city had to do with the way kids were raised. In her view, parents in the neighborhood often set bad examples for their children. In her graduation ceremony, for example, some parents got into fights in front of their children, and police came and arrested two parents and three kids. Loraine believed these kinds of incidents set very horrible examples to children. She elaborated on the effect of a lack of good parental role model on children: "It used to be when kids were fighting, parents would come out and say, 'stop, don't do that.' Now, parents come out and say, 'Kick his ass! Kill him! Kill him! Kill him!' Oh, I see the parent came out the house, screaming."

The Exodus: "I'm Tired of Fighting this Place"

As the children's school experiences became more and more negative, the neighborhood also became more and more dangerous to live in. In 2004 and 2005, Scott and Rod witnessed a few more shooting incidents and drug raids from their porch. They saw blood, police, specially trained dogs, and they watched the reports on the news. When Scott and Rod could not go out to play and had to stay indoors all the time to keep safe, Loraine and Stanley decided that it was time for them to move out of the city. Rod was particularly happy about the decision as the hope of going to a better place kept him fighting off the racism he experienced in school. He kept saying to Loraine, "Mom, it's okay. I don't care that they pick on me . . . I just ignore them because I know next year, I will be in a real school."

Since the children had so many problems in school then, Loraine had to go to the school to talk to the principals all the time. The frequent visits to the schools had made her feel very fed up and frustrated with what was occurring in the city and the schools, "You know what . . . I really got tired of trying to fight this place. I used to go in weekly and go straight to the principal, and when she saw me come in, she would turn around and run because she knew I had another complaint, and she didn't want to hear it . . . I get to the point where I'm just done. I just don't want to do it any more. It's almost over, and I don't have to deal with it any more."

Finally, what happened during Hurricane Katrina in 2005 helped the family make their final decision to leave. Loraine realized that in some sense her family was in a similar situation to those stuck in New Orleans. She describes the revelation: "You're stuck. It's like the people in Louisiana during the hurricane. They all got shipped out and they can't come back because they can't afford it. So they lost everything. And the families that can get out are getting out; and ones that are left there are ones that can't afford to go anywhere . . . People say, 'Why didn't they leave?' 'You know it was coming, why didn't you leave?' You know what? When you don't have any money, where do you go?"

In 2006, Loraine secured a much better job which paid more money than her previous job at the local supermarket and thus the family could afford to live in a suburb where it was safer and had better schools. In May 2006, they put their house up for sale and were ready to move to the suburb where Stanley's brother, Gary, lived. Scott and Rod were very excited about the move. In early June, Rod was counting the days, "I have ten more days in school. I am going to a field trip tomorrow . . . next week and then two days!" Scott was also counting the days and was complaining again about the school. Loraine kept telling him, "Just deal with it for another couple of weeks."

In August 2006, the Sassanos sold their house and bought a duplex in the suburb. Scott and Rod loved their new schools and the new community very much. They made some friends and often played outside. Loraine believed that freedom to play was the biggest difference for the children. She was also very optimistic about what the suburban schools could do for Scott's low grade point average and his Spanish, which he failed in the city school: "The schools here won't let that happen. No, they won't."

The Claytons: The Mobile Family

The Mobile Family and the Schools

Pauline Clayton grew up in Buffalo's East Side, which is predominantly a low-SES African American community. She attended school up to the twelfth grade but never graduated. After high school, she left home and settled in the West Side. Pauline had a baby and became a single mother. After that, Pauline had another baby by the same father. At the outset of this study, Pauline, twenty-nine, was a mother of three. In 2005, she became pregnant with her current live-in boyfriend's second baby. Her boyfriend, a second-generation American of Pakistani and Italian immigrant parents, was a carpenter who was then on a disability leave. He also had a son from his previous relationship, who was living with his mother in another state. Pauline and the children were supported by social welfare and they did not own a car.

Pauline was very busy with the three children every day. On a typical day, she woke up at 7:30 a.m. to get Kate, her first daughter, who was in fourth grade, ready for the school. After that, she took care of Josh, who was three years old, and her baby daughter, who was eight months old in 2004. Pauline cleaned the house, fed and bathed the children, and changed their clothes. Josh, born with chronic asthma and receiving steroid treatments, was always very hyper, thus complicating her task of caring for him and Kate. Before lunch, Pauline usually let them watch some cartoons or she just played with them. In the afternoon, she usually took the baby to see her mother, who was living nearby, or walked to the store to get something for supper.

Having grown up in the harsh East Side, Pauline did not have a good experience in school and did not finish high school. She went to an auto-mechanic high school attended mostly by male students. She described her experiences as "very negative" and that very little learning took place because of a lack of pedagogical caring. She recounted those experiences:

> Then you were allowed to smoke on the bus and in class . . . so learning, the teacher just really did not care . . . High school was horrible, I was a teenager. I did not graduate; I dropped out. It's brutal . . . teachers, they did not care at all . . . If you do the work, you do it; if you don't, you don't . . . Because of the teachers, because of the environment, because of the violence in the high school, definitely nobody cares. So [teachers thought], why should I?

Pauline had difficulty with reading comprehension in school, so she often asked the teachers for help, but "nobody really wanted to help" her. For example, when she asked, "I had a difficult time understanding, and would you please explain to me?" The teachers basically told her, "You are not the only

Table 5.2 The Clayton Family Profile (as of 2004)

Name	Age	Occupation	Education	Languages	Others
Pauline	29	Supported by social welfare	Dropped out of high school	English	Grew up in the East Side; had bad experiences in school but holding high expectations for her children
Brian		Home mechanic	Dropped out of high school	English	Second-generation offspring of Pakistani and Italian immigrants; had bad experiences in school
Kate	10	Student	Rainbow Elementary	English	Dislikes the school; moved schools a few times
Josh	3	NA	NA	English	Has chronic asthma
Baby daughter	8 months	NA	NA	English	NA

student in this class." Her boyfriend, Brian, had also had a bad experience in school. He dropped out of school when he was in the eleventh grade. Though he wanted to become an interior designer or get into a computer-related job, he was unable to do so. He then "wasted a couple of years after school," and started to learn home improvement skills from his father, such as repairing refrigerators and air conditioning, and painting.

Given her own as well as her boyfriend's negative schooling experiences, Pauline believed it was extremely important that her daughter Kate have a good teacher in the school and that her school experiences should be positive:

> If [it's] something she has to do, I don't want it to be miserable for her. I want her to make the best of it and I want it to be the best time of her life." She also had very high expectations for her children, "The higher, the better . . . college . . . everything that I didn't have. I had such a poor school . . . horrible experience. I want her to be happy. That's for all three of my children. I don't want them to go through what I went through . . . I don't want them to have to live in a poor community, just go to any school that you have to go to because it's there. I don't want that for my children.

Through the interviews, I learned that the family had moved at least three or four times in the past four years prior to this study; as a result Kate had changed her school three times. Through our conversation and my observations, however, it turned out that their constant moving was not always related to the school quality but often a result of the family's economic situation and other factors related to the so-called culture of poverty in the West Side. According to the parent liaisons Marilyn and Nelli, one of the characteristics of the subculture of poor and working-class people living in the social welfare system is that they keep moving from one rental place to another, often leaving behind many of their household belongings even though they need to buy them in their new place. Pauline was also caught in an unfortunate situation—she wanted to move to a better neighborhood but her economic situation would not allow her to do so. When Kate was in preschool, Pauline learned of a good Head Start program, so she moved to a neighborhood that was closer to the program. Kate brought home books to read from the program. Pauline still had happy memories about Kate's experiences with the Head Start program: "I got her started in that, and on the way home, I encourage her to sing a song they learned in class . . . like that ABC song, [recognizing] different animals, recognizing good or bad days. They started with Kate, then I taught her [more]." She was very proud that Kate taught those songs to her brother and even to the baby. Kate's positive experience with Head Start made Pauline decide to send Josh to a Head Start program as well.

After the Head Start Program, Pauline enrolled Kate in Rainbow Elementary for the first grade. However, Kate's experience in the school was very negative, similar to Pauline's own story in school. First, the school allowed someone else to take Kate home without Pauline's permission. Pauline did not know the person well; it was just someone to whom she said hello. When she went to the school to pick up Kate, the school had no idea where she was and with whom she left the school. That was a very scary experience for Pauline. Even worse, Kate did not like the school. She felt like the teacher was nasty and mean to her, and every day she came home crying, "I don't like the school. I don't like the teacher!" Realizing that her daughter's attitude was quite different, not what it used to be, Pauline discussed the problem with the principal, but the situation did not change, so she decided to transfer Kate to another school.

Pauline enrolled Kate in a nearby elementary school made up of mostly Hispanic children. Pauline described that the school program was more academically focused. She noted, "It was basically just about schooling—math and reading—just about learning." The school was an "awesome" experience for Kate, who "loved her teacher and the school." Pauline described Kate's positive experience, "[The school] gave Kate all of her. She had a wonderful teacher who just always recognized Kate's strength, always saying like, 'Kate, you are doing really good, you are doing good.' You know, just a push, 'Are you doing good, Kate? You can do it.'"

Kate's report cards from the school showed that, in the second and third grade, Kate was constantly absent from school. During the 2001–2002 school year, she was absent for sixteen days and was tardy ten times. In the spring 2003 semester, she was absent for nine days. The report cards also showed that Kate was struggling with reading and writing but was very strong in math. As for reading, the report card indicated that she had some deficiencies in higher-level reading abilities such as comprehension, using prediction and confirmation strategies, and retelling. As for writing, she was struggling with conventions, writing independently, and constructing connected sentences on a topic. In the third grade, although her performance had been satisfactory, Kate's report cards showed that her grades in English Language Arts remained in the lower B range, which was lower than her other subjects such as math. As a result, Kate only qualified for the merit roll.

Even though Kate liked the school, the family moved again to another rental place in the West Side. This time it was because Pauline did not like the neighborhood. In our interview, Pauline described how horrible it was to live there because Kate was not able to play outside. Even when she could go out occasionally, she was not allowed to go far out of Pauline's sight. Pauline remembered, "We don't go out at night; we just locked the door. I don't walk to the store which was like a couple of streets. So if she has to go out of the house, she will go with parents or friends."

After being in the elementary school for two years, Pauline returned to the Rainbow School community. When Kate found that she had to go back to the school, she cried and refused to go. She protested, "I'm not going to that school! I don't like the teachers there! They are nasty and mean!" Through a lunch supervisor in the school whom Pauline befriended, she came to know that the teacher who used to teach Kate had left the school and there would be a new teacher for the fourth graders. She was anxious about the new teacher and wondered whether Kate would have the same bad experiences as two years previously. At this time, she was ready to go straight to the principal again if Kate had similar problems. To her relief, the new teacher was wonderful. Pauline explained at length how one teacher could make a world of difference:

> It depends on the teacher. The teacher shows them interest, and lets Kate know, "You are doing right or you're wrong." She's a wonderful teacher. And she gave them a focus point, and Kate stays on, which was very good. Some teachers have a child bouncing and bouncing and bouncing, and the child gets confused, whereas she keeps the child on a point. And she calls me to let me know how Kate behaves during the week, [things] you don't know back and forth. I'm very grateful for her help.

Also, when Pauline went to a PTO meeting, she was actually asked to go to the classroom to have a one-on-one conference. Pauline was very impressed, "[The teacher] sits me down. She shows me everything. She talks to me." The biggest lesson Pauline learned from her bad school experiences is that she was not learning when a teacher moved quickly from one topic to another. She was very pleased that Kate's new teacher was not like that. In fact, from Kate's homework, she learned that the teacher not only used project-based learning, but also focused on those projects in depth. She described, "In the beginning, basically everything was about African Americans, and then switched to Indians. While she teaches them different cultures, she didn't just bounce and bounce, they stuck with it through the whole year, which was really good, because I can still see [that] Kate is still learning about the Indian or African American culture and things like that."

Pauline was also very impressed with the international and multicultural aspects of the school. Since she did not know much about other countries such as China, Japan, and Russia, it was difficult to answer her children's questions about such topics. She was very pleased that Kate often came home and told her about the different cultures that she studied. Pauline spoke highly of the multicultural teaching in the school: "They are awesome. I think that's great . . . She learns about many cultures . . . very well for all the cultures. That's [what] the school do, everything, Arabic, because my boyfriend has Arabic, so better when there's something I want the rest of the family to know. Like the African

American and the white and the Spanish, it's great . . . not just center on one culture."

Like many other parents, Pauline used to attend the annual international festival at the school. Even though Kate stood out from other students as she was a white minority, Pauline thought it was a great experience for her: "We just went there for a culture festival. We look and see Kate. She's the only one white there . . . She is the only one white there that stands out, but I think it's great because she looks at other people and recognizes their differences and they look at her, and recognizes her differences. And they still get along, so it's great to teach each other."

In the fourth grade in the Rainbow School, Kate continued to miss a lot of classes. Her spring 2004 report cards showed that she had missed fourteen days in the first seven weeks, though I do not know the reasons for these absences. However, she remained on the merit roll. Kate's writing sample (Figure 5.1) indicated that her early struggles with reading and writing were still persisting. In a written response to a reading on the Indian culture (see the writing sample), Kate's writing was satisfactory but needed improvement in conventions such as capitalization and punctuation, and in providing contexts of concepts and non-references, which was related to her reading comprehension.

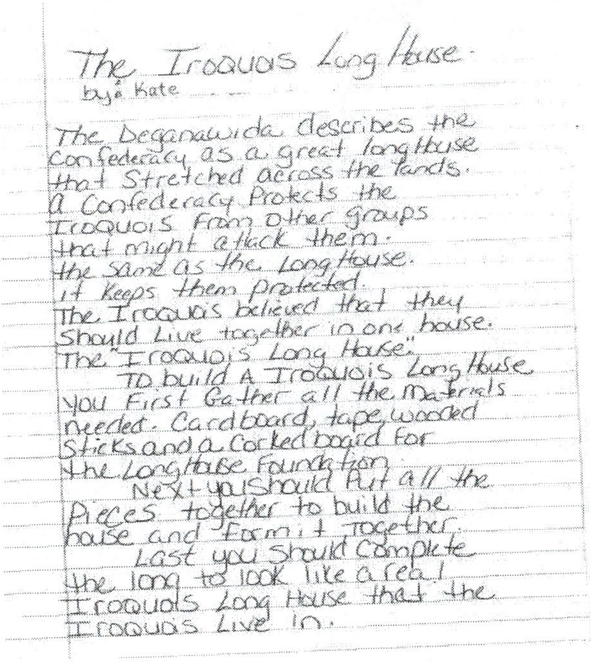
The Iroquos Long House.
by Kate
The Deganawida describes the
Confederacy as a great longhouse
that Stretched across the lands.
a Confederacy Protects the
Iroquois From other groups
that might atack them.
the same as the Long House.
it Keeps them protected.
The Iroquois believed that they
Should Live together in one house.
The "Iroquois Long House"
To build A Iroquois Long House
you First Gather all the Matrials
needed. Cardboard, tape, wooded
Sticks and a Corked board for
the Long House Foundation
Next you Should Put all the
Pieces together to build the
house and Form it Together.
Last you Should Complete
the long to look like a real
Iroquois Long House that the
Iroquos Live in.

Figure 5.1 A Sample of Kate's Written Response to Reading.

Even though Kate was happy attending Rainbow Elementary School, Pauline decided to move again as she and her boyfriend were still not happy about the neighborhood. Their current neighborhood was "more decent" than the last one they had lived in, but "still not good." Pauline explained, "Right in this block, you see there's a high school over there. A lot of adults are aware of after school hours, always fighting. In the morning, it's always fighting . . . so there're certain hours I need to know where she's at all the time." Also, Pauline's boyfriend Brian was urging her to consider enrolling Kate in East Camp, a magnet school that they heard was more academically focused. Brian said, "I've always told her that [Kate] is good and somewhere like East Camp was good for her. She doesn't want to push her, but that wouldn't exactly be pushing her." Pauline was convinced and tried to get Kate into that school. In 2004, Kate was on the waiting list. However, Pauline was aware that Kate wanted to go to the Academy for Visual and Performing Arts (grades 5–12) where she could specialize more in dancing. Pauline rationalized that she might let her choose that school if she could get her admitted: "I have to make sure that this is really what she wants to do." Later it turned out that they, especially Brian, might have been misinformed about the schools, in particular about East Camp. The State assessment results in 2005 showed that academically East Camp was one of the lowest performing schools and was much lower than the Academy of Visual and Performing Arts. For instance, the 2005 eighth grade assessment results indicated that in the latter school 45 percent of the students met state standards in English Language Arts (ELA) and 46 percent in math, but in East Camp only 29 percent of the students met state standards in ELA and 23 percent in math.

In the spring of 2005, after attending Rainbow Elementary School for one year, Pauline and the children moved to a community outside the West Side where many white, working-class families were living. Being pregnant with her fourth baby, it was hard for Pauline to live far away from her extended family without a vehicle. Even though the new community might be a little better and they were away from the high school violence, the houses on the street were very run-down and unkempt. The family settled in the lower level of a house which looked very bleak and in much worse condition than their previous apartment. The window panes were patched from outside with cardboard boxes and wood panels and in the front of the house was a big pile of junk. Though the new house was far from the Rainbow School, Kate continued to go to the school for the time being, using the public bus services. The Claytons did not stay in this place long, however. Not long after, they moved again and changed their phone number. Since then, I've lost contact with the family.

The Claytons' Home Literacy Practices

At home, Pauline recognized that Kate was struggling with reading and writing. She noticed that Kate read "but was not really interested in reading." Kate was able to talk about (or retell) what she had read, but had difficulties constructing responses to reading. In Pauline's words, "Her weakness was actually writing it down, reading and writing it down." Kate often got very frustrated when she had to write a book report as she was unable to express her thoughts. She also had difficulties in spelling, though she was better in grammar, as Pauline notes. That was why Kate preferred to do projects such as posters, which required less writing and included art works. For example, in a project called "My Earth," Kate produced a layer booklet with the shapes of rivers and mountains. Unlike the piece shown earlier, which required more writing and a connection with what she had read, all that she needed to do was to write a sentence on each layer of her booklet such as "My Earth has oceans" or "My Earth has plains" (Figure 5.2).

In order to help Kate become interested in reading, Pauline made sure that she read with her almost every day. When Kate encountered some difficult words, Pauline usually asked her to "sound it out." If Pauline herself did not know the word, she would ask her boyfriend or call her mother for help. Pauline also participated in several reading programs that were sent home from school, for example "Reading Across America" and "Parents as Reading Partners." The goal of these programs was to get children away from TV and do something more educational with their parents. They required parents to read with their children for a certain number of hours per week and submit a brief description of what they read. Pauline and Kate participated in about six

Figure 5.2 A Sample of Kate's Writing in a Project.

of these programs. She described how they read together: "We would read, first I would read a page, she would read a page, or she would read the book to me, and I would read a book to her. Well, if we do a couple of books a day, maybe we do a few hours, but next day, we only do for ten minutes, fifteen minutes." They were very proud of their achievements. The awards and certificates from these programs were hanging on the wall over Kate's bed. Pauline believed that, through these programs, Kate's reading was "improving highly." First, she noticed that Kate was beginning to become an independent reader and she was able to read on her own "instead of mom just reading for her." Another improvement was that the independent reading made Kate become more interested in books and "she [started] to like reading." In fact, Pauline was pleased that Kate was starting to read more than she expected.

Since Pauline did not have time to take the children to the library, she sometimes allowed Kate to go to the library with her friends, where they would just take some books and read there for a while. Sometimes Kate checked out books to bring home to read. Most of the books that the Clayton family owned (e.g., the Dr. Seuss series) had been given by others as gifts. Occasionally, Pauline bought books from the schools for Kate and Josh. Most of the time, Pauline read the children bedtime stories at night.

Though Pauline kept trying to help Kate, many times, she also felt helpless about Kate's struggle with reading: "I just don't know what to do. I don't know what to say." She just tried her own way: "I'm sitting there and reading to her, read it to her, giving her advice to think, it should be said like that, this is what you should say, why do you say that, or what do you think we should say like this? You let me know, and we go over it, and then it becomes very easy. She needs a little push . . . just say 'let's do it this way. Kate, what do you think?' And she'll tell me."

In addition to assisting with homework, sometimes Pauline used an encyclopedia to help Kate practice writing. As she described, "[We] go through them, look at the pictures and recognize the different names and draw pictures the other day. I go and buy them like art sets, pencils, and crayons. We'll just sit down and go through a dictionary, or encyclopedia." Pauline also encouraged Kate to keep a diary, but she made a point not to read it unless it was an entry they wrote together. Pauline believed that keeping a diary is very good not only for writing, but also for expressing feelings: "It's very good. She expresses her feeling, who was her friend . . . if somebody did something to make her mad, she expressed her anger." She is very pleased that Kate is "a very open child," who tells her everything, and they "share everything."

In addition to reading and writing, Pauline was also helping with Kate's math and science homework. Every day when Kate came home, "The first thing she got to do is the homework." Pauline would ask Kate about her day at school so that she can learn about the material covered in class as well as how her day went in general. After her homework was completed, Kate (and Josh) would go down the street to play at her friend's house for a couple of hours before they came home for supper. Even though her class had a lot of math and science homework, Kate loved these subjects, and was very interested in the projects assigned as homework in these subjects. However, at times, the homework in these subjects was very hard for Pauline to assist with because of her own limited educational experiences. She often turned to her boyfriend for help. Brian, who had not finished high school either, also found some of the homework challenging and difficult. Moreover, they found that there was often little instruction given to parents on what they were supposed to do. Pauline complained, "A lot of times Kate came home from school, there was nothing explaining [what to do] . . . nothing when you look up the book . . . we just want to know to teach what page and where to find information at." She suspected that either Kate forgot to bring the instructions home or the teachers rushed it at the end of the day and did not tell the students what pages to use to find information. To Pauline, this lack of communication was very frustrating; a few times, she had to call the teacher or whomever they could find in school to get help.

Besides these reading, writing, and homework activities, Pauline was also sending Kate to dance lessons twice a week to learn pop and jazz dances, in which she was interested. This was why Kate wanted to go the Academy of Arts and Performances when she advanced to the fifth grade or to a middle school. Apart from these activities, Pauline could not afford anything else. The Claytons mostly stayed at home during the week nights; on weekends, Pauline often took the children to see their grandma. Pauline could not afford to go to the zoo, to the museums, or to other sports activities. She took Josh to see a baseball game once, and that was a very nice treat for him. The family did not have a computer, so the children could not play video games. Even though they had a TV and VCR, they rarely used them. The children mostly watched cartoons and some young teen shows. Sometimes, Pauline encouraged them to watch educational programs such as *Dora the Explorer*, a children's cartoon show that teaches children how to count, how to recognize different shapes, and even how to speak both English and Spanish. Pauline was very pleased that Kate even picked up some Spanish words from the show. However, the children were not allowed to watch TV when they were reading or doing their homework.

Outside the school, Pauline seldom had contact with other parents or other people except for her extended family. She noted that she preferred to "stay on [her] own." Though she had not much thought about her view on the value of education, her limited contact with the African and Vietnamese parents gave her a sense that they had different attitudes toward their children's education. For example, she stated that "the Somalian parents cared less about the children's education." According to her, even when their children dropped out of the school and were supposed to go back to school, the parents did not care. They let the children hang out with teenagers and do whatever they wanted. Pauline commented, "These parents basically did not care. Nowadays that says a lot of things." In contrast, Pauline seemed to regard the Vietnamese as much more appreciative of the opportunities in America. She described a Vietnamese child that she knew: "I guess they had a really rough time over there. The school wasn't good. So when he came to Buffalo, came to US, he had an opportunity to learn more. He told me, he absolutely loves that. The school said that he is a very smart child. He knows several languages."

Conclusion

The two white families' stories illustrate contrasts and similarities in their home literacy practices. They seem to be similar in terms of parental involvement in homework and in ensuring the children's safety. In both families, literacy practices emphasized a "sustained talk" (Hicks, 2002) among family members along with cooperation and relationship-building. Both families believed in the power of open discussion and conversation in transferring knowledge and values. The parents (i.e., the Sassanos) engaged the children in diverse types of talks at the dinner table or in other contexts about different topics ranging from school life to sex, drugs, and crimes in the neighborhood. Like the Treaders in Rogers' (2003) study, home literacy practices in these two families were processes of apprenticeship through which children learned not only the meaning of reading and writing, but also social roles. In the Sassano family, for example, reading was considered a family activity in which everyone was involved either by reading on their own or by reading with each other. In the Clayton family, working on reading contests or school projects together was a family norm.

These home literacy practices are different from school literacy practices that emphasize individual mastery and decontextualized practices. As Loraine's son Rod pointed out, their schools "don't do like that. They let you sit and work on your own. And sometimes you're not allowed to talk." In Kate's case, her inability to read independently persisted in the school whereas her mother helped her as her reading partner at home. Their home literacy practices clearly demonstrate a mismatch between school and home.

In addition to their home literacy practices, the parents are also similar in their expectations for their children, their dispositions toward their racial status in the community, and to some extent their views on the other ethnic groups (e.g., of the Africans and the Asians). The families' experiences seem to suggest that being white is not an advantage in the inner city—their children are equally disadvantaged in the schools as the other children whom the schools have failed and are still failing. Their children were not necessarily the highest achievers in the schools. Like the children in the other ethnic families, they (except Rod) were also struggling with English language reading and writing and/or other subject matters. Like other ethnic minority groups, they also experienced racism within their local context, though of a different kind. And, like the others, they suffered from the substantial lack of pedagogical caring in the schools. Furthermore, like the other families, they also experienced a level of ethnic solidarity. Both families stayed within their own kinship networks outside school and seldom interacted with other parents or people in the community. Like the others, this was their choice—"they draw boundaries of what signifies acceptable networking at the borders of their own community" (Fine & Weis, 1998, p. 158).

Despite the above similarities, the two families differ in their family stability, socio-economic status and social mobility, and hence in their social and cultural capital. All of these factors inform us that being poor primarily matters, and the poorer they are, the worse it is for their children. The Sassano family, with two working parents, owned their own home and had stayed in the same neighborhood. On the other hand, the Clayton family constantly moved—they moved six or seven times and the children changed four or five schools in five years. Undoubtedly, this constant change and lack of stability had a negative impact on the children's academic progress and adjustment to school life. Furthermore, in the Sassano family, Loraine went back to school (a community college) to upgrade her education and eventually, her education allowed the family to move out of the West Side. Pauline Clayton, on the other hand, continued to have more children, which probably resulted in more financial stress. Though she wanted to move out of the West Side, her deteriorating financial situation kept her moving around the West Side, unable to escape. Even though she had attempted to move out, her situation, far from being improved, became worse with a new baby, no transportation, and being further away from her extended family. In a sense, these family stories suggest that having "the tenacity to move on" (Weis, 2004) alone is not enough for inner-city poor whites to break the cycle of the "culture of poverty." Unlike the freeway women in Weis's (2004) study, who came from a more stable white working-class community and relied heavily on social networks/friendships to obtain jobs, they cannot just pick up the pieces and move forward. They need to do much more on their own if they want to come out of the hard life. They need to take serious actions to upgrade their education and their employment—to make real changes to their lives—beyond the superficial changes of addresses and schools.

The difference in the financial capital of the two families had also affected their social and cultural capital and, in turn, the families' access to literacy resources (Li, 2007; Li & Christ, 2007). In terms of social capital, the Sassano family's kinship relations included Loraine's mother-in-law, who could provide the family with financial aid when needed, and Stanley's brother, a member of the upper middle class who not only provided financial support and educational input but also instilled in the children the ideologies of white privilege (i.e., he could do whatever he wanted and get whatever he wanted). The Clayton family, however, did not have such a family network. Pauline's mother was also living in the West Side and was able to provide only occasional babysitting and homework support. The two families also differed significantly in their cultural capital. The Sassano family, with a steady income and financial support from extended family, were able to enjoy the white advantage: they were active in Boy Scouts; they took regular vacations; they were able to afford whatever books they wanted or those that were popular such as the Harry Potter series; they had the latest gadgets and technologies such as computers, MP3s, video games; and they could afford regular entertainment such as renting movies, bowling, camping, and other outings. The Clayton family, however, could not share most of these advantages: they did not have a car or a computer, and they could not afford any of the luxuries that the Sassano children had. Their home literacy practices, therefore, were much more limited in variety and scope than those of the Sassano children.

Lastly, an important point that the two families' stories suggest here is that, as a white minority, the families exhibit similar interpretations of being white in relation to other ethnic minorities. Both families (though more explicitly expressed in the Sassano family) saw themselves as whites who have great respect for other cultures. At the same time, like other ethnic groups, they (especially the Sassanos) have internalized the prevalent racial hierarchy by problematizing the "African American other," and sometimes the Puerto Ricans, as the Sassano children considered them as the same race. Though they did not single out the African Americans as the sole source of the problems in the West Side, they regarded them as one of the origins of the problems plaguing the West Side. For example, like the white working-class women in Fine and Weis's study (1998), Loraine Sassano recognized that that there was "white trash," but believed that mostly the African American/black kids were causing problems and were involved in gangs. Further, in her (as well as her children's) view, the African Americans (and the Puerto Ricans) started the problem; the whites and the Africans followed suit because of the conforming culture in the community. Interestingly, the family did not include the Asians in these discussions. In the Sassano family, the Asians were considered the children's friends and their friendly academic competitors in school. In the Clayton family, the Africans were seen as indifferent to their children's education whereas the Asians were seen as smart kids who valued their opportunities in America. Pauline's different perceptions of the two groups suggest that, even though she appreciated the multicultural nature of Rainbow Elementary, she had little knowledge about the beliefs, attitudes, and experiences of other cultures, especially the African refugees.

Like the Sassanos, she held a very stereotypical image about the Africans and the Asians, submitting to the dominant racial hierarchy, even in the values of their languages. Though she understood that the African families knew several languages, she did not see their being "multilingual" as valued as that from an Asian culture. In addition, her indifference to the difference between the Africans and the African Americans suggests that, to the poor whites, race continues to be simply about skin color. These familiar views demonstrate that, in contemporary urban America, the dominant racial discourse continues as an unbreakable constant that is being reproduced and, in a sense, reinforced.

The two families' experiences signify two accounts of how race, ethnicity, and, in a sense, gender are configured in their daily lives as urban whites, and how they are configured differently in each family. As Weis (2004) points out, these lived reconfigurations are "under the control of those who produce them" (p. 111). In the families' stories, we can also see that the social and economic contexts (both familial and societal) are also pivotal in shaping their lived configurations of race, class, and ethnicity. That is, both the individuals and the social forces (those structural and cultural forces that are related to race and class) are at work when the families produce their race and class relations. The Sassano family had more family capital (financial and social) that enabled them to have more control over resources necessary for moving up whereas the Clayton family were more constrained by their socio-economic context and were unable to think themselves out of the condition they were in. Therefore, the lived configurations are not just under the control of the individuals; they are also highly subject to the social and economic context in which the individuals are situated. It is, as the two families' experiences suggest, the alignment and misalignment between the individuals and the social forces that produces qualitatively different racial and class fractions even within one ethnic group.

In the next chapter, I discuss the meaning of these lived reconfigurations and the tensions and resistance that resulted from the misalignment between the individuals and the social forces across the three different racial groups.

6

Multicultural Families and Multiliteracies: *Tensions, Conformity, and Resistance to Urban Schooling*

The problem of the twentieth century is the problem of the color-line—the relation of the darker to the lighter races of men in Asia and Africa, in America and the islands of the sea.

—W. E. B. Du Bois, *The Souls of Black Folk*

In the preceding chapters, I have described the rich complexity of home literacy practices within the six culturally and racially diverse families as they make sense of their daily relations in terms of race, ethnicity, class, and gender in their inner-city living condition. I have also illustrated their productions of such relations across cultural groups, their interaction with schools within and beyond the context of an inner-city neighborhood, and the consequences of these relations and interactions. In this chapter, I discuss the cultural contestations and tensions that arise from the families' struggles to conform to and resist the dominant discourses as they reconfigure their race, class, and gender relations within the urban context. I argue that these ubiquitous reconfigurations are systematically contradictory and nonsynchronous in nature and the intersections of these reconfigurations within the families' different social and familial contexts shape qualitatively different literacy and living among the various groups of America's "rainbow underclass."

To recap, the Vietnamese families' home literacy practices are characterized by Vietnamese cultural ways of knowing. Both families value the Vietnamese language and enforce high expectations, obedience, and appropriate gender roles on their children. Though the parents try to be "the quiet Asian" and do their best to support their children's learning, not all of their children fit the "new whiz kids" model of minority stereotypes. In fact, some of them are failing in school; and some, torn between the contradictory values of school and home, are experiencing serious psycho-social stress.

Similarly, in the Sudanese families, the parents try to enforce Sudanese ways of learning at home while fighting school practices that they regard as a hindrance to their children's academic progress. They encountered a wide range of cultural differences, not only in curriculum and instruction but also with educational values and beliefs, the role of teachers, schools and community in educating children, and expectations for the children. In addition, as Sudanese, they have to negotiate their ethnic identity in relation to the racialized black identity in the community and in America.

The white families' home literacy practices, characterized by sustained talk, cooperation and relationship-building, also differ from the school practices that emphasize individual mastery and decontextualized practices. As a racial minority in the inner-city neighborhood, the families exhibit similar interpretations of race relations as the Vietnamese and Sudanese families. But to them, being white, working-class, and/or poor adds an additional layer of complexity to their daily literacy practices and living.

These stories demonstrate that the families exhibit what Baumann (1996) calls a "discursive dual competence" that turns literacy, culture, race, ethnicity, and class into terms of contestation. As for literacy and schooling, on the one hand, all the families have distinct home literacy practices that reflect their cultural ways of knowing; on the other hand, their aspirations for their children are to acquire mainstream literacy practices so that they can transcend their class boundaries. However, all the families experience serious cultural mismatches in literacy practices between home and school. In terms of race and ethnicity, all the families share the same established interpretation of racial relations and hierarchies (especially concerning African Americans) in the inner city, but, at the same time, they separate themselves from the racialized identities of their culture and ethnic group. That is, the racially different families "engage in a dominant discourse and at the same time, deny its essential equation" when it concerns the very stereotypes of their own racial and ethnic identities (Baumann, 1996, p. 145). Similarly, in terms of class, even though the families live in a low-SES community, they reject the childrearing practice of "accomplishment of natural growth" commonly associated with the low-SES groups (Lareau, 2003). Instead, they actively strive to cultivate/accumulate middle-class cultural capital for their children's schooling through limited resources available to the lower-class individuals. These complex discursive dualities suggest that the families' lived reconfigurations in urban America are "matters of social contention . . . and cultural contestation" (Baumann, 1996, p. 189). Located between two different worlds of discourse, the families try to construct their own position by conforming to and/or resisting the discursive realities.

In the heart of these dualities of conformity and resistance, as their stories suggest, "race continues to be a ready-made filter for interpreting events, informing social interactions, and grounding identities and identification" at home, in school, in the inner-city community and beyond (Furgenson, 2000, p. 17). On the one hand, the families internalize and conform to the dominant racial discourses that prescribe the social and class organization in America's inner city; that is, they participate in the reproduction of the racial hierarchy by racializing other ethnic groups and endorsing the racial stereotypes. On the other hand, they resist the others' essentialization of their racial identities and practices. In this sense, each racial group has "two souls, two thoughts, two unreconciled strivings, two warring ideals in one . . . whose dogged strength alone keeps it from being torn asunder" (Du Bois, 1903, p. 1).

These "unreconciled" dualities suggest that, unlike the twentieth century (as described by Du Bois, quoted at the beginning of this chapter), in twenty-first-century urban America, the problem is not just the color line, but also the culture line, the class line, and the power line. In the pages that follow, I examine the tensions and consequences that arise from the dualities of conformity and resistance. I first discuss the tensions around the literacy and culture duality—the cultural conflicts around literacy practices, parental involvement, gender roles, and the politics of difference underlying the mismatches between school and home. I argue that urban schooling is a culturally contested terrain in which the power struggle between school and home is in a constant flux. I also discuss the complexities of urban living in relation to the duality of gender politics in the six families. I explain that reconfiguration of gender roles in the inner city is dependent on both culture and context; that is, how the families negotiate "new gendered practices" in the urban context is influenced by their previous cultural and economic experiences. These new gendered practices also shape profoundly how they raise the next generation. Following this, I examine the race and ethnicity duality—the intricate relationships among race, ethnicity, and urban socialization that further alienate/marginalize the families into their respective socio-cultural and racial locations. Finally, I examine the duality of class positioning that contributes to the miscommunication and disconnection between school and home. I argue that these members of America's "rainbow underclass" do not ascribe to the "culture of poverty" or choose inadequate schools; rather, it is the "make-believe" school curriculum (one that lacks multicultural substance) as well as the various levels of ideological hegemony that put them at a class disadvantage.

Home Literacies, Culture, and Urban Schooling

As I mentioned in chapter 1, literacy is an identity kit—it comprises cultural ways of behaving, interacting, valuing, thinking, believing, speaking, and is often tied to a particular set of cultural values and norms (Gee, 1989, 1996). Literacy is therefore inseparable from culture and cultural practices (Li, 2006). Culture, however, has dual meanings by its nature. Its more static properties include a set of values, traditions, norms, customs, arts, history, folklore, and institutions that a group of people—unified by race, ethnicity, language, nationality, or religion—share. This set of learned activities defines a collective identity for the group and their general behaviors and ways of life. In this sense, culture is a marker of both sameness within a cultural group and difference across cultural groups. On the other hand, culture contains a dynamic aspect that is not monolithic or unchanging, as it signifies "the particular ways in which a social group lives out and makes sense of its given circumstances and conditions of life" (McLaren, 1998, p. 175). Culture, in this sense, is seen as a shifting sphere of multiple and heterogeneous borders where different histories, languages, experiences, and voices intermingle amid diverse relations of power and privilege (Giroux, 1992, 2005). For many immigrant families who live in a new culture, these dual aspects of culture signify both the past, the culture of origin, and the present, the new socio-cultural reality within the host society. However, the two aspects are not irreconcilably divided. Rather, as Bhabha (1994) points out, "the borderline work of culture demands an encounter with the 'newness' that is not part of the continuum of past and present" (p. 13). It creates an in-between identity, a hybrid cultural space that requires translation between the past and the present and between the individual and the collective; it represents "a difference within" and an emergence of interstices that bridges the home and the world beyond it (Bhabha, 1994).

For the six families who are border-crossers, literacy is a process of cultural translation and transformation. This process is, however, not without contestation as the families often fail to translate between the past and the present. All the six families experience various degrees of cultural (and/or class) displacement and disjunction, which in turn results in different levels of "fracturing" in literacy practices (Vélez-Ibáñez & Greenberg, 2005). First, as their stories suggest, their home literacy practices are shaped by their culture of origin—especially for the four immigrant families—and also by the increasing demands of English literacy as the children go to school. The four immigrant households are characterized by extensive use of their first languages (e.g., Vietnamese, Bari, and Dinka). The parents, with various levels of English proficiency, often do not speak English at home. Their first language use is typically an oral tradition, commonly limited to household situations. As Vélez-Ibáñez and Greenberg argue, the outside demand on the shift from home languages to English interrupts or fractures children's literacy development, "because public schools demand an English literacy 'script' be followed, the comprehensive abilities of the parents are either unrecognized or are intentionally denied as being efficacious" (2005, p. 64).

For the immigrant families, this process of fracturing results in two consequences. One is widening generational cultural gaps between the parents and the children, as the latter are encouraged to embrace English literacy at the cost of their own heritage languages. As the families' home literacy practices suggest, the immigrants are multilingual and literate in their home languages.

They read and write different materials and texts in their first languages for different purposes in their everyday lives. All the parents want their children to be literate in their first language; however, only the older siblings have the ability to speak in their native language, whereas the younger children increasingly refuse to learn to speak it or to associate themselves with their first-language identities. The other consequence is that the parents are unable to participate or participate effectively in the children's school work. In some cases, when the children fail to learn English in school, the parents who do not speak English themselves succumb to this process of fracturing by not speaking/teaching their first language to their children for fear of interfering with their English learning. Dao and Lynne Phan, for example, in order to help Chinh learn English, try not to teach Chinh Vietnamese or converse with him in their first language. Instead, they try to talk to him in broken English, which they think contributed in part to Chinh's heavily accented broken English. Though Chinh believed that he was American and spoke "American," he was doubly disadvantaged as he was fluent neither in English nor in Vietnamese.

In some cases, this literacy fracturing also occurs in school settings when the teachers fail to understand students' language, cultural backgrounds, and their specific needs in language and literacy learning. Even though Chinh Phan, for example, could/did not speak Vietnamese and the family did not consider him as an ESL learner, he was assigned to an ESL class by his teacher. Similarly, the Myer children, though they came from Sudan and did not speak any Arabic, were sent to an Arabic-speaking teacher for help. This profound lack of knowledge about the students' language and cultural backgrounds is another catalyst for literacy fracturing that has not only contributed to the children's underachievement but also added to the psycho-social stressors they experience in schools.

Another example of such cultural (mis)translation is the common message that the parents often receive from school—"read with your child." In the Vietnamese families, for example, the parents' inability to speak English has prevented them from participating in the children's initial literacy activities or being able to be involved in their homework. They were unable to "read" to their children as the teachers had demanded, nor could they "read" in the way the teachers implied—the Eurocentric, parent–child shared reading. For them, "read with the children" means the children read and the adults supervise, as the parents often speak little English and with a heavy accent that they do not want their children to acquire. Whereas the Phan family leaves the reading with their son Chinh to their daughter, Hanh, who corrects his reading rather than reading with him, the Ton family uses the traditional copying method rather than reading with their son, Dan, who, like Chinh, is also struggling in school. In the two Sudanese families, though Anne Torkeri had some time to spend with the children when she was laid off and was able to read with her daughter, Irene, reading is also an adult-supervised reading practice mainly based on copying. In the other African family, the Myers, the parents did not have time to read with the children on account of the hours their employment required.

In the two white families, cultural translation in literacy practices is also manifested differently. For the Sassano family, the translation is more about reading "for fun" or "for duty." Whereas the school emphasizes the efferent stance of reading, that is, reading for information and for the accomplishment of an assigned task, the Sassano children prefer a more aesthetic stance—reading for pleasure and/or for the lived experience through reading (Rosenblatt, 2004). Rod Sassano was sometimes able to make that translation as he understood the importance of doing homework, although his brother, Scott, was often unable to translate between the two stances. As a result, he is often reluctant to "read for reading's sake." For the Clayton family, the issue was connecting reading and writing. Considering the observation of the teacher, Evelyn, Kate Clayton's difficulty in writing meaningful responses to readings might be related to the schools' scripted writing curriculum, which encourages no personal connection. Pauline's encouragement for Kate to keep a diary might have helped her make this translation. It is worth mentioning here that Pauline's home reading practices with Kate, characterized by joint interactive reading between mother and child, is a successful translation of school and home practices.

Cultural (mis)translation is also required in many other aspects of the families' home literacy practices. As the immigrant/refugee families' experiences of differences between home and school demonstrate, the families have to cross many educational borders in urban schooling, including prejudice against them as a low-SES group, culturally different disciplinary practices, unsupportive school programs, and the dominant deficit model about their parental involvement and their children's achievement. As the stories in chapter 2 illustrate, middle-class residents inside or outside the inner city often look at the parents from a deficit model, believing that members of this inner-city "underclass" practice a "culture of poverty" that primarily causes their socio-economic and academic failure. However, the families' stories show that, though most of them are poor, they do not believe in or practice the deterministic view of the "culture of poverty." Instead, their efforts suggest that these families, though struggling with the economic pressure in the inner city, do set high expectations for their children, actively seek educational opportunities for their own as well their children's improvement, and are strongly involved in their children's education. All six families expect their children to do well in school and advance to higher education so that they can transcend their class limits. They also expect the school and the teachers to take more responsibilities to help their children achieve these goals. However, cultural (mis)translation of what parental involvement means and what roles the school and the parents should assume often becomes an obstacle for the children's academic progress.

Like the working-class families in Lareau's (2000) study, the inner-city families in this study also keep a distance between family life and schools. They believe that their main role is to provide basic conditions for their children and prepare them for school by teaching them good manners and rudimentary life skills to deal with the inner-city environment. They also believe that the main role of the schools is to educate their children by teaching them the mainstream literacy practices that they will need to succeed in America and by taking good care of them at school. For example, since the Phan family could not handle the demands that Rainbow Elementary placed on them to assist their son, they decided to enroll Chinh in a Catholic school, hoping that the school would teach him English and supervise his studies on behalf of the family. However, to their surprise, the Catholic school demanded even more family involvement at home, even though they had to pay more for it. Similarly, the Ton family did not teach their young son, Dan, the necessary "emergent literacy" that is required for school readiness before he went to school. As a result, Dan was left behind in first and second grade, before the family realized that they were in fact expected to be involved. Since they did not have much time or expertise in English, they relied heavily on the Vietnamese teacher in school to help. Similarly, in the Myer family, the parents provided moral support by being a good role model for the children, hoping that the children would be well taken care of and learn English and good behavior at school. However, to their surprise, the children (especially the older ones) were assigned to classes that did not match their levels of language proficiency. Some of them even learned foul language in school and were sent home for inappropriate behavior that they believed the children acquired at school. Similarly, the Sassano family focused on teaching the children how to deal with violence, sex, drug, and alcohol issues in the city and hoped that the schools would teach the children the right things such as responsibility and respect. However, they were disappointed with the teachers losing students' assignments repeatedly and their indifference to reversed racism against their children or lack of respect among students. As Loraine Sassano noted, in the suburban schools the teachers "would not allow that to happen."

The perceived lack of "care" in the inner-city schools is shared across the families. Caring, according to Noddings (1992), means that teachers must be sensitive to the suffering, desires, and needs of the students and must strive to protect them from harm and promote their welfare. It requires teachers' attentiveness, empathy, and responsiveness (Thompson, 1995). Without these caring attitudes and actions, schooling can be subtractive in that it circumvents the students' cultural resources and identities, thereby compromising students' ability and desire to achieve success (A. Valenzuela, 1999). The children and the families in the study were left on their own to navigate border-crossing in the school and they were allowed to fail or fall through the cracks, unlike their suburban counterparts. If they fail to successfully translate between school and home, as Hanh Phan hinted about her brother, Dan, they are going to be left behind.

Gender Roles, Border-Crossing, and Urban Living

Another aspect of cultural translation significant to the families' literacy practices is the creation and recreation of gender roles in their daily interactions. Again, the translation of gender role plays out differently in the immigrant and the white households. For the immigrant families, consistent with previous studies (e.g., Baluja, 2002; Dion & Dion, 2001; A. Valenzuela Jr., 1999), the parent generation tends to reconstruct the traditional gender roles in the host society—the domestic code that defines women's domestic and childcare responsibilities and husbands' responsibility for financial support and decision-making. However, as the family stories reveal, the economic demands of surviving in the inner city put much more responsibility on the women while the men's roles remain unchanged. The women not only have to follow the domestic code from their countries of origin but also take on part of the men's responsibilities of financial support and decision-making to help the family make it in America. They often do so without the social support networks of extended families and friends that they used to have in their countries of origin. As a result, they are left alone in dealing with the increasing demands on them such as helping with their children's homework, while they themselves struggle with learning a new language and adapting to a new environment.

All the four women in the immigrant families, for example, were responsible for childrearing and housework, working in multiple low-wage occupations such as salon technician or factory worker. However, their jobs are often insecure, which places a further stress upon the women. Anne Torkeri, for example, was laid off as a family worker and later was forced to enter a factory job. These women's experiences suggest that, like their white working-class counterparts described in Weis (2004), their border-crossing has necessitated their working side by side with men in the home/family and public spheres—both to supplement the home income and to raise the next generation. However, unlike their white working-class counterparts, they are still doing the "hard living"—their low wages cannot afford them the "accomplishment of a still potentially stable and relatively affluent" lifestyle (Weis, 2004, p. 140).

The immigrant families' newly constructed gender patterns in the host society have significant impacts on how they raise their next generation. The parents' gender adaptation has shaped their expectations of their sons' and daughters' behavior and academic achievements. In the four families, the older daughters are socialized into the double roles of their mothers and the older sons into those of their fathers. That is, the older daughters in the families are all expected to follow the traditional gender role of their heritage culture: helping with household chores and at the same time doing well in school so that they can get better jobs in the future. It is worth noting here that the position of the child in the family affects parents' expectations of girls' academic achievements. For example, family aspiration for Hanh Phan's school achievement was very high, because she is the eldest child and her brother showed less academic ability. In Nyen Ton's case, being the second child, her parents were ambivalent about their aspiration for her and focused all their high expectations on her elder brother, Mien. Similar patterns were also seen in the two Sudanese families.

In addition to high expectation, similar to findings in Mexican immigrant households, the older daughters in the Vietnamese and Sudanese families take on various domestic roles such as tutors (when children serve as translators and teachers for their parents and younger siblings), advocates (when children intervene or mediate on behalf of their households during difficult transactions or situations), and surrogate parents (when children undertake nanny or parent-like activities) (A. Valenzuela Jr., 1999). In the two Vietnamese households, the girls (Hanh and Nyen) are expected to excel in school and also help with their younger brothers' school work, besides doing household chores. Hanh even played an advocate role for her parents with regard to her brother's schooling through questioning the NCLB policy and demanding more school support. Similarly, the older girls in the two Sudanese families, Abok and Nina, both helped their parents raise the younger siblings and cook and at the same time were expected to do well in school. The older boys, however, were exempted from domestic duties and responsibilities. Although the boys were expected to excel academically they had fewer behavior restrictions—they could go out and socialize whereas the girls were not allowed to do so. Most of the girls are expected to stay home all the time, but the boys, like Mien and Owen, are "always going somewhere." Hanh Phan was not allowed to go anywhere except grocery shopping with her parents, and was not even allowed to talk to her friends on the phone, whereas her brother did not have these kinds of restrictions.

The double standards placed on the second-generation girls have significant implications for their cultural translations between home and school, since the two have different codes for their expected behaviors. Unlike the home milieu, the schools often do not have similar differentiated gendered expectations for boys and girls and the children are exposed to more gender equality. The girls are also exposed to peers who do not have the culturally specific gender expectations posed on them at home. Whether they are able to negotiate the differences between school and home will have significant influence on their psycho-social well-being. Furthermore, as Dion and Dion (2001) note, the difference has potential implications not only for parent–child relations but also for the development of ethno-cultural identity among adolescents and young adults. Hanh Phan, for example, struggled with the different gender expectations between school and home and between her and her brother. Her struggles caused her psycho-social stress in relationship with her father and in her self-perception as Vietnamese. On the other hand, Nyen Ton was able to negotiate the differences by recreating her own personal connections with her peers at home. For example, she was not allowed to go out like her brothers but she invited her friends over to her home instead so that she still could maintain her friendships outside home. This negotiation has allowed her to adhere to traditional gender behaviors without experiencing psycho-social stress. Succeed or not in the gender translation, as Lee (2005) points out, the struggle over gender roles is central to the stories of immigrant students.

Gender roles are, however, played out differently in the two white families. Pauline Clayton, as a single mother who managed to survive on welfare support with four kids, represents a case of "hard living." Though I do not know her full story, her case seems to be similar to that of "Suzanne" in Weis's (2004) study. During her high school years, Pauline attended a male-dominated school and faced discrimination because of her gender. Her story of having grown up in the East Side and circling around inside the West Side (and having children from different fathers) despite her hope of moving out is very much like Suzanne's story. Like Suzanne, she was pursuing her desired freedom and independence from men and at the same time she had serious financial trouble and could not get away from her particular low-SES "habitus"—the West Side. Therefore, for Pauline, it was also "at some level her 'choice' to remain part of her collective of origin while pushing at the boundaries of gendered possibilities" (Weis, 2004, p. 128). Unfortunately, it is not clear whether or how her choice influences her daughters and sons in their day-to-day practices.

In the Sassano family, gender practices are much more in alignment with their consciousness of the economic reality. The family, with a double income and a stable home, represents what Weis (2004) calls "a settled living." Unlike the immigrant families, in which the men and women followed their specific roles while women were shouldering part of the men's financial responsibility, the Sassano family did not have such clearly defined gender roles. Unlike the immigrant families, in which men did not help with household chores, Loraine and Stanley shared their domestic chores and childrearing responsibilities. Stanley took care of the house, cooked, and supervised the boys. When Loraine became busier at her new job, Stanley continued to take on more responsibilities. As Loraine noted, both of them participated in the housework. This "settled living," exemplified by Stanley's participation in domestic chores is, as Weis (2004) argues, a reconfiguration of the traditional white working-class gender dynamics marked by hegemonic male dominance and is a new domestic unit that breaks the old masculine/feminine binaries. It is "one that is now produced, or accomplished, through altered family form and destabilized notions of masculine/feminine . . . It is the new domestic unit of wage earner/child rearer as it operates in the new economy that not only destabilizes old hegemonic notions of the masculine/feminine binary but also allows this all to work" (p. 103).

This new form of gender dynamic has also influenced the way the Sassano parents raise their two boys, Rod and Scott. As their home literacy practices suggest, they engaged their two sons in a process of socialization that pushed the gender boundaries to its extreme—a process of total domestication and independence. The boys were taught to do all kinds of domestic chores with their mother and father, including cooking, sewing buttons, doing laundry, and cleaning. They participated in all kinds of housework every week. In the family, their chores were clearly outlined every week and they rotated so that they had diverse experiences. As their mother noted, "They can do all the things a woman can do. They don't need a woman when they grow up." Therefore, unlike the immigrant families, who socialized their children into hegemonic traditional gender roles, the Sassano parents had prepared their children for ultimate independence and unlimited gender possibility that completely breaks away from the traditional specifications of gender roles and of the masculine/feminine binaries. In this sense, the Sassano family was restructuring their gendered future and preparing them with confidence so that "they can survive any situation, if they choose not to be with a woman," as their mother said proudly. That is, they are not only prepared for the "settled living" that the Sassano parents have accomplished but also for the "hard living," if they don't end up "settled."

Though it is not generalizable that every white working-class family socializes their children in this gender-preparedness, it is interesting to see the difference in gender socialization between the immigrant and the white families. While the immigrant families try to recreate the old gender hierarchy that maintains the hegemonic male dominance and creates a double burden for the females in their next generation, the white families are trying to break this male/female binary. The differential gender socialization will inevitably influence the boys' and girls' preparedness for their future living, settled or hard. Though the double burden creates more stress in the immigrant daughters' growing-up process, it may have positive effects on them, since the demands will afford them a certain degree of independence and autonomy which better prepares them for the future, like the Sassano boys. The immigrant sons, however, are more likely to be disadvantaged by growing up with a hard-line gender ideology, since they will not be prepared for a new landscape of cultural and economic future that will differ drastically from their fathers' generation.

Therefore, for the next generation, class mobility is intrinsically linked with their ability to reconfigure gender relations. In a sense, gender reconfiguration has become the linchpin on which class reconfiguration rests for the sons and daughters of America's "underclass," especially those of immigrant families. In her study on Asian immigrants in America, Espiruti (1999) concludes that the patriarchal authority of Asian immigrant men, particularly those of the working class, has been challenged by the social and economic losses that they suffered in their transition to the status of men of color in the United States. On the other hand, the recent growth of female-intensive industries—and the racist and sexist "preference" for the labor of immigrant women—has enhanced women's employability over that of some men. This gender reconfiguration is further intensified and complicated by the erosion of working-class (i.e., male) laboring jobs in contemporary America within the context of a globalized economy that affects all races who are part of the working-class economic sector, including the whites, the African Americans, and the immigrant groups. Within this new gendered economy, the next generation of men and women, like the children in the six families, then, must rework their culturally embedded gender roles and sensibilities to adapt to this changing economic structure if they wish to move up the class ladder that is also racially stratified.

Race, Ethnicity, and Inner City Border Work

As I mentioned earlier, the families' literacy and living in the inner city are related not only to the politics of cultural and gender differences but also to those of race and ethnicity. The discourse of race and race relations in the United States has been centered on the black and white dichotomy (Lee, 2005; Weis, 2004). The established racial discourse is that the white has been constructed as *the* "good American" whereas the African Americans are constructed as *the* "black other," whose ethnic identity is often considered as a social stigma, especially for those in inner-city America. As Meacham (2001) notes, within the considerable chaos of American identity, the one predictable constant has been that those things regarded as "black" or of black cultural origin are on the bottom of the social order (p. 179). The constructed "black other," in turn, offers an "other" against which the "good" white is reproduced, revealed, and reinforced. Waters (1999) describes this dominant racial stereotype:

For most nonblack Americans the image of blacks as poor, unworthy, and dangerous is still potent, despite the very real success of many black Americans and the growth of a sizable black middle class. The existence of an urban underclass of poor blacks who exhibit "ghetto-specific behaviors," no matter how small a proportion of black people in America they actually are, reinforces and shores up cultural stereotypes American whites developed long ago to justify and shore up slavery itself.

(pp. 342–343)

On the margins of the black and white dichotomy, Asians are constructed as the industrious, quiet, law-abiding, and successful "model minorities" who can make it on their own and as "honorary whites" who are acceptable to and yet different from whites in the racial formations of the society (Li, 2005a; Walker-Moffat, 1995). This phenomenon of artificial acceptance is believed to be a form of "cultural racism" that operates without overt reference to either race itself or the biological notions of difference (Appiah, 1996; Waters, 1999).

How do the different ethnic groups cope with these established racial discourses? The stories of the six families' literacy and living in the inner city suggest that these racially and culturally diverse families all conform to these dominant racial discourses and at the same time resist the social stigma associated with their own race or ethnic groups. The duality of conformity and resistance thus makes race and ethnicity a significant social and cultural category that is situationally constructed (Fordham, 1996). This means that, depending on the families' individual race and ethnicity, their social class, and their socio-cultural and historical experiences, each family will have different modes of conformity and resistance—each will construct a shared, but at the same time different, racial positioning.

All the six families conform to the "good whites" and "bad blacks" racial hierarchy with the Asians on the margin outside the scope of an "other". The families all attributed the problems of violence and drugs in the inner city to the underclass blacks. They are labeled as "troublemakers" who have caused the deterioration of the city environment. The Vietnamese families, for example, even though they have not met any bad African Americans in their daily interactions, consider that it is the blacks who are creating problems in the neighborhood. Similarly, the Sassano family believes that the sources of the social ill in the city are the blacks and their newly converted partners, Puerto Ricans. The Sudanese families acknowledge the same reality but believe that it is because the African Americans do not value the chances they have in America. In contrast to other studies (e.g., Lee, 2005), in which whiteness is the standard against which all others are judged, in this study, blackness is the other standard against which all others are judged. In this sense, this shared racial imagining around the undesired blackness is "the social glue that maintains existing racial practices" (Fordham, 1996, p. 64).

Therefore, I argue that, in inner-city Buffalo, it is not just the white middle class, as commonly perceived, who do the racial border work; the minorities (including the poor whites) also engage in day-to-day racial border work—"the setting up of physical and psychological borders related to who lives where, who associates with whom in school, who and what is valued" (Weis, 2004, p. 105). This is neither surprising nor uncommon. As Freire (1970) illustrates, the minorities "have adapted to the structure of domination in which they are immersed and have become resigned to it" (p. 32).

The conformity, however, is not without contestation. As Freire (1970) points out, a particular problem is the duality of the minorities (or the oppressed)—they are contradictory, divided beings, shaped by and existing in concrete situations of oppression and violence. This duality therefore allows them to deviate from conformity in the form of resistance and distancing. Like the other ethnic groups in several other studies (e.g., Chinese and West Indians), the Sudanese and Vietnamese believe that discrimination and prejudice are something they can and must overcome as immigrants through hard work and success (Li, 2002, 2006; Waters, 1999). Therefore, they develop "immigrant identities" that differ from the dominant group's identities, but their identities are not necessarily opposed to the dominant identities when conforming to and internalizing the prevalent racial discourse (Waters, 1999, p. 142). Similarly, the white families, situated at a lower class location than the white middle class in the suburbs while living as a racial minority in the inner city, also assume this duality of identities that is different but not opposed to the mainstream racial discourses. In this sense, these six families, coming from different backgrounds, all have a certain degree of autonomy in identifying or not identifying with a specific racial group in a particular social and cultural context.

The Sudanese families, for example, are well aware of the dominant discourse against the blacks and try to differentiate themselves from the blacks. To them, race is a cultural category—it's not about skin color but about how one behaves to others, especially to whites. The parents, for example, differentiate themselves from the African Americans because they have cultural roots in Africa, unlike the African Americans. They also believe that they can overcome racism based on skin color by "doing good" and respecting others, such as white policemen. The children also believe that they differ from African Americans because they "behave differently" and eat different foods. Unlike African Americans, who often develop "oppositional identities" against the dominant group (Ogbu, 1986; Waters, 1999), the Sudanese families believe in making it through academic achievements—learning to read and write, going to school and college, and seeking better job opportunities—what white

America defined as its prerogatives (Fordham, 1996). Although the Sudanese families reject the "undesirable" cultural traits associated with African Americans, they do not oppose their children acquiring African American accents; this is possibly because being able to speak English without a heavy foreign accent, in a sense, symbolizes a step toward becoming "American."

Indeed, the Africans are seen as very different from the native-born African Americans. As Marilyn observes, "There are no similarities other than the color of their skin." Some of the teachers also noted that African kids are "more motivated" than African Americans. Ideally, this should enable them to merit inclusion in American society and become a model minority, but for the Sudanese families this is often not the case. As Waters (1999) points out, the status of the group often does not improve even if they distance themselves from the underclass black image. Rather, there is often a boomerang effect because they are still subjected to cultural and vulgar racism: "because being black is a racial identity, people with certain somatic features—dark skin, kinky hair—are defined as blacks by other people regardless of their own decision about how they wish to identify" (p. 342). Waters (1999) further explains that being black is often associated with the stigmatized image that they are "poor, criminal, hostile, or nasty" regardless of their socio-economic backgrounds (p. 343). The fact that the Sudanese families are also at the bottom of the socio-economic ladder, therefore, will make it increasingly difficult for them to overcome the negative images associated with being black, whether or not they choose to identify with African Americans.

At the other end of the spectrum, the white families are also placed in a contradictory racial (and class) location. As white, but working class and poor, they are not in the official poor black and white middle-class dichotomy. Furthermore, as remaining whites in the inner city, they are a racial minority, not a majority. Their identity is therefore that of "being not-black, not-Asian, not-Latino . . . not-'ethnic' as well as not-rich-white" (Perry, 2002, p. 182). Because of this unique identity, they experience *reversed racism* in the school and the community. They see/experience at first hand what it is like to be disrespected and racialized as other racial minorities. As Loraine notes, they "got to taste what is like to be on the other side."

Like the white students in Perry's (2002) study, these white families are put in situations in which their power and privileges are threatened by other racial majorities in the inner city. As a result, their perspectives on race issues and racialized groups have become "conflictive, stereotypical, and defensive" (p. 183). The families equate black skin with the welfare people, seeing the blacks primarily through the "culture of poverty" spectrum. The Sassanos also believe that African Americans along with the newly arrived Puerto Ricans are the cause of the problems whereas other groups, such as the Africans and some of the poor whites, just follow suit. The Asians, again like the common stereotypes, are left out of these racial frameworks—they are good friends of the whites and high achievers. Although endorsing the dominant racialization, the Sassanos distance themselves from the racialization process by critiquing several other racial groups such as Puerto Ricans, Africans and African Americans, as well as their own race. Therefore, they appear to be "neutral" and "objective." Through this neutral stance and the inclusion of other racial groups in their critique, the Sassano family engages in a new racialization process that stretches the existing racial dichotomy. Implicit in this new process, the "stretched" racial others are associated with welfare dependency, depravity, criminality, and ghetto behaviors whereas the distanced white middle-class outsiders are associated with independency, goodness, righteousness, and self-discipline. This "stretching" is also highly context dependent. Just as the Sassanos extend the racial "other" to several different racial groups in the community in which they reside, others expand it to other ethnic groups in their particular communities. For example, in Weis's (2004) study, the white working-class men and women interpreted race relations around the Yemenis in their community. In Waters's (1999) study, the West Indians were inscribed as racially different by the whites. Similarly, in Kim's (2000) study, Koreans are racially triangulated between blacks and whites in a way that conceals the politics of the white dominance. This racial stretching work suggests that the white working class and poor "continues to fix race—their own as well as others—they expand the racial 'other' in significant ways, making it possible to center on whiteness without necessarily having to engage a constructed black other" (p. 175). Central to this process, however, whiteness continues "to be asserted and inscribed as *good* in a grown-up world of valued family and community living space" (Weis, 2004, p. 174, italics original).

Consistent with their racial alignment, the strategy that the Sassano parents teach their children to combat the new racial order is to continue distancing themselves from the mainstream discourse and to be neutral. They are taught to leave the matter alone—"to do their own thing" and "not to conform." This distancing allows them to develop an "us" and "them" boundary and stay within one boundary while indifferent to the other. It is therefore a new form of avoidance, thus constructed, enabling them "to retain a sense of power and agency" that is similar to that of their suburban white counterparts (Fordham, 1996, p. 39).

On the margin, the existence of Asians (and the Hispanics) "becomes a way of 'stretching' the existing United States racial dichotomy—a dichotomy that rests largely along a black–white continuum" (Weis, 2004, pp. 174–175). Like the whites and the Sudanese, the Vietnamese also internalized the dominant racial discourse—the good whites, the troublemaking blacks, and the smart Asians. Their racial interpretation is, however, conflicted. The Ton family, for example, believes that not all the blacks are bad, as some of the blacks they know are not bad. They also believe that the whites are in the power position and that racial discrimination against the Vietnamese indeed exists. They, however, take a "blame the victim" approach as they believe the discrimination exists because the Vietnamese are not good at English; that is, they associate race with language and literacy abilities.

Similarly to the Vietnamese in previous studies, the two families maintain clear ethnic boundaries and try to prevent their children from becoming "part of the wrong part of America," that is, not to be assimilated into the urban black culture (Zhou & Bankston, 1998, p. 229). The Ton family rely heavily on the ethnic community to shield their children from becoming part of the inner-city culture (even though the children like Mien enjoy rap music) whereas the Phans lock themselves in from the outside world. Whether or not they socialize within their co-ethnic networks, the two families maintain the racial borders through their ethnic culture. As Zhou and Bankston (1998) write:

> Becoming integrated into a low-income, disadvantaged neighborhood means becoming part of a social group that is alienated from middle-class America and that integration offers few opportunities for becoming part of the American mainstream. In this situation, the ethnic community acts as an alternative to the marginalized segment of the society. Through their families, young people become part of the ethnic community, and the ethnic community enables them to bypass the troubled, marginalized neighborhood that surrounds them and to concentrate on the chief opportunities offered them, public schooling.
>
> (p. 229)

It is worth noting here that, even though the families internalize the Asian model minority stereotypes, as their stories demonstrate, not all the children are successful in school. They themselves seem to be ambivalent about this fact. In Chinh Phan's case, the family blamed the school for his failure whereas the Ton family blamed the lack of preschool experiences for Dan Ton's difficulties in school. Further, they seem to reject a "pan-Asian identity." For example, Hanh and Chinh Phan were very distressed when they were called Chinese. These examples suggest that, although the Vietnamese families conform to mainstream racial and ethnic discourses, they at the same time reject some essentializations about their own ethnicity and culture.

Social Class, Power, and Resistance to Urban Schooling

Omi and Winant (1986) argue that racial dynamics must be understood as determinants of class relationships and indeed class identities, not as mere consequences of these relationships (p. 37). Social class is not just a concept that is defined by one's position in economic relationship and production system in a society, but also a sociological process through which people live their lives (Anyon, 1980; Li, 2005b; Walkerdine, Lucey, & Melody, 2001). Wright (1997, 2003) theorizes these two faces of social class as objective and subjective class locations. Objective class location answers to the question of "how are people objectively located in distribution of material inequality?" It tends to be defined in terms of material standards of living usually indexed by income or wealth, that is, how people earn their money and how much of it they have (Hout, 2006; Wright, 2003). Subjective class location answers the question of "how do people locate themselves and others within a social structure of inequality?" This aspect of social class is contextually dependent upon how individuals understand class distinctions and how they position themselves in relation to these distinctions within a social system. The objective and subjective aspects of social class are important for understanding the immigrant families as well as the white families, who often made multiple transitions across time, space, and different social systems. On account of the dramatic change in their lives, their subjective and objective class locations may not match, which may situate them in contradictory class locations.

In the case of immigrant families, Fuligni and Yoshikawa (2003) point out that, since many of their socio-economic features were developed in their countries of origin, their socialization and behavior patterns are more closely tied to their native class locations than to the norms of contemporary American society. Therefore, immigrant groups' subjective class location in America may not reflect their objective class location (and vice versa) thanks to their dual frame of references in two countries and two class systems.

The four immigrant families' story of parenting in inner-city America suggests that their current income level and occupation, their objective class location, is not a determinant factor that shapes immigrants' parenting practices. Instead, it is the complex workings of the families' current class location, their prior class location, their cultural practices, as well as the neighborhood and school conditions that influence how the parents educate their children and get involved in their schooling. The two Sudanese families, for example, all came from a middle-class background in their country and experienced a serious status drop after settling in America. The fathers, who were once a lawyer and an accountant, are now a mechanic and a meat slicer. The mothers, who used to be a teacher and a pre-service teacher, are now factory workers. Their middle-class backgrounds in their home country, however, remain to shape their high expectations for their children and their knowledge base of what schools should be like. Contrary to the popular deficit views of the refugee families, the Sudanese parents valued education highly and tried to provide their children with a better learning environment as much as possible by making personal sacrifices. They expected their children to earn a college degree, become successful and have a better quality of life in the future. They wanted their children to take advantage of the opportunities available to them in the US in order to make their dreams come true. In this sense, they have become the new "middle-class poor people" in America (Sampson, 2003, p. 124).

The families' middle-class backgrounds also afforded the parents the ability to search for different resources to facilitate their children's extracurricular activities (though in a more limited way) and to fight with the school about ESL programs and other policies. The cultural values that emphasize discipline and respect for elders have shaped their expectations of their children's behavior in school and home and how they educate their children to combat the racism against Africans or blacks in general. However, their efforts are clearly overshadowed by the poor and unsafe neighborhood and school conditions. In order to keep them safe and protected, they have to enforce strict discipline and parental control over their children's whereabouts. They also make more conscious efforts to get involved in their school work at home.

More importantly, they (especially the Torkeri family) managed to (re)work the school system in order to overcome the poor school conditions. The parents, being actively involved and gravely concerned, tried their best to learn about the system and work it through their own "struggles." Although the goal of the ESL programs in public schools is to improve non-native students' English proficiency so that they can engage in the English-dominant mainstream class and do well in academic subjects, in the parents' opinion, the structure of the existing ESL programs do the opposite, in that they take the students away from regular instruction. In Anne Torkeri's words, "If they miss like this, they will have nothing . . . [not] even the foundation!" Therefore, she tried to fight against the ESL programs in the schools by petitioning to remove her children from the ESL list. In addition, she (along with some other parents) repeatedly raised these concerns to the schools. Unfortunately, these concerns were rarely addressed and school programs remain unchanged. The family's story of fighting against the ESL programs in the two urban schools demonstrates the unequal power relations between the school authorities and minority parents whose first language is not English. Minority parents, like the Torkeris, who are marginalized in society, are often powerless to make changes in school programs and are excluded from decision-making processes concerning their children's education (Fine, 1993; Li, 2005b).

Similarly, the Vietnamese families in this study were also at a contradictory class location. Unlike the Sudanese families, these families came from a low-SES background in their home country, but are now making a middle-class income in the US. Their middle-class income is, however, a misguided read on their financial status as both families also support their extended families in Vietnam. It is very common for immigrants (regardless of their levels of income) to send portions of their income as remittances to the relatives in their native countries. In 2005, the World Bank officially estimated that immigrants in developed countries sent home more than $223 billion to their families in developing countries – a figure more than twice the level of international aid (World Bank Group, 2006). The unique patterns of immigrants' household expenditure suggest that traditional associations among parent income, parenting, and children's development may not apply to immigrant families (Fuligni & Yoshikawa, 2003). The Vietnamese families' inflated income level, however, deprived them of services from school. Chinh Phan, for example, was denied extracurricular support because his family income was above the federal poverty line. The barriers in the children's school adjustment and the schools' failure to listen to their voice suggest that they are examples of refugee and immigrant children who are "overlooked and underserved" in our school system (Ruiz-de-Velasco & Fix, 2001).

In the two white families, class conflicts play out differently. The Sassano family holds middle-class values but lives a working-class life in the inner city. They were able to accumulate cultural capital through their own cultural activities (e.g., vacations, reading, and Boy Scouts activities). Like the middle-class Prescott parents in Lareau's (1989, 2000) study, they actively supervised and intervened in the children's schooling. For example, they checked their homework and made sure it was done. When a teacher lost her son Scott's homework, Loraine Sassano went to the school to request help and eventually got the vice-principal to resolve the issue. As Loraine noted, she made sure that the teachers knew that she was always available if they needed her. They also took active measures at home, for example taking the children's computer and games out of their room to help them concentrate on studies. The family also utilized their upper-middle-class social networks such as their successful uncle, Gary, as a model for the children to follow. This middle-class "cultural capital" or "habitus" suggest that there is also a mismatch between the family's subjective and objective class locations. It is not surprising that, as Loraine moved from a working-class job as a clerk in a grocery chain to a nursing aide in a big hospital, they were able to step up the class system and move to a middle-class suburban neighborhood.

Though the Clayton family also wanted to transcend their class limit and move out of the inner city like the Sassanos, they could not escape a downward spiral because of several differences. Like the Sassanos, Pauline Clayton also held high expectations for their children and was concerned with their academic achievement and well-being. However, as Lareau (2000) points out, class differences in family educational activities are not just matters of values and concerns. Pauline, herself a high school drop-out, lacked not only the knowledge base to help with her child's school work, but also necessary social supporting networks and basic income and material resources that the Sassanos possessed. Therefore, for Pauline, having the tenacity alone did not help her move out her class boundary. As her story suggests, she might be able to move beyond the temporary physical border of her class, but she might not be able to move beyond the social border of her class since none of the class indicators such as income, education, occupation, and social relations has changed for the better.

Therefore, as Lew (2006) notes, it is important to distinguish the variability of social class and network orientations. All in all, the families' stories contradict the theory that parents' social class systematically shapes/determines children's life experiences and outcomes. Rather, as the families' stories suggest, despite their lower SES status in the US, their homes are print-rich environments with a wide range of literacy materials such as textbooks, storybooks, workbooks, encyclopedias, sports magazines, newspapers, flyers, computers, games, and TV; and the families use the literacy resources for a variety of purposes such as pleasure, school, shopping, and everyday living. The families' literacy and living cannot be understood through the common belief that the parents set a clear boundary between adults and children and between home and school, and rear their children by "accomplishment of natural growth" (that is, letting the children be) (Lareau, 2003). In reality, the parents are actively involved in the children's homework and literacy development, engaged in "concerted cultivation" to utilize available resources to ensure children's success in school, and at times become their strongest advocates in school. Despite these efforts, many of the children still fail and struggle in school. The families' struggles against the schools suggest that these members of America's "rainbow underclass" do not ascribe to the "culture of poverty" or choose inadequate schools; rather, it is the various levels of power imbalance, the hidden curriculum in school work associated with the SES status of their community (i.e., knowledges, skills, and resources made available to them in school), as well as the "make-believe" school curriculum (one that lacks multicultural substance), that put them at a class disadvantage.

Though there is a substantial difference across classes in child upbringing at home, as Lareau (2003) argues, the above findings suggest that we need more elaborated frameworks when we talk about immigrant families. The families' differential home practices within their socio-cultural contexts suggest that traditional class analysis that focuses exclusively on parental education, occupation, and income does not work for some minority families. Rather, a more contextualized approach that emphasizes family history, race, culture, and locality will be more appropriate in understanding how social class works for some minority groups. Without this broader lens of analysis, we will stop short of understanding how the families really operate (Kotchick & Forehand, 2002).

Conclusion

In this chapter, I discussed the meaning of the families' literacy and living as "discursive dual competence" that turns literacy, culture, race, ethnicity, and class into a field of contestation. Though I explored the tensions within the dualities of literacy, culture, gender, race, and class separately, as the stories demonstrate, these tensions overlap and intersect in the various fields of differences. As Bhabha (1994) argues, the social articulation of difference is, from the minority perspective, a "complex, on-going negotiation that seeks to authorize cultural hybridities that emerge in moments of historical transformation" (p. 2).

The complexities of the tensions between and among dualities and their consequences suggest that the operation of literacy, culture, race, gender, and class relations at the levels of daily practices in an inner-city context is systematically contradictory and nonsynchronous (McCarthy, 1988). Rather than essentializing the minority groups as homogeneous entities, I have paid special attention to contradiction, discontinuity, and nuance within and between embattled social groups. I have striven for a critical understanding of the individual group's experiences in relation to other groups of color—"the varying diversity they might encounter—those involving relations of ethnicity, race, gender, *and* class" (Hicks, 2002, p. 4, italics original). I pointed to the contradictory interests, needs, and desires that help us understand each family's educational, cultural, and political behaviors and define their encounters with other groups in their everyday living, in educational settings, and in society (McCarthy & Crichlow, 1993). This nonsynchronous approach is important in understanding the unpredictable dynamics of the struggles of "America's underclass". As McCarthy (1988) writes:

> The issue of culture and identity must be seriously incorporated into a nonsynchronous approach to racial domination in schooling—not in the sense of an easy reduction to beliefs and values, or benign pluralism ("We are all the same because we are different.") of the multicultural paradigm, but in terms of a politics that recognizes the strategic importance of the historical struggles over the production of knowledge and the positioning of minorities in social theories and educational policies.
>
> (pp. 276–277)

Researching the six culturally diverse families' literacy and living from this approach suggests that we need to rethink the existing practices of minority education to address the lived realities of "America's underclass". We also need to redefine the structures of dominant discourses that are becoming the "limit-situations" for their success (Freire, 1970, p. 89). In the next chapter the implications of the families' inner-city literacy and living for teachers and policy makers are considered.

7

Culturally Contested Literacies and the Education of America's "Rainbow Underclass"

The very possibility of cultural contestation, the ability to shift the ground of knowledges, or to engage in the "war of position", marks the establishment of new forms of meaning, and strategies of identification.

—**Homi K. Bhabha**, *The Location of Culture* **(1994)**

The six inner-city families' nonsynchronic literacy and living suggests that the mismatches and difficulties they experience are not just isolated events of individuals or a matter of deficiencies in social structure. Rather, they are products of dialectic interactions between the individual, the community, and the society. The rich complexities of resistance and conformity within each family mirror various levels of cultural contestation, contradiction, and asymmetry of power and privilege that shape the meaning of their family lives and school experiences, and make it problematic at the same time. They, as part of the very fabric of the America's inner city, are involved not only in the reproduction of racial, cultural, economic, and gender hierarchy but also in the emergence of new substructures that can help them transcend the sticky web of constraints limiting them to their "assigned" socio-cultural location. However, as their stories indicate, despite the parents' overwhelming commitment, persistence, and concerted cultivation, the sticky web of dominant discourses and the contradictions both within and between home and school cultural sites still hold them in place of failure and disadvantage (Giroux, 2001; Rogers, 2003). To overcome the adversities of cultural and contextual barriers—the sticky web of constraints or limit-situations in the inner city—they need to become successful cultural translators who can move across diverse physical and social borders and rewrite the hegemonic domination of certain discourses instead of just reproducing it.

However, as the families' stories of conformity and resistance demonstrate, they are often left on their own to "self-help" in navigating the muddy terrains of inner-city environment and schooling. As the complexities of their dual positioning and the difficulties in their struggles to overcome the barriers indicate, this self-help model—one that mainly relies on the families' individual empowerment and agency—is not enough. They also need strategic assistance from multiple parties in the community including the local government, schools, teachers, and policy makers. The concerted efforts from diverse sides have to be both comprehensive and pragmatic—an approach that "links educational issues to environmental issues, one that responds to the problems confronting schools in concert with those facing the local community" (Noguera, 2003, p. 144). That is, to improve the schooling and living of "America's underclass," we need more than the families' and the neighborhood's self-empowerment. Noguera continues to argue that we also need strategic assistance from more influential institutions such as the government and the schools to change the learning environment of the inner-city communities and the power structure within the institutions.

Improving the social context of learning—the inner-city socio-economic environment—is a daunting task that has not been fulfilled satisfactorily by the federal or local governments for decades. Noguera (2003) points out that, though they live in the wealthiest nation on earth, many of America's inner-city communities have not been able to achieve sustained economic growth and social stability; and that the economic policies of the federal government (and state and local governments) have also failed to address the current urban poverty epidemic. These are precisely the problems that have plagued the city of Buffalo for decades—the local government and community have failed to revitalize the socio-economic environment and improve the quality of life for its low-SES residents. As I indicated in chapter 2, the newly elected mayor and superintendent, as well as the local community organizations such as The Buffalo Joint Schools Construction Board and The Citizens for a Better Buffalo, are joining forces in solving the persistent urban problems such as drugs, violence, and social instability. Their efforts, though just begun, have given the local residents a sense of optimism and hope.

In addition to these initiatives in improving the urban environment, we also need efforts to change the power relationships within the schools. Li (2006) posits that, to alter the existing power structure and to meet the educational needs of minority families, change must occur reciprocally between school and home, between teachers and parents. For this reciprocal change, efforts must be made in two other critical areas. The first area is culture work within the school system to reinvent the make-believe curriculum that is void of multicultural substance. Drawing on Li's (2006) pedagogy of cultural reciprocity and Giroux's (2005) border pedagogy, I propose a culture pedagogy that aims to redesign school literacy practices to enable students to become successful border-crossers who "engage the multiple references that constitute different cultural codes, experiences, and languages" (Giroux, 2005, p. 21). I make recommendations for teachers, educators, and policy makers who are committed to develop a more empathetic understanding of the students' lives outside the school. The second area is strategic assistance for minority families to help them liberate themselves from the process of social reproduction that further marginalizes them. For this, I return to Freire's problem-posing education, which emphasizes dialogue, consciousness-raising, and limit-acts— "those directed at negating and overcoming, rather than passively accepting, the given" (p. 89). These two areas of work *must* be done simultaneously and synchronously with the environmental initiatives in the community.

Culture Pedagogy, Literacies, and Urban Schooling

As indicated in the last chapter, cultural translation between home and school is of great significance to the immigrant families and their children's literacy and living. For them, the process of cultural translation is a highly contested process that often results in various levels of displacement and fractures in their daily experiences—from their language use and gender roles to home literacy practices, school expectations, and parental involvement. The displacement and fractures, which are often cultured, raced, gendered, and classed, have affected the children's learning experiences in and out of school. Therefore, helping minority students gain the abilities and skills that enable them to translate the differences among diverse domains of border-crossing, especially those within the dualities discussed in the last chapter, should take a critical place in minority education. As Apple and Weis (1983) insist, "Investigating the role [culture] plays and struggling to promote progressive elements of it becomes of great consequence" (p. 22).

For this end, I propose a new pedagogical framework that I call *culture pedagogy* to empower educators with the theoretical foundation upon which they can develop new curricula to help students to become successful cultural translators. Similar to Giroux's (2005) border pedagogy, culture pedagogy treats culture as a vital source for reshaping the politics of identity and difference. Culture, as Bhabha (1994) notes, has become a very uncomfortable, disturbing practice of survival and supplementarity between the past and the present, between the public and the private. Unlike border pedagogy, which focuses more on the analysis of ideologies, culture pedagogy has a greater emphasis on the actions that result from such analysis. That is, culture pedagogy builds on border pedagogy by drawing attention not only to students' competence (that is, knowledge building) but also to their performance (that is, production and action based on the knowledge acquired) in understanding the politics of differences. Two steps are central to the culture pedagogy: one is cultural reconciliation and the other is cultural translation.

Cultural reconciliation involves helping students recognize the "unreconciled" dualities and the consequences of the contested literacies. To help students do so, teachers and educators need to know more about students' lived realities and the socio-cultural contexts of their learning in and out of school. For the inner-city teachers and educators, who often live in the suburbs or outside of the community where they teach, getting in touch with students' literacy and living is of critical importance. Li (2006) suggests that teachers must take a culturally reciprocal approach in minority education, by which teachers and families mutually learn each other's cultural knowledge. To be culturally reciprocal, teachers and educators must "find effective ways to collect student social and cultural data outside school as we cannot teach when we do not know who we are teaching" (Li, 2006, p. 211). In effect, direct contact with and systematic study of students' families and communities should "become the basis for curriculum planning and instruction, rather than unfounded generalizations or unconfirmed information" (Mercado, 2005, p. 147). This data collection process will not only help teachers reconcile cultural differences between home and school but also enable them to help students understand the discursive dualities surrounding their own lives. Only when teachers come to a deep and comprehensive understanding of the school and home cultural practices can they help minority students come to terms with the cultural contestations. And only by doing so can teachers establish positive relationships with the students and really *care for* them.

Teachers' reconciliation with cultural contestation will help them redesign school literacy practices and avoid fracturing minority students' literacy experiences. For example, the literacy and living of the six families in this study suggest that teachers must abandon the scripted, one-size-fits-all curriculum to address the diverse levels of literacy fracturing in the minority families. First, teachers and schools must value students' first language and culture and treat them as "funds of knowledge." In fact, the National Reading Panel's reviews on second language research concluded that children's literacy learning in their first language (L1) is beneficial to their second language (L2) learning (August & Shanahan, 2006). Therefore, having L1 support in school, written and/or oral, will de-fracture students' literacy experiences and successfully involve parents in the process of educating their children, especially those who are not proficient in English. Mercado (2005) believes that, with the cultural knowledge of their minority students, teachers will be able to "build on and support bilingualism, multidialectalism, biliteracy, and language play for learning in the school" (p. 147). At least, teachers will be able to assign students to the right services. For example, if teachers have basic information about the Sudanese children's language and literacy backgrounds, they will help them find support in Dinka instead of assigning them to an Arabic-speaking teacher.

In literacy instruction, teachers will also be able to individualize the curriculum by addressing the different kinds of literacy fracturing. For example, with the refugee families, who have different cultural and pedagogical traditions and different levels of English proficiency, teachers must use a variety of methods and materials. For this, they need to provide explicit and scaffolded instruction that clearly sets the goals, tasks, reading texts, and learning processes, synchronized with students' proficiency levels and their learning styles. For the Myer children, who had no prior English backgrounds, this might mean that teachers need to listen to the parents' plea to place them in beginners' English classes. Or, as the teachers interviewed by Evelyn suggest, the school may need to set up some transitional classes for these children instead of mainstreaming them upon their arrival into their age-level classes. For the native-born white children such as Scott and Rod, individualized literacy instruction means that they need to be allowed to read from an aesthetic stance that goes beyond filling worksheets and answering text-based questions. In terms of the writing curriculum, students must be encouraged to make connections with their personal experiences and their cultural backgrounds.

Further, teachers may need to rethink the current homework assignments such as home reading. Again, the assignment needs to be tailored to individual families' home practices. For parents with good English proficiency and with enough time available, teachers can require such assignments as home reading, but with very specific explanation to the parents about the most beneficial ways to read with the children. This may require teachers to provide a model for parents or explain in writing how to conduct such a reading. As Li (2002) notes, sometimes families from different cultural backgrounds may have different notions of what it means to "read with a child," since teachers often imply the white middle-class ways of interactive reading without recognizing that parents may not share similar notions. For parents who have very limited English proficiency and available time on account of their financial status, teachers should provide bilingual reading materials and/or multicultural literature if possible. Further, offering after-school tutoring on homework and one-on-one reading might be necessary. The two Vietnamese children whose parents were not proficient in English, for example, would have benefited tremendously from this kind of after-school service.

Another important part of the curriculum redesign is to help students recognize the cultural contestations in their lives and learn how to reconcile with them. González (2005) argues that the school site should provide students with an ideological space not only for the development of bilingualism and biliteracy but also for multidiscursive practices and readings of the world. This means that students need to read not only the direct environment such as their community but also the world beyond it such as the dominant society in which their existence is "either ideologically disparaged or ruthlessly denied" (Giroux, 2005, p. 25). Teachers can help students to read their own worlds by engaging them in "analyzing how ideologies are actually taken up in the contradictory voices and lived experiences of students as they give meaning to the dreams, desires, and subject positions that they inhabit" (Giroux, 2005, p. 24). To do so, teachers must use students' cultures and literacies as texts in literacy education. This means that literacy teaching must be built on students' histories, languages, memories, and community narratives that are gendered, classed, and raced. Further, as Giroux (2005) argues, literacy education must also allow space for cultural remapping. That is, students not only need to learn how to analyze their lived cultural experiences but also need to develop abilities to explore alternatives that may rewrite their learning trajectories— from those on the margins and prescribed as failures to those in the center and with the promise of academic success. Only when they develop these abilities can they achieve the true sense of cultural reconciliation. Freire (1970) calls this practice "co-intentional education," in which teachers and students "are both Subjects, not only in the task of unveiling the reality, and thereby coming to know it critically, but in the task of re-creating that knowledge" (p. 56).

The process of cultural remapping is also a process of cultural translation. Bhabha (1994) posits that cultural translation does not simply revalue the contents of a cultural tradition or transpose values "cross-culturally." Rather, according to him, it is "to introduce another locus of inscription and intervention, another hybrid, enunciative site, through an active process of doubling and splitting contradictory identities within the dualities" (Bhabha, 1994, pp. 241–242). The previous process of cultural reconciliation provides teachers and students with a repertoire of knowledge base or competence to move across the in-between spaces. To know when to double or split within the dualities and create a new hybrid, they need not only to master the codes within major domains of differences or dualities but also to develop skills to know when and how to switch codes in order to gain race, class, and gender advantage that remaps their future. Bartlett (2001) defines this competence (i.e., the knowledge about cultures/dualities) as one that is "to be thrust into cultural interstices linguistically armed and culturally knowledgeable" (p. 30). In addition to gaining this competence, students' performance (i.e., the ability to enact) in this cultural translation is of critical importance—they need to be aware of the concept and consequences of "oppositional identities" and at the same time to develop strategies that help make choices and decisions that lead to neither ethnic flight (distance from one's own language and culture) nor identification (resistance to mainstream literacy and culture), but a third space that is characterized by "aporetic coexistence" of different codes at different social contexts. As Bhabha (1994) argues:

> What is at issue here is the performative nature of differential identi-
> ties: the regulation and negotiation of those spaces that are continu-
> ally, *contingently*, "opening out", remaking the boundaries exposing the
> limits of any claim to a singular or autonomous sign of difference—be

it class, gender, or race. Such assignations of social differences—where difference is neither One nor the Other but *something else besides the in-between*—find their agency in a form of the 'future' where the past is not originary, where the present is not simply transitory. It is, if I may stretch a point, an interstitial future, that emerges *in-between* the claims of the past and the needs of the present.

(p. 219, italics original)

Cultural translation is therefore not some happy consensual mix of diverse cultures; it is the strategic, translational transfer of tone, value, signification, and position—a transfer of power—from an authoritative system of cultural hegemony to an emergent process of cultural relocation and reiteration (Seshadri-Crooks 2000). It involves continual interface and exchange of cultural performances that in turn produce a mutual and mutable recognition (or representation) of cultural difference. As Jordan (2002) describes:

Cultural translation is a holistic process of provisional sense making. It implies trying to render accessible and comprehensible, first to the self and then to others, one's experience of aspects of ways of life – either one's own life made strange, or lives which are different from one's own. We are constantly involved in translating self to other and other to self . . . It reinforces the importance of starting with the self, making strange of one's own practices and learning to articulate them afresh from another, more reflexive, stance . . . learning to live another form of life and speak another kind of language.

(pp. 99–101)

Jordan (2002) further cautions that performing cultural translation is "not a question of replacing text with text (although this may well form part of the endeavor) but of co-creating text, of producing a written version of a lived reality, and it is in this sense that it can be powerfully transformative of those who take part" (p. 98).

Pedagogically, cultural translation requires teachers to rethink what and how major questions in literacy education are asked and how diversity should be addressed in their classrooms. For example, Bhabha (1994) suggests that, instead of asking "what might have been" in the cultural translation, it is more fruitful to pose questions such as "what could have been." If the former focuses on the "conditions of an obscene past," the latter symbolizes "the conditionality of a new birth" that allows the possibility of cultural hybridity (p. 245). It means that teachers must teach students to ask questions such as: Where do I belong in this present? In what forms do I identify with or distance from "us" or my first language and culture? And in what forms do I identify with or distance from "them" or the Others? In addition, they must also engage students in constant inquiry into how their present might interface with their future.

In terms of addressing diversity, the cultural translation requires teachers to abandon the "hallway multiculturalism" currently practiced in many inner-city schools—the happy mix of different cultures at face value by simply adding ethnic content such as the foods, folkways, and holidays approach (Hoffman, 1996). As noted above, cultural translation involves developing competence to challenge one's own self and one's own ways of seeing the world; therefore, the popular multiculturalism and make-believe curriculum will not work. Hoffman (1996) argues:

> Culture cannot and should not be artificially inserted, bits and pieces, into everything and anything in the guise of multiculturalizing it; indeed, infusing culture in the curriculum in this way is at best futile and at worse damaging, for it encourages us to think of culture as simply something that can be dissected, categorized, and inserted into convenient slots. Rather, it requires a holistic and a comparative perspective that allows students to draw their own conclusions and abstractions from evidence, rather than being [forced] proper attitudes or principles (such as "All cultures are equal/special"), that in the end mean nothing without a grounding in a knowledge base or context.
>
> (p. 555)

Similarly, Bhabha (1994) concurs that the popular multiculturalism represents an attempt both to respond to and to control the dynamic process of articulating cultural difference and administering a *consensus* based on a norm that propagates cultural diversity. It is for a token effect of including differences, rather than opening up opportunities for negotiating identities and differences discursively constructed in daily lives. Therefore, instead of clinging on to practices that are futile and damaging, it is necessary to approach minority literacy education from a new perspective—an interstitial perspective that allows "liminal" negotiation of cultural identity across differences of race, class, gender, and cultural traditions. Bhabha (1994) illustrates this perspective:

> It is in the emergence of the interstices—the overlap and displacement of domains of difference—that the intersubjective and collective experiences of *nationness*, community interest, or cultural value are negotiated. How are subjects formed "in-between," or in excess of, the sum of the "parts" of difference (usually intoned as race/class/gender, etc.)? How do strategies of representation or empowerment come to be formulated in the competing claims of communities where, despite shared histories of deprivation and discrimination, the exchange of values, meanings

and priorities may not always be collaborative and dialogical, but may be profoundly antagonistic, conflictual and even incommensurable? ... Terms of cultural engagement, whether antagonistic or affiliative, are produced performatively. The representation of difference must not be hastily read as the reflection of *pre-given* ethnic or cultural traits set in the fixed tablet of tradition. The social articulation of difference, from the minority perspective, is a complex, on-going negotiation that seeks to authorize cultural hybridities that emerge in moments of historical transformation.

(p. 2)

This interstitial perspective, therefore, allows teachers and students to move beyond the make-believe curriculum and examine the cultural hybridities—to develop knowledge about different cultural ways of seeing the self–other relationship and to explore new alternative versions of self (Hoffman, 1996). It is "not simply a discourse about 'diverse others,' but rather is a practice that engages both self and other, students and teacher, in rethinking constructions of identity, culture, representation, and power" (Asher, 2005, p. 1081). To work from this perspective, as Hoffman (1996) suggests, teachers must approach culture as children do—as genuine and natural explorers who are able to transform and to be transformed by their encounters and to productively use methods of transcultural sensitization and reflective cultural analysis, paying particular attention to their own framework in cultural observation and interpretation. Teaching literacy through this interstitial perspective will transform students' lives and help them connect the present with the past and the future. In its deepest sense, "it concerns the opening of identities— exploring new ways of being that lie beyond our current state.... It places students on an outbound trajectory toward a broad field of possible identities" (Wenger, 1998, p. 263). Asher (2005) describes this kind of new social imaginary in education:

Imagine then a multiculturalism that engages the "possibility of a cultural hybridity" and recognizes identities and cultures as fluid, dynamic, negotiated at the intersections of race-class-gender-culture. Imagine then students and teachers in teacher education and in K–12 classrooms participating in critical, self-reflexive, pedagogical processes that go beyond essentialized representations of diverse "others" toward engaging the interstices at which self and other are located.

(p. 1083)

Curriculum redesign for cultural reconciliation and translation, however, should not be limited to individual teachers' efforts only. Rather, as Li (2006) suggests, it should be a school- and district-wide endeavor. As indicated in the families' experiences with schools, teachers often follow the protocol and respond to parents that "this is the system and we can't do anything about it." In addition, in the current educational climate, issues of time, resources, and opportunities for collaboration are chronic problems that teachers face. Without institutional support at local, state, and even federal levels, teachers' abilities to enact these recommendations will be limited. In any case, teachers alone cannot change the structural inequities. Schools, district administrators, and policy makers must attend to culture pedagogy as a policy agenda. Efforts at the policy level will enforce structural changes and create a school- and district-wide culture that is truly and systematically responsive to minority cultural differences. González (2005) maintains, "There is no doubt that schools can be sites of interpellation, reproducing dominant discourses of power and control. But they can also be sites for reimagining the role of public education, for fostering informed citizenship, and for listening to the voices of students" (pp. 173–174). Li (2006) calls for a policy of mutual literacy accommodation in which both teachers and students modify their literacy practices for achieving high levels of academic success. As Li (2006) explains, this policy requires that schools make use of the languages and literacies of students in teaching and students use the school literacy and culture for learning. To support the continuity of the children's literacy experiences, for example, school districts can consolidate neighborhood resources to provide bilingual literacy supports for each minority group. As a powerful institution, schools can also resist the structural constraints such as urban apartheid, drugs, violence, and biased social stereotypes that portray the minority groups as an unworthy "underclass." For this, schools need to advocate/demand federal and state programs aimed at improving the systemic inequities—including childcare, medical insurance, preschool programs, after-school services, summer classes, and bilingual education (Bhimji, 2005). In addition, school districts can initiate parental empowerment programs as a policy agenda. These programs, consistent with the culture pedagogy for teachers and students, must be designed to help parents understand their dual positioning and cultivate their ability to explore alternative versions of their daily realities.

Culture Pedagogy, Problem-Posing Education, and "Underclass" Parents: Literacy for Empowerment

The education agenda for language minority literacy should not be limited to improving children's school achievement or changing school practices, but should also include the literacy needs of the families (McKay, 1993). As indicated in the families' stories, the parents are dual cultural beings who both resign themselves to and resist the dominant discourse on race, class, gender, and ethnicity. That is, being minorities, they are part of both the oppressed and the dominant groups; and their dual positioning has influenced how they raise their next generation. Their resignation to the dominant discourses has made them both the victims and victimizers of the social inequity that often limits their children's educational advancement. Though some of them, like the Torkeri family, occasionally opposed the limit-situations, their oppositions were sporadic and therefore not always successful. Therefore, there is a need for districts and schools to provide strategic assistance to help the parents go beyond blind conformity and counteract their limit-situations. Given the heavy burdens that inner-city teachers are already shouldering, this outreach can be carried out by community–school liaisons and professionals trained for facilitating home–school partnerships, but it must be an integral part of school and district efforts.

One way to provide such strategic assistance is to provide a new kind of family literacy programs that aims to help parents become aware of their realities and take actions to change them. In this new literacy program, literacy is not treated as isolated language skills but more as ways of interacting, reflecting, rethinking, and reforming their lived realities—as tools of empowerment. This program will not follow the traditional *transmission of school practices* model that aims to teach minority parents how to raise their children to internalize white middle-class values and literacy practices (Auerbach, 1989; McKay, 1993). Rather, it should adopt Freire's problem-posing approach, which involves parents in a dialogue, encouraging them to be conscious of their own limit-situations, dualities, literacy practices, and subsequently their own actions that emerge from such reflections and dialogues. Valdés (1996) describes the difference of this empowerment approach from the transmission model:

> In an empowerment approach to "fixing the problem," programs would be designed to help parents understand that, as opposed to what many school personnel often claim, their children's futures and school success are dependent on a complex set of factors for which they, as parents, are not responsible. If such empowerment programs were successful, parents would no longer accept blame for being "uninvolved," "uninformed," or "uneducated" parents.
>
> (p. 194)

Therefore, rather than following a prescribed medical model in which parents are rarely engaged in diagnosing problems (Sigel, 1983), the new literacy programs will be more like open-ended, ongoing practices focusing on issues and themes brought forward *by* the parents about their own lived realities and ways to transform them. Freire (1970) posits that the starting point for organizing the program content must be the present, existential, concrete situation reflecting the aspirations of the people. Program developers must utilize certain basic contradictions (e.g., the gender, racial, and class contradictions described in the last chapter) to expose this situation as a problem setting and challenge parents to sophisticate their responses—not just at the intellectual level but at the level of action (Freire, 1970, p. 85). Thus, the parents' views, "impregnated with anxieties, doubts, hopes or hopelessness," become the content of the themes (Freire, 1970, p. 82). For the inner-city parents, such themes can include their views on their dual identities in culture, race relations, gender roles, and socio-economic status; their shared concerns for the neighborhood such as racism, violence, drugs, and social welfare problems; and issues concerning their children's schooling such as ESL programs, reading homework, and parents' role in education.

Starting with the parents' view on the very limit-situations in which they are submerged is of critical importance to assist parents to reconcile the dualities within their own consciousness and become successful cultural translators for themselves and for the next generation. As Asher (2005) argues, the awareness emerging from this process may be construed as a consciousness of one's own particular "borderlands." Thus, integrating rather than resisting/distancing one's encounters with difference into one's consciousness is a productive process that deconstructs the binary of self and other. Freire (1970) cautions that program developers and policy makers should go not to teach, to transmit, or to give anything to the people, but rather to learn with them about their lived realities:

> The task of the humanists is to see that the oppressed become aware of the fact that as dual beings, "housing" the oppressors within themselves, they cannot be truly human. This task implies that revolutionary leaders do not go to the people in order to bring them a message of "salvation," but in order to know through dialogue with them both their *objective situation* and their *awareness* of that situation—the various levels of perception of themselves and of the world in which and with which they exist.
>
> (p. 84)

There is no doubt that conducting this kind of new literacy program is not an easy task. As the families' diverse cultural, linguistic, and socio-economic backgrounds imply, there are significant obstacles to reach the parents and to create such programs that can cater to their diverse backgrounds and needs. To overcome these obstacles, program developers and educators must break the conventional transmission/medical model to address themes that are part of the parents' concrete reality and diversify strategies to provide parents with concrete support (Lareau, 2000).

First, as cultural workers, program developers and educators must use the languages and literacies of the parents when they conduct the programs and use the parents' lived realities as texts. Therefore, these programs cannot be like the school's make-believe curriculum based on a one-size-fits-all approach. They must be diversified according to parents' lived realities. In terms of language communication, the programs can use interpreters or bilingual parents for help. According to Title VI of the Civil Rights Act of 1964, all schools receiving federal funding are required to provide interpreters for parents to facilitate communication. In addition, the NCLB Act states that communication with immigrant children's parents should take place in the parents' native language. Providing parents with support in their first languages will overcome what immigrant and refugee parents consider "an insurmountable barrier" and reduce their anxieties in participating in these thematic investigations (BRYCS, 2007).

Second, program developers must, as Freire (1970) suggests, "become integrated with the people, who are co-authors of the action that both perform upon the world" (p. 183). That is, program developers must become the parents' advocates and allies in implementing actions or limit-acts derived from their thematic investigations. Otherwise, parents will consider these kinds of programs as simply paying lip service and as having no power to change anything and therefore will lose their motivation and desire to participate further. For example, in investigating racism and race relations in the school and the community, parents may come up with tasks (e.g., increasing intra-cultural contacts and communication) to overcome racism against blacks as well as reversed racism against the working-class and poor whites. The program developers and educators must become part of the team with the parents to fulfill those tasks. Similarly, following investigations on class issues, parents may make the schools recognize their objective and subjective class locations and change education services for the children from income-based to needs-based. The program developers and educators can help the schools to monitor the children's needs and provide support that might have been denied to some children in need (e.g., Chihn and Dan in this study). When they discuss ESL programs, program developers and educators may need to help the schools and districts listen to the parents' voices and redesign their ESL programs and policies to address the parents' and students' concerns about missing regular classes. As the parents suggest, after-school ESL programs might be more beneficial for students who need to master both English and academic content at the same time.

Lastly, program developers and educators should not work alone in this endeavor. They must utilize resources available in the community such as the Vietnamese, the Sudanese, and the white communities to help them organize such programs. They must, through these efforts, build strong social support and parent networks within and across ethnic communities. By building these networks, they can help parents change the communities from alienated islands in the urban ghetto to interdependent communities that collaborate with each other and with schools to improve their life conditions and their children's literacy practices.

Conclusion

In this book, I have described the complex discursive conditions of the six families' literacy and living as they cross the culture, race, class, and gender borders in America's inner city. As promised in chapter 1, I have moved their voices and experiences from the margin to the center and exposed their efforts and frustrations as they respond to the American inner-city living conditions. I have not, as Giroux (2005) cautioned, romanticized their everyday life as merely an embodiment of cultural diversity—a happy mix of multicultural families. Rather, I have treated their lives as a contested terrain and a site of struggle filled with contradictions and complexities as well as possibilities for convergence and compromises in and around issues of literacy, race, class, gender, and schooling. I have proposed a culture pedagogy to *rework* "the relationship between differences as it is constituted within subjectivities and between social groups" (Giroux, 2005, p. 165). As illustrated in this chapter, culture pedagogy requires dialogical cultural practices that help reconcile and translate between those seemingly irreconcilable differences.

In contrast to other approaches, in this book, I have made prominent the role that the minority families play in invoking the race, gender, class, and culture boundaries as well as in crossing the borders in their particular socio-cultural, historical, and economic circumstances. I have problematized the meaning of their experiences in both invoking and crossing these boundaries. I have seen their experiences of inner-city literacy and living as "immediate struggles" to show that they are active cultural beings and border-crossers (Foucault, 1982). As Foucault describes:

> They are struggles which question the status of the individual: On the one hand, they assert the right to be different and they underline every-thing that makes individuals truly individual. On the other hand, they attack everything that separates the individual, breaks his links with others, splits up community life, forces the individual back to himself and ties him to his own identity in a constraining way.
>
> (1982, pp. 211–212)

However, by making the families' contradictory locations prominent in crossing borders, I do not intend to convey a "blame the victim" message or to downplay the role of schools and other powerful institutions in shaping their experiences and placing them in their current locations. Rather, by situating their immediate struggles within larger socio-political contexts, I join other researchers such as Lee (2005), Weis (2004), and Willis (1977) and consider the contradictions and contestations within the families as legitimate and valuable critiques of the social inequity inherent in their lived realities and the role that schools and other powerful institutions play in shaping their choices and agencies. I believe these moments of critique are of great significance to our understanding of the lives of "America's underclass" and their next generation, who have been rendered invisible and unworthy of attention in the society. These moments help us understand how these marginalized groups, like those historically at the center stage, "actually take up particular subjective positions . . . and what the conditions are that make it impossible for [them] to take up, live, and speak particular discourses" (Giroux, 2005, p. 172). More importantly, these moments of critique offer us insights to and hopes for a *newness* in minority education—new understandings, new meanings, new strategies, and new possibilities for a better social imaginary.

Notes

Chapter 1

1 The real city name is used in the book. However, all street names, the names of the schools the children attend, and the names of all participants in this study are pseudonyms.

Chapter 2

1 Evelyn was interviewed for this project. She also helped collect some data for this project. In addition, she interviewed five teachers in the school as one of her course projects in a local university. She does not wish her real name to be revealed, so I do not cite her paper. Rather, I indicate that some quotes came from her interviews with the teachers.

References

AAPIP (1997). *An invisible crisis: The educational needs of Asian Pacific American youth*. New York: Asian American/Pacific Islanders in Philanthropy.

Alvarez, A., & J.E. Helms (2001). Racial identity and reflected appraisals as influences on Asian Americans' racial adjustment. *Cultural Diversity & Ethnic Minority Psychology*, 7(3), 217–231.

Anyon, J. (1980). Social class and the hidden curriculum of work. *Journal of Education*, 162(1), 67–92.

Anyon, J. (1981). Social class and school knowledge. *Curriculum Inquiry*, 11(1), 3–42.

Appiah, A. (1996). Race, culture, and identity—misunderstood connections. In *Color conscious: The politics of morality of race*. Ed. A. Appiah & A. Gutmann. Princeton, NJ: Princeton University Press, pp. 30–105.

Apple, M., & L. Weis (1983). Ideology and practice in schooling: A political and conceptual introduction. In *Ideology and practice in schooling*. Ed. M. Apple & L. Weis. Philadelphia: Temple University Press, pp. 3–24.

Asher, N. (2005). At the interstices: Engaging postcolonial and feminist perspectives for a multicultural education pedagogy in the South. *Teachers College Record*, 107(5), 1079–1106.

Auerbach, E. R. (1989). Toward a social-contextual approach to family literacy. *Harvard Educational Review*, 59, 165–181.

August, D., & K. Hakuta (1997). *Improving schooling for language minority children: A research agenda*. Washington, DC: National Academy Press.

August, D., & T. Shanahan (2006). *Developing literacy in second-language learners: Report of the national literacy panel on language-minority children and youth*. Mahwah, NJ: LEA.

Bakhtin, M. M. (1981). *The dialogic imagination: Four essays by M. M. Bakhtin*. Austin, TX: University of Texas Press.

Baluja, K. F. (2002). *Gender roles at home and abroad: The adaptation of Bangladeshi immigrants*. New York: New Americans LFB Scholarly Publishing LLC.

Bartlett, T. (2001). Use the road: The appropriacy of appropriation. *Language and Intercultural Communication*, 1(1), 21–39.

Baumann, G. (1996). *Contesting culture: Discourses of identity in multi-ethnic London*. Cambridge, UK: Cambridge University Press.

Bell, D. (1992). *Faces at the bottom of the well: The permanence of racism*. New York: HarperCollins.

Bell, T. (2000). Buffalo, New York teachers defy anti-strike law. Retrieved March 1, 2007, from www.wsws.org/articles/2000/sep2000/buff-s09.shtml.

Bettie, J. (1995). Class dismissed? *Roseanne* and the changing force of working-class iconography. *Social Text,* 45(14), 125–149.

Bhabha, H. K. (1994). *The location of culture.* New York: Routledge.

Bhimji, F. (2005). Language socialization with directives in two Mexican families in South Central Los Angeles. In *Building on strength: Language and literacy in Latino families and communities.* Ed. A. C. Zentella. New York: Teachers College Press, pp. 60–76.

Bourdieu, P. (1977). Cultural preproduction and social reproduction. In *Power and ideology in education.* Ed. J. Karabel & A. H. Halsey. New York: Oxford University Press, pp. 487–511.

Bourdieu, P., & J. C. Passerson (1977). *Reproduction in education, society and culture.* Beverly Hills, CA: Sage.

Brand, D. (1987). The new whiz kids: Why Asian Americans are doing so well, and what it costs them. *Time,* August 31. Retrieved May 31, 2006, from www.time.com/time/magazine/article/0,9171,965326-1,00.html.

Brantlinger, E. (2003). *Dividing classes: How the middle class negotiates and rationalizes school advantage.* New York: Routledge and Falmer.

BRYCS (2007). *Spring 2007 spotlight: Involving refugee parents in their children's education.* Retrieved March 16, 2007, from www.brycs.org/brycs_spotspring2007.htm.

Buffalo Geek (2006). The Dr. James Williams backstory. Retrieved December 27, 2006, from http://buffalogeek.wnymedia.net/archives/category/buffalo-schools/.

Buffalo Public Schools (2006). *News: Governor's 06–07 budget allocation.* Retrieved February 20, 2007, from www.buffaloschools.org/News/NewsInner.aspx?PID=420

Caplan, N., M. H. Choy, & J. K. Whitmore (1992). Indochinese refugee families and academic achievement. *Scientific American,* 266(February), 36–42.

Carspecken, P. F. (1996). *Critical ethnography in educational research: A theoretical and practical guide.* New York: Routledge.

Centrie, C. (2004). *Identity formation of Vietnamese immigrant youth in an American high school.* New York: LFB Scholarly Publishing.

Chung, C. H. (2000). English language learners of Vietnamese background. In *New immigrants in the United States: Readings for second language educators.* Ed. S. L. McKay & S. C. Wong. Cambridge, UK: Cambridge University Press, pp. 216–231.

Chuong, C. H. (1999). Vietnamese American students: Between the pressure to succeed and the pressure to change. In *Asian American education: Prospects and challenges.* Ed. C. C. Park & M. M. Chi. Westport, CT: Bergin & Garvey, pp. 183–200.

City-Data.com (2007). *Buffalo, New York.* Retrieved May 16, 2007, from www.city-data.com/city/Buffalo-New-York.html.

Clark, W. A. V. (1986). Residential segregation in American cities: A review and interpretation. *Population Research and Policy Review,* 5(2), 95–127.

Collins, J., & R. K. Blot (2003). *Literacy and literacies: Text, power, and identity.* Cambridge, UK: Cambridge University Press.

Council of the Great City Schools (2000). *Reforming the Buffalo Public Schools: Final report of the Buffalo Public Schools.* Retrieved December 27, 2006, from http://www.cgcs.org/management/Reports/BuffaloPublicSchool.pdf.

Creswell, J. W. (2005). *Educational research: Planning, conducting, and evaluating quantitative and qualitative research,* 2nd edn. Columbus, OH: Pearson.

Cummins, J. (1989). *Empowering minority students.* Sacramento, CA: CA Association for Bilingual Education.

D'Andrade, R. D., & Strauss, C. (eds.) (1992). *Human motives and cultural models.* Cambridge, MA: Cambridge University Press.

Darder, A. (1995). The politics of biculturalism: Culture and difference in the formation of Warriors for Gringostroika and The new Mestizas. In *Culture and difference: Critical perspectives on the bicultural experience in the United States.* Ed. A. Darder. Westport, CT: Bergin & Garvey, pp. 1–20.

Department of Community Development (2003). *Buffalo weed and seed initiative.* Retrieved January 3, 2007, from http://ojjdp.ncjrs.org/pubs/gun_violence/profile03.html.

Dillaway, D. (2006). *Power failure: Politics, patronage, and the economic future of Buffalo, New York.* Amherst, NY: Prometheus Books.

Dimitriadis, G. (2001). *Performing identity/performing culture: Hip hop as text, pedagogy, and lived practice.* New York: Peter Lang.

Dimitriadis, G. (2003). *Friendship, cliques, and gangs: Young black men coming of age in urban America.* New York: Teachers College Press.

Dion, K. K., & K. L. Dion (2001). Gender and cultural adaptation in immigrant families. *Journal of Social Issues,* 57(3), 511–521.

Du Bois, W. E. B. (1903). *The souls of black folk.* Chicago, IL: A. C. McClurg.

El-Haj, A. (2006). Race, politics, and Arab American youth: Shifting frameworks for conceptualizing educational equity. *Educational Policy,* 20(1), 13–34.

Eisenbruch, M. (1988). The mental health of refugee children and their cultural development. *International Migration Review,* 22(2), 282–300.

Encyclopedia of American History (2006). *Buffalo.* Retrieved December 27, 2006, from www. answers.com/topic/buffalo.

Erickson, F. (2001). Culture in society and in educational practices. In *Multicultural education: Issues and perspectives.* Ed. J. A. Banks & C. A. McGee Banks. New York: John Wiley, pp. 31–58.

Espiruti, Y. L. (1999). Gender and labor in Asian immigrant families. *American Behavioral Scientist,* 42(4), 628–647.

Feagin, J. (2000). *Racist America: Roots, current realities and future reparations.* New York: Routledge.

Fine, M. (1993). [Ap]parent involvement: Reflections on parents, power, and urban public schools. *Teachers College Record,* 94(4), 682–710.

Fine, M., & L. Weis (1998). *The unknown city: Lives of poor and working class young adults.* Boston, MA: Beacon Press.

Finn, P. J. (1999) *Literacy with an attitude: Educating working-class children in their own self-interest.* Albany, NY: SUNY Press.

Foner, N. (1997). The immigrant family: Cultural legacies and cultural changes. *International Migration Review,* 31(4), 961–974.

Fordham, S. (1996). *Blacked out: Dilemmas of race, identity, and success at Capital High.* Chicago, IL: University of Chicago Press.

Foucault, M. (1972). *The archeology of knowledge.* New York: Pantheon books.

Foucault, M. (1978). *The history of sexuality: Volume I.* Trans. Robert Hurley. New York: Vintage.

Foucault, M. (1982). Afterword: The subject and power. In *Michel Foucault: Beyond structuralism and hermeneutics.* Ed. H. L. Dreyfus & P. Robinow. Chicago, IL: University of Chicago Press, pp. 208–226.

Freire, P. (1970). *Pedagogy of the oppressed*. New York: Seabury Press.

Freire, P. (1975). *Cultural action to freedom*. Cambridge, MA: Harvard Educational Review

Fuligni, A. J., & H. Yoshikawa (2003). Socioeconomic resources, parenting, poverty, and child development among immigrant families. In *Socioeconomic status, parenting, and child development*. Ed. M. H. Bornstein and R. H. Bradley. Mahwah, NJ: Lawrence Erlbaum Associates, pp. 107–124.

Furgenson, A. A. (2000). *Bad boys: Public schools in the making of black masculinity*. Ann Arbor, MI: The University of Michigan Press.

Gallimore, R., & C. Goldenberg (2001). Analyzing cultural models and settings to connect minority achievement and school improvement research. *Educational Psychologist*, 36(1), 45–56.

Gee, J. P. (1989). Literacy, discourse, and linguistics: Introduction. *Journal of Education*, 171(1), 5–17.

Gee, J. P. (1991). What is literacy? In *Rewriting literacy: Culture and the discourse of the other*. Ed. C. Mitchell & K. Weiler. New York: Bergin & Garvey, pp. 3–11.

Gee, J. P. (1996). *Social linguistics and literacies: Ideology in discourses*. London: Taylor & Francis.

Gee, J. P. (1999). *An introduction to discourse analysis: Theory and method*. London: Routledge.

Gilmore, P. (1991). "Gimme room": School resistance, attitudes, and access to literacy. In *Rewriting literacy: Culture, and the discourse of the other*. Ed. C. Mitchel & K. Weiler. New York: Bergin & Garvey, pp. 57–76.

Gimpel, J. G. (1999). *Separate destinations: Migration, immigration, and the politics of places*. Ann Arbor, MI: University of Michigan Press.

Giroux, H. (1992). *Border crossing: Cultural workers and the politics of education* (first edn.). New York: Routledge.

Giroux, H. (2001). *Theory and resistance in education*. West Port, CT: Bergin & Garvey.

Giroux, H. (2005). *Border crossing: Cultural workers and the politics of education* (second edn.). New York: Routledge.

Gitlin, A., E. Buendía, K. Crosland, & F. Doumbia (2003). The production of margin and center: Welcoming-unwelcoming of immigrant students. *American Educational Research Journal*, 40(1), 91–122.

Goetz, J. P., & M. D. LeCompte (1984). *Ethnography and qualitative design in educational research*. New York: Academic Press.

Gold, S. (1999). Southeast Asians. In *A nation of peoples: A sourcebook on America's multicultural heritage*. Ed. E. R. Barkan. West Port, CT: Greenwood Press, pp. 505–519.

Gold, S. (2004). From Jim Crow to racial hegemony: Evolving explanations of racial hierarchy. *Ethnic and Racial Studies*, 27(6), 951–968.

Gold, S., & N. Kibria (1993). Vietnamese refugees and blocked mobility. *Asian and Pacific Migration Journal*, 2(1), 27–56.

Goldenberg, C., & R. Gallimore (1995). Immigrant Latino parents' values and beliefs about their children's education: Continuities and discontinuities across cultures and generations. In *Advances in motivation and achievement: Volume 9*. Ed. M. Maehr and P. R. Pintrich. Greenwich, CT: JAI, pp. 183–228.

González, N. (2005). Beyond culture: The hybridity of funds of knowledge. In *Funds of knowledge: Theorizing practices in households, communities, and classrooms*. Ed. N. González, L. C. Moll, & C. Amanti. Mahwah, NJ: Lawrence Erlbaum, pp. 29–46.

Gorz, A. (1982). *Farewell to the working class*. London: Pluto Press.

Grieco, E. (2004). *The African foreign born in the United States*. Migration Policy Institute. Migration Policy Institute. Retrieved March 22, 2005, from www.migrationinformation.org/Usfocus/display.cfm?id=250.

Gutiérrez, K., Rymes, B., & Larson, J. (1995). Script, counterscript, and underlife in the classroom: James Brown versus "Brown v. Board of Education." *Harvard Educational Review*, 65(3), 445–471.

Hall, S. & Jefferson, T. (eds.) (1976). *Resistance through rituals: youth subcultures in post-war Britain*. London: Hutchinson.

Hayward, P. W. (1994). Pre-resettlement preparation: Needs and issues of refugees. *Proceedings of the Conference of East African Refugee Service Providers*. Arlington, VA.

Healey, J. F. (2003). *Race, ethnicity, gender and class: The sociology of group conflict and change*. Thousand Oaks, CA: Fine Forge Press.

Heath, S. B. (1983). *Ways with words: language, life, and work in communities and classrooms*. New York: Cambridge University Press.

Hicks, D. (2002). *Reading lives: Working-class children and literacy learning*. New York: Teachers College Press.

Hiestand, B., & M. Maloney (2005). *Buffalo, N.Y., activists rally against KKK racism*. Retrieved December 27, 2006, from www.workers.org/2005/us/buffalo0728/index.html.

Hoffman, D. M. (1996). Culture and self in multicultural education: Reflections on discourse, text, and practice. *American Educational Research Journal*, 33(3), 545–569.

Hout, M. (2006). *How class works: Objective and subjective aspects of class since the 1970s*. Paper presented at the conference "How Class Works," New York University (April 21, 2006), New York.

Jordan, S. A. (2002). Ethnographic encounters: The processes of cultural translation. *Language and Intercultural Communication*, 2(2), 96–110.

Kibria, Z. (1993). *Family tightrope: The changing lives of Vietnamese Americans*. Princeton, NJ: Princeton University Press.

Kim, C. J. (2000). *Bitter fruit: The politics of Black–Korean conflict in New York City*. New Haven, CT: Yale University Press.

Knapp, M. S. & S. Woolverton. (2004). Social class and schooling. In *Handbook of research on multicultural education*, 2nd edn. Ed. J. A. Banks & C. A. M. Banks. San Francisco: Jossey-Bass, pp. 656–681.

Kotchick, B. A., & R. Forehand (2002). Putting parenting in perspective: A discussion of the contextual factors that shape parenting practices. *Journal of Child and Family Studies*, 11(30), 255–269.

Krieg, E. J. (2005). Race and environmental justice in Buffalo, NY: A ZIP code and historical analysis of ecological hazards. *Society and Natural Resources*, 18, 199–213.

Krysan, M., & R. Farley (2002). The residential preferences of blacks: Do they explain persistent segregation. *Social Forces*, 80(3), 937–980.

Lam, B. T. (2003). *The psychological distress among Vietnamese American adolescents: Toward an ecological model.* Unpublished doctoral dissertation, Columbia University, New York.

Lam, W. S. E. (2004). Second language socialization in a bilingual chat room: Global and local considerations. *Language Learning & Technology,* 8(3), 44–65.

Lareau, A. (1989). *Home advantage: Social class and parental intervention in elementary education.* London: Falmer.

Lareau, A. (2000). *Home advantage: Social class and parental intervention in elementary education,* 2nd edn. New York: Rowman & Littlefield Publishers.

Lareau, A. (2003). *Unequal childhoods: Class, race, and family life.* Berkeley, CA: University of California Press.

Lave, J., & E. Wenger (1991). *Situated learning: Legitimate peripheral participation.* Cambridge, UK: Cambridge University Press.

Le, T. L., & J. L. Warren (2006). Self-reported rates and risk factors of Cambodian, Chinese, Lao/Mien and Vietnamese Youth. In *Beyond the 'Whiz Kid' stereotype: New research on Asian American and Pacific Islander youth.* Los Angeles: UCLA Asian American Studies Center.

Lee, S. (2005). *Up against whiteness: Race, school and immigrant youth.* New York: Teachers College Press.

Lee, P. W., & S. L. Wong (2002). At-risk Asian and Pacific American youths: Implications for teachers, psychologists and other providers. In *Asian and Pacific Islander American education: Social, cultural, and historical contexts.* Ed. E. H. Tamura, V. Chettergy, & R. Endo. South El Monte, CA: Pacific Asia Press, pp. 85–115.

Lee, V., & D. Burkam (2002). *Inequality at the starting gate social background differences in achievement as children begin school.* Washington, DC: Economic Policy Institute.

Lew, J. (2006). *Asian Americans in class: Charting the achievement gap among Korean American youth.* New York: Teachers College Press.

Lewis Mumford Center (2001). *Ethnic diversity grows, neighborhood integration lags behind.* Retrieved May 31, 2006, from http://mumford1.dyndns.org/cen2000/WholePop/WPreport/page1.html.

Li, G. (2000). Family literacy and cultural identity: An ethnographic study of a Filipino family in Canada. *McGill Journal of Education,* 35(1), 1–27.

Li, G. (2002). *"East is east, west is west"? Home literacy, culture, and schooling.* New York: Peter Lang.

Li, G. (2003). Literacy, culture, and politics of schooling: Counternarratives of a Chinese Canadian family. *Anthropology & Education Quarterly,* 34(2), 184–206.

Li, G. (2004). Perspectives on struggling English language learners: Case studies of two Chinese-Canadian children. *Journal of Literacy Research,* 36(1), 31–72.

Li, G. (2005a). Other people's success: Impact of the "model minority" myth on underachieving Asian students in North America. *KEDI Journal of Educational Policy,* 2(1), 69–86.

Li, G. (2005b). *Asian-American education across the class line: A multi-site report.* Buffalo, NY: GSE Publications, SUNY Press.

Li, G. (2006). *Culturally contested pedagogy: Battles of literacy and schooling between mainstream teachers and Asian immigrant parents.* Albany, NY: SUNY Press.

Li, G. (2007). Home environment and second language acquisition: The importance of family capital. *British Journal of Sociology of Education,* 28(3), 285–299.

Li, G., & T. Christ (2007). Social capital and home literacy engagement: Case studies of low-SES single mothers' access to literacy resources. *English in Education*, 41(1), 21–35.

Lincoln, Y. S., & G. E. Guba (1985). *Naturalist inquiry.* Beverly Hills, CA: Sage.

McBrien, J. L. (2005). Educational needs and barriers for refugee students in the United States: A review of literature. *Review of Educational Research*, 75(3), 329–364.

McCarthy, C. (1988). Rethinking liberal and radical perspectives on racial inequality in schooling: Making the case for nonsynchony. *Harvard Educational Review*, 58(3), 265–279.

McCarthy, C., & W. Crichlow (1993). Introduction: Theories of identity, theories of representation, theories of race. In *Race, identity, and representation in education.* Ed. C. McCarthey & W. Crichlow. New York: Routledge, pp. xiii–xxiv.

McCarthy, C., A. Rodriguez, S. Meeham, S. David, C. Wilson-Brown, H. Godina, K. E. Supryia, & E. Buendia (2005). Race, suburban resentment, and the representation of the inner city in contemporary film and television. In *Beyond silenced voices: Class, race, and gender in United States schools*, revised edn. Ed. L. Weis and M. Fine. Albany, NY: SUNY Press, pp. 117–132.

McKay, S. L. (1993). *Family agenda for second language literacy.* Cambridge, UK: Cambridge University Press.

McLaren, P. (1998). *Life in schools: An introduction to critical foundations of education,* 3rd edn. New York: Longman.

McLaren, P. (2003). *Life in schools: An introduction to critical pedagogy in the foundations of education,* 4th edn. New York: Allyn & Bacon.

Meacham, S. (2001). The clash of "common senses": Two African American women become teachers. In *The skin that we speak: Thoughts on language and culture in the classroom.* Ed. L. Delpit and J. K. Dowdy. New York: The New Press, pp. 179–202.

Mercado, M. (2005). Seeing what's there: Language and literacy funds of knowledge in New York Puerto Rican homes. In *Building on strength: Language and literacy in Latino families and communities.* Ed. A. C. Zentella. New York: Teachers College Press, pp. 134–147.

Meyer, B. (2006). Brown gives himself an "A" after first year as Buffalo mayor. *Buffalo News*, December 20. Retrieved December 30, 2006, from www.buffalonews.com/editorial/20061230/1045951.asp.

Migration News. (2005). *Welfare, licenses, Sudanese.* Retrieved March 1, 2005, from http://migration.ucdavis.edu/mn.

NEAP (2005). *National assessment of educational progress: The Nation's report card.* Retrieved October 15, 2006, from http://nationsreportcard.gov/reading_math_grade12_2005/.

Nguyen, H. H., L. A. Messe, & G. E. Stollak (1999). Toward a more complex understanding of acculturation and adjustment: Cultural involvement and psychosocial functioning in Vietnamese youth. *Journal of Cross-Cultural Psychology*, 30(1), 5–31.

Nieto, S. (2002). *Language, culture, and teaching: Critical perspectives for a new century.* Mahwah, NJ: Lawrence Erlbaum.

Niman, M. (2006). Niman: Anti-Indian racism in New York's anti-casino movement. *Indian County*, September 22. Retrieved December 30, 2006, from www.indiancountry.com/content.cfm?id=1096413699.

Noddings, N. (1992). *The challenge to care in schools.* New York: Teachers College Press.

Noguera, P. (2003). *City schools and the American dream: Reclaiming the promise of public education*. New York: Teachers College Press.

Ochs, E. (1986). *Culture and language acquisition: Acquiring communicative competence in a Western Samoan village*. New York: Cambridge University Press.

Ogbu, J. (1986). Class stratification, racial stratification, and schooling. In *Class, race and gender in American education*. Ed. L. Weis. New York: State University of New York Press, pp. 163–182.

Oh-Willeke, S. J. (1996). *Moving beyond the model minority myth: First and second generation Korean women in Buffalo and the culture of successing oneself*. Unpublished master's thesis, State University of New York at Buffalo.

Omi, M., & H. Winant (1986). *Racial formation in the United States: From the 1960s to the 1980s*. New York: Routledge.

Ong, A. (1999). Cultural citizenship as subject making: Immigrants negotiate racial and cultural boundaries in the United States. In *Race, identity, and citizenship: A reader*. Ed. R. Torres, L. Miron, and J. Inda. Malden, MA: Blackwell Publishing, pp. 262–293.

Orellana, M. F. (2001). The work kids do: Mexican and Central American immigrant children's contribution to households and schools in California. *Harvard Educational Review*, 71(3), 366–389.

Orellana, M. F. (2003). Responsibilities of children in Latino immigrant homes. *New Directions for Youth Development*, 100, 25–39.

Pan, E. (2006). *The U.S. immigration debate*. Retrieved January 4, 2006, from www.cfr.org/publication/10210/us_immigration_debate.html#8.

Perry, P. (2002). *Shades of white: White kids and racial identities in high school*. Durham, NC: Duke University Press.

Portes, A., & R. G. Rumbaut (1996). *Immigrant America: A portrait*, 2nd edn. Berkeley, CA: University of California Press.

Portes, A., & R. Rumbaut (2001). *Legacies: The story of the immigrant second generation*. Berkeley, CA: University of California Press.

Portes, A., & Zhou, M. (1993). The new second generation: Segmented assimilation and its variants. *Annals AAPSS*, 530, 74–82.

Povell, M. (2005). The history of Vietnamese immigration. *American Immigration Law Foundation*. Retrieved May 31, 2006, from www.ailf.org/awards/benefit2005/vietnamese_essay.shtml

Purcell-Gates, V. (1996). Stories, coupons, and the TV guide: Relationships between home literacy experiences and emergent literacy knowledge. *Reading Research Quarterly*, 31(4), 406–428.

Quinn, N., & D. Holland (1987). *Cultural models of language and thought*. New York: Cambridge University Press.

Rey, J. (2002). Buffalo Niagara minorities fall further behind in economic race. *Buffalo News*, August 14. Retrieved January 4, 2006, from http://mumford.albany.edu/census/othersay/BN81402.pdf.

Rogers, R. (2003). *A critical discourse analysis of family literacy practices: Power in and out of print*. Mahwah, NJ: Laurence Erlbaum.

Rosenblatt, L. M. (2004). The transactional theory of reading and writing. In *Theoretical models and processes of reading*. Ed. R. B. Ruddell & N. J. Unrau. Newark, DE: International Reading Association, pp. 1363–1398.

Ruiz-de-Velasco, J., & M. Fix (2001). *Overlooked and underserved: Immigrant children in U.S. secondary schools.* Washington, DC: Urban Institute.

Rutledge, P. J. (1992). *The Vietnamese experience in America.* Bloomington, IN: Indiana University Press.

Sampson, W. A. (2002). *Black student achievement: How much do family and school really matter?* Lanham, MD: Scarecrow Press.

Sampson, W. A. (2003). *Poor Latino families and school preparation: Are they doing the right things?* Lanham, MD: Scarecrow Press.

Schieffelin, B. B., & E. Ochs (1986). Language socialization. *Annual Review of Anthropology,* 15, 163–191.

Scott, E., & M. Linsky (1999). A time of reckoning: Crisis in the Buffalo Public School System. *Journal of Cases in Educational Leadership,* 2(3), 22–50.

Seshadri-Crooks, K. (2000). Surviving theory: A conversation with Homi K. Bhabha. In *The Pre-occupation of postcolonial studies.* Ed. F. Afzal-Khan, & K. Seshadri-Crooks. Durham, NC: Duke University Press, pp. 369–379.

Shipler, D. K. (1997). *A country of strangers: Blacks and whites in America.* New York: Alfred A Knopf.

Sigel, I. E. (1983). The ethics of intervention. In *Changing families.* Ed. I. E. Sigel and L. M. Laosa. New York: Plenum, pp. 1–21.

Sigelman, L., & S. A. Tuch (1997). Metastereotypes: Blacks' perception of whites' stereotypes of blacks. *Public Opinion Quarterly,* 61, 87–101

Siu, S.-F. (1996). *Asian American students at risk: A literature review.* Report No. 8. Baltimore, MD: Johns Hopkins University, Center for Research on the Education of Students Placed at Risk (ED 404 406).

Sokoloff, B., J. Carlin, & H. Pham (1984). Five year follow up of Vietnamese refugee children in the United States. *Clinical Pediatrics,* 25, 565–570.

Spindler, G., & L. Spindler (1982). *Doing the ethnography of schooling: Educational anthropology in action.* Berkeley, CA: University of California Press.

State Education Department (2002). *The New York State School Report Card For School Year 2000–2001.* Retrieved November 15, 2005, from http://emsc33.nysed. gov/repcrd2002/.

Streater, A. (2005). *Salary rankings watched closely by districts.* National Center for Policy Analysis. Retrieved January 10, 2007, from www.ncpa.org/prs/ cd/2005/20050828.htm.

Suárez-Orozco, C., & M. M. Suárez-Orozco (2001). *Children of immigrants.* Cambridge, MA: Harvard University Press.

Taylor, H. L., Jr., & S. Cole (2001). *Structural racism and efforts to radically reconstruct the inner-city built environment.* Paper presented at the Forty-third Annual Conference, Associate of Collegiate schools of Planning, Cleveland Ohio, November 8–11, 2001.

Thomas, J. (1993). *Doing critical ethnography.* Newbury Park, CA: Sage.

Thomas, V. (2006). West Side becomes war zone. *Buffalo News,* July 16.

Thompson, L. (1995). Teaching about ethnic minority families using a pedagogy of care. *Family Relations,* 44(2), 129–135.

Tran, A. N. (2003). *Acculturative stressors affecting Vietnamese American adolescents and their parents.* Unpublished doctoral dissertation, Pacific Graduate School of Psychology, Palo Alto, California.

US Census Bureau (2000). www.census.gov/census2000/states/ny.html (accessed March 30, 2005).

US Department of Housing and Urban Development (2004). *State of the Cities Data Systems (SOCDS)*. Retrieved March 15, 2007, from www.socds.huduser.org.

Valdés, G. (1996). *Con respeto: Bridging the distance between culturally diverse families and schools: An ethnographic portrait*. New York: Teachers College Press.

Valdés, G. (1998). The world outside and inside schools: Language and immigrant children. *Educational Researcher,* 27(6), 4–18.

Valdés, G. (2001). *Learning and not learning English: Latino students in American schools*. New York: Teachers College Press.

Valenzuela, A. (1999). *Subtractive schooling: U.S.–Mexican youth and the politics of caring*. Albany, NY: State University of New York Press.

Valenzuela, A., Jr. (1999). Gender roles and settlement activities among children and their immigrant families. *American Behavioral Scientist,* 42(4), 720–742.

Vélez-Ibáñez, C., and J. Greenberg (2005). Formation and transformation of funds of knowledge. In *Funds of knowledge: Theorizing practices in households, communities, and classrooms*. Ed. N. González, L. C. Moll, & C. Amanti. Mahwah, NJ: Laurence Erlbaum, pp. 47–71.

Vygotsky, L. S. (1978). Interaction between learning and development. In *Mind in the society: The development of higher psychological processes*. Ed. M. Cole, V. John-Steiner, S. Scribner, & E. Souberman. Cambridge, MA: Harvard University Press, pp. 79–91.

Walker-Moffat, W. (1995). *The other side of the Asian American success story*. San Francisco, CA: Jossey-Bass Publishers.

Walkerdine, V., H. Lucey, & J. Melody (2001). *Growing up girl: Psychosocial explorations of gender and class*. New York: New York University.

Waters, M. C. (1999). *Black identities: West Indian immigrant dreams and American realities*. Cambridge, MA: Harvard University Press.

Weis, L. (1990). *Working class without work*. New York: Routledge.

Weis, L. (2004). *Class reunion: The remaking of the American white working-class*. New York: Routledge.

Weis, L., & C. Centrie (2002). On the power of separate spaces: Teachers and students writing (righting) selves and future. *American Educational Research Journal,* 39(1), 7–36.

Weis, L., & M. Fine (2004). Introduction. Compositional studies in four parts: Critical theorizing and analysis on social (in)justice. In L. Weis & M. Fine, *Working method: Research and social justice*. New York: Routledge, pp. xv–xxiv.

Wells, G. (1986). *The meaning makers: Children learning language and using language to learn*. Portsmouth, NH: Heinemann Educational Books.

Wenger, E. (1998). *Communities of practice: Learning, meaning and identity*. Cambridge, UK: Cambridge University Press.

Wertsch, J. V. (1991). *Voices of the mind: A sociocultural approach to mediated action*. Cambridge, MA: Harvard University Press.

Whitehouse, M., & C. Colvin (2001). "Reading" families: Deficit discourse and family literacy. *Theory Into Practice,* 40, 212–219.

Willis, P. (1977). *Learning to labor: How working-class kids get working-class jobs*. Westmead, UK: Saxon House Press.

Wong, R. S. (1998). Multidimensional influences of family environment in education: The case of socialist Czechoslovakia. *Sociology of Education,* 71, 1–22.

Wong-Fillmore, L. (1991). Language and cultural issues in the early education of language minority children. *The Yearbook of the National Society for the Study of Education,* 90(1), 30–49.

World Bank Group (2006). *05 world development indicators.* Retrieved October 27, 2006, from http://devdata.worldbank.org/wdi2005/Cover.htm.

Wright, E. O. (1997). *Class counts: Comparative studies in class analysis.* Cambridge, UK: Cambridge University Press.

Wright, E. O. (2003). Social class. In *Encyclopedia of social theory.* Ed. G. Ritzer. Thousand Oaks, CA: Sage.

Wu, P. H. (2002). *Yellow: Race in America beyond black and white.* New York: Basic Books.

Zhou, M. (2001). Straddling different worlds: The acculturation of Vietnamese refugee children. In *Ethnicities: Children of immigrants in America.* Ed. R. G. Rumbaut and A. Portes. Berkeley, CA: University of California Press, pp. 187–228.

Zhou, M., & C. L. Bankston III (1998). *Growing up American: How Vietnamese children adapt to life in the United States.* New York: Russell Sage.

Zuckerman, M. (2002). Our rainbow underclass. USNews.com. Retrieved November 17, 2005, from www.usnews.com/usnews/opinion/articles/020923/archive_022696.htm.

Index

Academy for Visual and Performing Arts 152

accomplishment of natural growth 6, 18, 162, 181

acculturation: and integration of immigrant and minority groups 8; process 10, 11–12, 93

achievement gap 9, 58

adaptation 10; cultural 12; parents' gender 169

adjustment 10, 42; to life in the US, 23, 97; to school life 157; to US schools 104

African Americans 3, 8, 27, 28, 30, 32, 35, 94, 118, 125, 142, 172–5; community 29, 146; poor and working class 3

African refugees 7, 93, 104, 158

Africans 35, 142, 158, 175, 179

"Afro-Americans" 100, 103

American: culture 13, 78; dream 27, 59, 98, 117; mainstream 12, 13, 59; schools 105, 106, 124, 125

annual international festival 49, 139, 141, 151

Anyon, Jean 16, 17

"anti-gaming" movement 32, 33

anti-Indian racism 32

Apple, M. and Weis, L. 185

apprenticeship 24, 156

Arabic 95, 97, 103, 118, 124, 165

Asher, N. 191, 194

Asian: Americans 10, 59; at-risk 11; East Asian immigrants 58; immigrants 59, 172; parents 86; Southeast 11; students 73, 91

Asians 8, 29, 36, 59, 80, 158, 173, 175, 176; poor and working class 58; Southeast 58

assimilation 7, 22, 44; downward 10; segmented assimilation 7, 8, 11

Bari 95, 103,

Bartlett, T. 188

Baumann, G. 162

Bhabha, Homi 164, 182, 183, 185, 188, 189, 190

Black Chamber of Commerce 29

black(s) 7, 8, 30, 32, 34, 43, 79, 80, 81, 91, 94, 101, 102, 143, 173, 174, 175; being 101, 175; community 30, 35, 93; immigrant 94, 126; people 98, 101, 105, 142; students 118, 142

"black other" 93, 95, 131, 172, 176

blackness 94, 173, 174

"blame the victim" 177, 196

border pedagogy 184, 185

Bourdieu, P. 17; and Passerson, J. C. 17

Boy Scouts 3, 134, 136, 158

Brantlinger, E. 18

Brown High School 43

Buffalo 1, 8, 13, 27, 28, 31, 32, 33, 37, 40, 60, 93, 115, 127, 129; city of; 27, 28, 31, 37, 184; economy 28; inner city 174; north 28, 29, 36, 99; public school districts 39; public schools 37, 39, 40, 47; racial divide 31; racial segregation 32; school system 37, 38, 41; teachers 40

Buffalo Fiscal Stability Authority 40

Buffalo Joint Schools Construction Board 41, 184

Buffalo News 31, 65

Canada 60, 61, 82

Canisius High School 37

capital: cultural 6, 17, 125, 157, 158, 162, 180; discontinuity between school and home cultural 17; financial capital 157; social 89, 157

Caplan, Choy, and Whitmore 59

caring 143, 146, 157, 167

Catholic charity 97 115

Catholic school 68, 167
Centrie, C. 71
Chinese 73, 177
Citizens for a Better Buffalo 32, 184
class 162, 181, 195; advantages 18;
    boundaries 162, 181; fraction 3, 4, 13;
    privilege 18, 127; reproduction 17;
    social 4, 16, 18, 29, 53, 74; stratification
    18; structures 16; systems 36, 127; 128;
    traditional class analysis 181
class location 174, 179; objective 178;
    subjective 178
Clayton family 24, 126, 128, 146–56, 157,
    158, 159, 166, 180; Clayton family
    profile 147
Claytons 2, 152, 155
co-constructors 16
co-ethnic settlement 7, 8
"co-intentional education" 188
Collins, J. and Blot, R. K. 19
communication 54, 140, 195; barriers 86;
    lack of 155; language 195
community college 2, 3, 117, 119, 124, 129,
    133, 139, 157
community service 99, 102, 136
Comprehensive Immigration Reform Act
    33
"concerted cultivation" 6, 8, 181, 183
content and thematic analysis 21
contestation 25, 162, 164, 174; cultural 162,
    183, 186
Council of the Great City Schools 40
culture 10, 11, 12, 15, 16, 19, 48, 49, 158,
    163, 164, 182, 185, 189, 190, 191;
    home 15, 118; of origin 11, 63, 164; "of
    poverty" 22, 25, 51, 148, 157, 163, 166,
    175, 181; pedagogy 26, 184, 185, 192,
    196; school 11, 17, 142, 143
cultural: clashes 12, 71, 93; conflicts 12, 25,
    75, 163; differences 26, 49, 94, 161, 186,
    192; (mis)translation 164, 165, 166, 167,
    168, 185, 188, 189, 190; "racism" 173;
    reconciliation 185, 188, 191; remapping
    188; "tastes" 17; translation between
    home and school 185; translators 25,
    26, 183, 185, 194; workers 194
curriculum 16, 38, 44, 48, 55, 107, 129; and
    instruction 9, 106; redesign 187, 191;
    school 17, 48; scripted 48
counternarratives 5

deficit model 166
Department of Community Development
    31

dialectical: interaction 6; thought, 5; view
    of schooling, 4
diary 154, 166
difference: between Afro-Americans
    and Sudanese people 100; between
    home and school 166, 186; in gender
    socialization 171; in schooling, 105–7,
    120–2
Dillaway, D. 29, 37
Dinka 118, 186
Dion, K. K. and Dion, K. L. 170
disappearance of working-class jobs 13
discrimination 10, 100, 170, 184, 177;
    against blacks 104; racial 10, 11, 73, 177
discourse 4, 5, 14, 183; against black 174;
    dominant 5, 6, 161, 174, 182, 192, 193;
    dominant racial 159, 162, 173, 176;
    literacy 4; primary 14, 15; of privilege
    loss 128; of race and race relations
    172; racial 32, 33, 34, 36, 172, 174;
    secondary 14, 15; socio-cultural; 15;
    sticky web of dominant 183; "sticky
    web of institutional" 6; "of suburban
    resentment and fear of encirclement"
    31
discursive: conditions 5, 196; "dual
    competence" 24, 162, 182; dualities,
    162, 186; elements 5, 6
diversity 10, 13, 45, 49, 141, 189, 190;
    cultural 49, 190, 196; ethnic 7
duality 25, 163, 174, 182, 185, 188,
    194; of class positioning 25, 163; of
    conformity and resistance 60, 161, 163;
    discursive 162, 186; gender politics 25,
    163; literacy and culture 163; of the
    minorities 174; race and ethnicity 25,
    163
Du Bois, W. E. B. 161, 163

East Camp 151
East Side 28, 29, 30, 37, 42, 146, 170
education 23, 24, 35, 49, 50, 51, 59, 61, 90,
    94, 100, 105, 106, 120, 125, 132, 133,
    155, 157, 178, 185, 191, 192; higher
    education 36, 71, 125, 166; importance
    of 50, 59, 105, 132, 133; problem-posing
    185, 192; value of 155
educational: borders 4, 166; experiences
    24, 155; values 22, 61, 125, 161
Egypt 95, 97, 104, 115
Elmwood Strip 36
empowerment 25, 93; and agency, 25, 183
ESL 43, 44, 46, 107, 108, 109, 110, 114, 123,

179, 195; classes 72, 108, 109, 110, 115, 123, 165; population 43; programs 22, 61, 76, 95, 107, 109, 110, 115, 119, 122, 123, 179, 195; pullout programs 107, 108, 114, 125; students 43, 44, 45, 67, 107; teachers 37, 44, 46, 48, 108, 110
Espiruti, Y. L. 172
ethnic: concentration 43; "flight" 11; identification 11; identity 162, 172
ethnographic: accounts 13; methods, 19
Evelyn 20, 43, 44, 45, 48, 49, 166
expectations: high 22, 23, 59, 61, 63, 64, 90, 148, 161, 166, 169, 178, 180; parental 86, 90, 104

family: activities 136; dinner conversation 137; literacy programs 193; stability 133, 157
Fine, M. and Weis, L. 158
Foucault, M. 5, 196
Fordham High 87
Freire, Paulo 1, 174, 185, 188, 193, 194, 195
frustration with the schools 72, 124
Fuligni, A. J. and Yoshikawa, H. 178

Gary 132, 133, 137, 145, 180
Gee, J. P. 14, 15
gender: adaptation 169; dynamic 171; expectations 170; inequalities 90; patterns 169; roles 163, 168, 170, 171, 185
generation gap 11, 12
generational: consonance, 12; cultural gaps 164; dissonance 12
Gimpel, J. G. 8
Giroux, Henry 188, 196
global economic structure 13
globalized economy 4, 172
González, N. 187, 192
Green High School 36, 43

Habitat for Humanity 99
"habitus" 17, 170, 180
Head Start programs 97, 111, 148
Hicks, D. 13
Hispanic: community 33, 35; people 33, 34; population 8, 3, 43; students 81
Hispanics 7, 29, 33, 34, 35, 81, 176
Hmong students 10, 59
Hoffman, D. M. 49, 190, 191
host society 10, 11, 164, 168, 169
Hurricane Katrina 145

identity 14, 164, 174, 175, 191, 196; adversarial 11; cultural 13, 23, 91, 94, 129, 190; ethnic 162, 172; formation, 6, 10, 24, 71; immigrant 94, 174; oppositional 10, 11, 174, 188; politics 125; racial 60, 163; social 15
immigrant: blacks 94, 126; children 9, 11, 57, 73, 126, 195; families 11, 23, 97, 110, 164, 168, 169, 170, 171, 178, 180, 181, 185; parents 11, 15, 50, 65, 104; youths 69, 70, 71
immigrants 6, 7, 8, 10, 28, 35, 93, 179, 180; and minorities 127; and refugees, 2, 4, 7, 8, 30, 36; Asian 58, 59, 172; African 35; East Asian 58; foreign born 4; Hispanic 42, 61; illegal 33; low SES 7, 8, 30, 66
influx of refugee and immigrant population 42
inclusionary–exclusionary process 48
integration 7, 8, 12
International Festival of Cultures 49
intersectionality of various social categories 13

Johnsons High 87
Jordan, S. A. 189

Kibria, Z. 63
Kim, C. J. 176
Krieg, E. J. 30

Lakeside High 39, 87, 129
Lam, W. S. E. 10, 15
language; and literacy learning 15, 165; first 11, 43, 66, 103, 164, 165, 186, 195; gap between parents and adolescents 12; instruction 107; minority learners 15, 16; second 11, 186; socialization 15, 16
Lareau, A. 21, 180, 181
learning disability 24, 67
Lee, S. 58, 170
Lew, J. 181
Lewis Mumford Center for Comparative Urban and Regional Research 29
Li, Guofang 184, 186, 187, 191, 192
literacy 4, 19, 163, 164, 191, 192, 193, 194; and living 4, 14, 25, 91, 161, 172, 173, 181, 182, 183, 186, 916; cultural models of 14, 15; education 188, 189, 190; fracturing 165, 186; instruction 186, 187; learning 15, 16, 186; problem-

posing 26; programs, 26, 193, 194; teaching, 46, 188
literacy practices 65, 67, 192; cultural mismatch in 162; daily 4, 91; "fracturing" in 164; home 64, 65, 67, 69, 82, 89, 112, 134, 137, 152, 156, 161, 162, 171; immigrant and minority groups' 15; mainstream 162, 167; school(ed) 156, 184, 186

McBrien, J. L. 12
McCarthy, C. 182
Madison Tech High school 39, 76, 86, 87, 129
"make-believe" school curriculum 25, 163, 181, 190, 191, 195
Marilyn 38, 42, 51, 52, 53, 54, 128, 148, 175
Marshall, Professor 20, 32, 34, 36, 39, 42, 53, 127, 129
masculine/feminine binaries 171
Meacham, S. 172
Mercado, M. 186
Michael Chang 63
Michael Niman 33
middle-class 53, 58, 127; African American parents 94; Asian immigrants 58; backgrounds 178, 179; Blacks 173; "poor people" 179; values and literacy practices 193; values and practices 13; ways of interactive reading 187; Whites 74, 174, 175
middle and upper-middle class: circle 37; tastes or activities; 17
Mimi 2, 81, 84
minority: experiences 4; families and children 25; parents 179, 193; school failure 6; students 10, 15, 22, 54, 185
miscommunication between the school and the home 108
mismatch 14, 23, 24, 162, 183; between children's learning experiences in school and at home 23, 126; between the family's subjective and objective class locations 180; between school and home 156; discursive 17
mobile family 146
mobility: class 172; downward social 3; geographic 8; socio-economic 8; upward social 7, 10, 58, 63, 94
model minority 36, 58, 90; Asian 177; stereotypes 161
multicultural: activities 48, 49; teaching 150

multiculturalism 48, 191; "hallway" 190; popular 190
Myer: children 165, 187; family 2, 23, 93, 114–24, 126, 167; family's expectation for the children 119; family profile, 116
Myers 118, 166

National Reading Panel 186
NEAP 9
Nelli 20, 33, 34, 35, 44, 51, 52, 53, 128, 148
Nichols School 37
No Child Left Behind (NCLB) 47, 68, 169, 195
Noddings, Nell 167
Noguera, Pedro 27, 184
nonsynchronous approach 182

Ochs, E. 15
Oh-Willeke, S. J. 59
Oliver School 39
Omi, M. and Winant, H. 177
"other" 93, 94, 172, 173, 176, 191; "African American" 158; "black" 93, 94, 95, 131, 172; "constructed" 4, 14, 91; "diverse" 191; racial 176
others 176, 178, 189, 191, 196
"overclass" 127; "an Anglo-Asian" 58

parents 18, 22, 50, 51, 52, 53, 54, 138, 156, 157, 161, 164, 165, 166, 167, 174, 178, 179, 181, 186, 187, 192, 193, 194, 195; middle-class 18; refugee 50, 126, 195; working-class and poor 18
parental involvement 49, 51, 68, 125, 138, 156
"Parents as Reading Partners" 139, 153
patriarchal authority of Asian immigrant men 172
Perry, P. 175
Phan: children 89; family 22, 57, 60–75, 82, 165, 167; family profile 62; family's belief in education 61; parents 61, 65, 89
Phans 61, 64, 66, 68, 177
Philippines 60, 75
policy of mutual literacy accommodation 192
Portes, A. and Rumbaut, R. 12
Portes, A. and Zhou, M. 12
poverty 8, 32, 51, 52; rate 8, 9, 29
power 5, 29, 192; codes of 11; relations 5; relationships 5, 126, 179, 184; struggle between school and home, 25, 163
power and privilege 175, 183;

contradictions and asymmetries of 5;
diverse relations of 164, 183
program developers 193, 194, 195,
psychological stress 72, 90
Puerto Ricans 35, 80, 81, 175
pull-out programs 44, 107
push-in programs 44

race 162, 172, 173, 174, 175; perception of
80; relations 79, 172, 176, 195
racial: concentration 36; dichotomy 59,
176; differences 53, 74; hierarchy 125,
158, 162, 173; imagining 93, 94, 125,
174; minority 141, 143, 162, 174, 175;
relations 32, 34, 162; relationship 81, 91;
resentment against the blacks among
whites 32; tensions between the white
and black populations 28
racialization 176
racism 31, 32, 81, 91, 94, 145, 157, 179, 195;
reversed 167, 175, 195
Rainbow Elementary (School) 3, 19, 22, 24,
43, 45, 47, 68, 76, 78, 89, 95, 109, 129,
141, 142, 148, 151, 152, 158, 167
reading 9, 24, 44, 46, 48, 67, 69, 82, 84, 89,
111, 134, 135, 139, 149, 151, 153, 154,
156, 165, 166, 187: home 166, 187
"Reading Across America," 153
real estate: business 30; markets, 30
refugee: camps 44; children 45, 95, 107;
children's needs 12; family 12, 21, 166,
178, 186; students 13, 42
refugees 2, 7, 8, 42, 57
reproduction of racial hierarchy 162, 183
resistance 11, 24, 125; conformity and 6,
60, 95, 125, 162, 163, 173, 183
Rey, J. 29
Rogers, R. 24, 156
role model 23, 102, 121, 122, 125, 133, 144,
167

Saigon Canada 82
Sassano: children 136, 158, 166; family
24, 128, 129–45, 156, 157, 158, 159,
166, 167, 170, 171, 173, 176, 180; family
profile 130; parents 171, 176
Sassanos 11, 145, 175, 176
Scott, E. and Linsky, M. 39
schools: affluent professional 17; budget
40; city 54, 143, 167, 190; counselors
73; executive elite 17; experiences 24,
141, 144, 148, 150, 177; in higher SES
communities 9; international 61, 68,

129; knowledge 16, 17; private 37, 38,
39, 127; public 14, 27, 37, 39, 47, 68,
110; serving students from low-income
families 9; suburban 37, 151, 167; urban
20, 179; working-class 16, 17
second generation 57, 59; acculturation 12;
girls 169; students 10
segregation 7, 8, 20, 22, 36, 37, 38;
economic and racial 38; patterns 22;
racial 32; racial and economic 8; racial,
economic, and residential 22, 36;
residential 7, 22
self-esteem 73
self-help model 25, 183
semi-structured interviews 19, 20
single-parent families 53
Siu, S.-F. 11
social circle 66, 75
Social Services office 131
State of the Cities Data System (SOCDS) 8
strategic assistance 184, 193
stereotypes 80, 90, 128, 161, 163, 175, 177,
192; racial 163, 172
stereotypical image 158
Suárez-Orozco, C. and Suárez-Orozco, M.
M. 9, 11
Sudan 118, 120, 121, 124; life in 103, 117;
"Lost boys of" 115
Sudanese: American 118; culture 103;
families 125, 161, 165, 169, 173, 174, 175,
178; identity 100, 102, 118; parents 95,
125, 178; refugees 1, 13, 93; traditions
102; ways 23, 102, 161
summer school 88, 97, 109
"sustained talk" 24, 156, 162

Taylor, H. L. Jr. and Cole, S. 32
teachers' union 40
tennis 63, 64, 65
tensions 22, 28, 182; between African
Americans and Africans 35; between
the union and school district 40;
between the whites and the non-whites
128
Thoi Bao 82
Title VI of the Civil Rights Act of 1964 195
Ton: children 89; family 1, 22, 57, 75–89,
165, 167, 177; family profile 77; parents
81, 89
Tons 20, 76
Torkeri: family 23, 93, 95–114, 193; family
profile 96
Torkeris 179

transmission model 193

underclass 58, 127, 166, 173, 175; "America's " 182, 184, 197; "rainbow" 3, 7, 10, 25, 161, 163, 181
urban schooling 6, 25, 126, 163, 166, 177, 185
US Census Bureau 57

Valdés, G. 193
Vélez-Ibáñez, C. and Greenberg, J. 164
Vietnam 57
Vietnamese 50, 57, 58, 59, 66, 69, 76, 79, 81, 82, 86, 165, 176, 177; adolescents 10, 59; community 76, 79, 89; culture 13, 22, 59, 61, 63, 90; families 89, 91, 132, 161, 165, 173, 177, 179, 180; females 71; immigration 57; newspaper 65, 82; parents 57, 59, 63, 155; refugees 57, 58, 59, 75; students 10, 13, 58, 82; teacher 76, 78, 86, 88, 89, 167; values 10, 60; way 78, 79, 90; youths 10, 11, 58, 60, 91

Walkerdine, Lucey, and Melody 18
WASPs 29
Waters, M. C. 94, 172, 175,
Wayne 44, 45, 46, 47, 48, 50, 51

Weis, L. 13, 157, 158, 159, 168, 170, 171, 176
Weis, L. and Centrie, C. 4
Weis, L. and Fine, M. 91
welfare system 129, 131, 132, 148
West Indians 94, 176
West Side 1, 28, 29, 31, 33, 34, 36, 42, 61, 128, 129, 133, 158; schools 22, 41, 42
whiteness 94, 127, 128, 173, 176
whites 7, 8, 10, 29, 30, 32, 34, 36, 37, 39, 43, 59, 74, 80, 81, 91, 101, 118, 127, 128, 131, 141, 143, 151, 156, 158, 159, 168, 170, 172, 175, 176, 177; dominance 91, 176; families 2, 3, 24, 127, 156, 162, 166, 170, 171, 174, 175, 178, 180; "flight" 29, 30, 31, 41; minority 151, 158; privilege 158; women 128; working and/or poor 127; working-class 13, 128, 162, 168, 171, 176
Willis, P. 17, 18, 196
within-group differences 59
Wright, E. O. 178
writing 24, 48, 65, 60, 134, 139, 140, 149, 151, 153, 166; writing curriculum 48, 166, 187

Zhou, M. 10
Zhou, M. and Bankston, C. L. III 59, 177